C000085774

From House to House

FROM HOUSE TO HOUSE

The Endless Adventure of Politics and Wine

The Times and Life of Sir David Mitchell

AN AUTOBIOGRAPHY

The Memoir Club

© David Mitchell 2008

First published in 2008 by
The Memoir Club
Arya House
Langley Park
Durham
DH7 9XE

All rights reserved.
Unauthorised duplication
contravenes existing laws.

British Library Cataloguing in
Publication Data.
A catalogue record for this book
is available from the
British Library

ISBN: 978-1-84104-191-9

Typeset by TW Typesetting, Plymouth, Devon
Printed by The Cromwell Press Ltd, Trowbridge, Wilts

In memory of Pam
and for
our descendants

Contents

List of Illustrations

Acknowledgements

With my grateful thanks to: Cyril Bleasdale OBE, Henri Duboscq, Christopher Green, Walter Harrison, Jim Hastings, Christopher Kirkham-Sandy, Philippe Marion, Bridget Marriott, Christopher Mitchell OBE, John Noulton, Valerie Steele CBE, LVO, Alan Watkins, the late Bernard Weatherill, PC, DL, Alan Whitehouse.

I acknowledge with gratitude the kind friends whose memories I have picked to make this as accurate a tale as it is, but where it falls short, the blame is entirely mine. Importantly, I cannot put down my pen without paying particular tribute and giving many thanks to Margaret Ireland who has catalogued my records, deciphered my handwriting, typed and retyped the chapters of this book with extraordinary patience. Without her assistance and encouragement I doubt this project would have been completed.

Foreword by Matthew Parris

As a young government backbencher in Mrs Thatcher's army after her 1979 victory I used to divide ministers into three categories: sharks, pilot fish and plankton. The sharks cut the waves and made the political weather. The plankton, unmemorable, interchangeable and infinitely expendable, drifted with the current. The pilot fish swam with the sharks, providing competence, quiet intelligence and sometimes cover.

David was a pilot fish, and one of the best. Known among ministers for his quick mind, pleasant manner and steady nerve, he did more than smooth the way: he delivered. In all the retrospective talk about Thatcher Dominatrix, and about the battles and warriors that her critical decade produced, it is easy but wrong to forget that her Government was from the start a complex and sometimes ambiguous amalgam of courage and caution, as reliant for its success on those who cried 'steady on' as those who cried 'forward'.

David's was a quiet talent and to that administration an important one. I knew him simply as a senior can-do minister with whom it was a pleasure to serve on standing committees on the many Transport measures which he led and where I sat as a junior backbencher interested in public transport and endlessly impressed by his grasp. I had never realised before reading this memoir that he had been Sir Keith Joseph's Parliamentary Private Secretary. Nobody can have had a greater need for a lieutenant with feet on the Westminster ground than the unworldly Keith, and the description David gives of his 'racehorse' of a master – compulsively sucking boiled sweets, and teeming with ideas like 'a bluebottle in a jam jar' – is spot-on. I shall now count Keith's words to his PPS on relinquishing his pursuit of the Conservative Leadership – 'I would not get the answers right often enough' – among the most moving testaments I have heard to that man's strange alloy of pride (even arrogance) with humility.

And an absolute gem of a chapter lies buried in this book: as unlikely a diversion as any student of modern politics is likely to encounter. David was, while an MP, also principal French wine-buyer for his family firm of El Vino. And instead of a bibulous account of gentlemanly ease, we find a fascinating ride through the vineyards of France and a beautifully crafted introduction to the art of wine tasting as well as the business of wine importing, such as would grace any lively beginner's guide. David writes of his customers in Fleet Street too – and one realises how much has been lost now we have a generation of politicians who know no other world but Westminster.

The world has changed since the political times David Mitchell brings back to life. His and his colleagues' work to raise the status of small business may be read today almost with incredulity because the things they were saying then seem so obvious now. His quote from the 1970's Inland Revenue Trade Union Leader, Cyril (later Lord) Plant: 'With all the means at our disposal we must destroy the capacity to pursue self employment', seems to come from another world.

Men like David Mitchell were part of the force that banished it. This typically modest, gentle, good-natured account of this part of that bigger story should be read as the tonic to Margaret Thatcher's gin.

Preface

The evening is warm; the sun setting into a calm sea, the waves gently lapping the sand immediately below my campervan. I am parked in an isolated spot on the Bay of Biscay. I tell myself I must soon make a start on the book the Memoir Club have commissioned me to write.

Overnight all has changed – now there are scudding black clouds, whilst a soughing wind shakes my little home and great waves buffet the beach. Change does not always come so quickly but, as in life, it can be the signal to move on, as I have, from market gardening to the wine trade and from backbench MP to Minister.

Amongst those who have urged me to write this story of my life were my good friend, David Trippier who was, like myself, a Minister in Margaret Thatcher's government; also, more locally, Alec Nelms my long time village barber, an unusual man brought up in the workhouse (at Old Basing) and married into the aristocracy, thus securing an entry in Debrett and who, at ninety two, was still cutting my hair. He said the village knows that I have had an interesting life, but not much about it, and are curious.

The pre Great Fire of London cellar at the Olde Wine Shades of El Vino in the City made an ideal backdrop for one of the tutored wine tastings I gave from time to time. Once I introduced myself, saying I had been a buyer of French wines for over twenty years and moonlighted as an MP for as long. During the buffet interval between white and red wines, I was approached by a gentleman saying he felt he should introduce himself as a constituent of mine. Oh dear! Before the tasting continued, I said I needed to issue a correction; in fact, I had been an MP for some twenty five years and moonlighted as a wine merchant! This little vignette encapsulated the dexterity required from time to time in concurrently pursuing two interesting and absorbing careers, those of wine merchant as seen from VINTAGE HOUSE, the headquarters of my family business, and of politics within the HOUSE OF COMMONS.

Family Tree

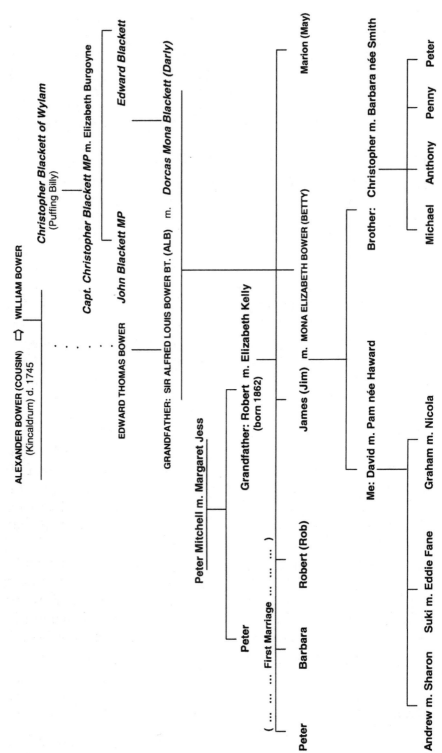

CHAPTER 1

Genes from forebears

*Previous generations introduced through the genes they
passed on / See family tree, one development of national and
international significance*

Aᴄᴄᴏʀᴅɪɴɢ ᴛᴏ ᴛʜᴇ ʜᴀᴛᴄʜᴇᴅ, ᴍᴀᴛᴄʜᴇᴅ ᴀɴᴅ ᴅᴇsᴘᴀᴛᴄʜᴇᴅ columns of *The Times* newspaper, I was born on 20 June 1928. This, for me, important event occurred at 4.30 in the afternoon in our recently acquired family home near Amersham, Buckinghamshire.

The house 'Sundials' in Finch Lane no longer exists. It was a pleasant, three-storey, middle-class house standing in an acre of garden. Later my father erected a wooden stable, a workshop and dog kennels in the orchard. This was to accommodate my Mother's passion for dogs and horses. She never disguised her priority for the four-legged young over the two-legged.

My ski-ing friend and fellow wine lover, Lord (Robert) Winston, one of the world's most respected medical academics, is wont to say 'It's all in the genes'. This truth was graphically illustrated for me when, after I became a parliamentary candidate, Christopher Blackett, a second cousin, wrote saying 'I see it has come out in the blood again'. Mystified, I enquired 'What?' and only then discovered that my maternal great grandfather and his elder son were both MPs in the 1800s.

So I start by recording something of the previous generations who endowed my genes, but if you are not interested in why one relative was dragged to jail with his hair tied to a horse's tail, nor how and why another built 'Puffing Billy', the world's first commercially successful steam locomotive, nor how a pub keeper's son became Lord Mayor of London – then skip this chapter and move on to page 17.

Father Mitchell

The first gene comes from my father's family. My great grandfather, Peter Mitchell, was a boilermaker from Govan on Clydeside. He lies buried in the Craigton cemetery whose directors undertook to 'keep and dress his lair from time to time each year in all time coming'. – Oh the Victorian confidence in an unchanging world! Peter married Margaret Jess – their second son Robert, my grandpa, was born in 1862. He entered the shipbuilding industry, becoming in his time the youngest member of the prestigious Institute of Naval Architecture (MINA), now the Royal Institute. He rose to become Manager of a substantial Clydeside shipyard; on its amalgamation with a bigger company, he lost out for the top job. So it was that in 1903 he moved to Middlesbrough-on-Tees as joint manager and later director of the well regarded[1] Harkess and Sons shipyard. His first contract (by me as I write) gave him joint responsibility with Wm Harkess for 'The oversight, control and management of the business' *but* 'In case of any difference of opinion between the two joint managers, the opinion of the said Wm Harkess shall prevail'!

The salary was £500 per year plus a commission. However, Grandpa had to buy in a shareholding and Grannie, my second gene, formerly a school teacher, dispensed with cook and housemaid to enable them to raise the money. She was born Elizabeth Kelly, one of four daughters of James Kelly the factor (Manager) of an estate at Kirkintilloch, later to become the Broomhill Home for the Relief of Incurables. From extant letters, it was a happy and very affectionate marriage.

During the 1914–18 war the shipyard was extremely busy on Admiralty work, incidentally displaying a notice:

> A wise old owl lived in an oak;
> The more he heard the less he spoke
> The less he spoke the more he heard.
> Friends, beware of that wise bird.

For many of their latter years, my grandparents used in the summer to take first a house and, later, rooms in the North East fishing port of Whitby overlooking its picturesque harbour. One incident, whilst there, reveals something of Grandpa's character. An active Presbyterian at home, he was also a regular Sunday worshipper while in Whitby. The townsfolk had greatly prospered both during and after the war with fishing, boatbuilding and holidaymakers. Taking round

---

[1] I have photographs of King George V, who was accompanied by Queen Mary, visiting the shipyard.

the collection plate one Sunday to the accompaniment of the hymn 'Take my silver, take my gold' he was affronted at the halfpennies and farthings put in, and stumped out of the church, never to return. Each Sunday he drove Grannie there and sat outside in the car, no doubt smoking his beloved pipe. If determination (or is it obstinacy?) is in the genes of my brother and myself, here could be its place of origin.

Grandpa married twice; his first wife died, having borne him two sons, Peter and Robert (shortened to 'Rob') and, between them, a daughter Barbara. Rob created a shock and mystery when, without a word, he just disappeared one night whilst staying with relatives in Hartlepool. Grandpa never rested in his efforts and hope of finding him. He advertised each year on the anniversary of Rob's disappearance and left him the reversionary interest in an eighth of his estate 'if he claims it within one year of my wife's death'.

There may be no connection, but the mystery deepens for, when my father died, his niece bought our family home 'Sundials' from his estate. She employed a daily help, a Mrs Brockie, whose first husband had been a Robert Mitchell, who had worked in Northern Ireland but was brought up in the North East, and was reticent about his family. He had, it seems, run away from home because he could not get on with his stepmother; he had a career in shipping and died of TB in the 1930s. It is a small world and it just may be . . .

Grandpa and Grannie had two children – my father, James (known as Jim), in October 1889 and his sister, Aunt May, born three years later. In many ways Father started out in his father's footsteps. The youngest MINA, like him, he had chosen shipbuilding and engineering, and trained with Wm Harkess where he was successively Assistant and General Manager. In 1918 the firm was sold, Grandpa retired but the new owners retained Father as General Manager. Sometime in the 1920s the firm went under during the great depression in shipbuilding.[2] He moved on to become the successful shipyard manager of Richardson, Duck and Co. at Stockton on Tees. This company also closed following a financial crash elsewhere.

About this time, 1925/6, Sir Isaac Pitman Publishers chose Father to write their text book on Shipbuilding. I cannot resist one extract in which he described preparation for launching: 'Some lady

---

[2] I have been unable to trace details, but the yard built *The Graceful*, one of the earliest ships to have the engine in the stern, allowing uninterrupted space for cargo.

generally tries to break a bottle on its stem which contained red wine when it entered the drawing office to be beribboned by the apprentice draughtsman'. I recall Father explaining that, in those days, wine bottles were sealed with wax. It was the task of the junior in the office to heat a knife, slice off the seal, draw the cork and pour out the contents for the seniors in the drawing office, make up a matching mixture of red ink and water, recork, reheat the knife and restore the wax seal to its place.

Pontresina was then a fashionable Swiss ski resort. There, in about 1922, Father met up briefly with a large family party amongst whom were Betty Bower and Margaret Spurrell. Later Betty described Jim Mitchell as 'that funny little man who had made a gawky schoolgirl feel grown up'.

Another time in Pontresina, Father helped out of a snowdrift an older man who had run off the piste. As a 'thank you' he was invited back to his hotel for a drink. He turned out to be F.R. Simms, the Managing Director of Simms Motor Units, makers of magnetos, dynamos, solenoid starters etc. – a substantial business. Taking a liking to Father and learning he was, now, unemployed, Simms offered him the job of his Assistant. Father worked there, managing branch and export business and some years later was nominated by Simms for the position of Joint General Manager of the Company. Then in 1934 a putsch took place. Old Simms was forced out in a boardroom row and, not long after, his 'blue eyed boy', my father, now aged forty two, was looking for another job.

After some months unemployed, Father secured a job as manager of a hat factory in Aylesbury, belonging to the Itas, two Austrian brothers. That continued until 1939 when the Itas brothers were arrested under the 18B Regulation (providing for aliens or potential enemy sympathisers to be imprisoned). The factory closed and once again Father was unemployed. The Admiralty asked him to return to shipbuilding, but he declined since he felt technology had moved on and he was out of touch. Eventually after, I think it was eighteen months, he joined Van Houten chocolate manufacturers where he was responsible for transport and their war effort department which assembled medical packs for air sea rescue and similar purposes.

Father was a reticent man, so it was only after his death that I learned a good deal more about him and his life. Only then I discovered he had been awarded the Royal Humane Medal for saving the life of a drunken seaman who fell into a dock. He was trustee for his uncle Peter Mitchell's estate as well as for his own father's. In each case there was a second marriage to a younger wife who outlived their husbands from the 1930s into the '60s. Both Wills provided a life interest to the widow, but the ravages of inflation destroyed their living standards, and Father personally helped out from his own strained finances. (He had 'jacked in' one pension, I suspect to pay for our school fees.) He retired at age sixty eight, suffering from high blood pressure. He lived life to the full in his remaining time. In May, 1959 he wrote to a friend that his life expectancy was five or, if he was lucky, ten years. As fate would have it, he died six months later, survived by his mother who followed him three months after. I wish I had known him better.

Part of his approach to life and, I dare say, his view of my generation, is perhaps summed up in a poem he wrote:

It Might Have Been

Have you seen the cherry blossom?
Or did you just not care
And let the shimmering beauty
Pass by unaware.

You've gone each week to the Pictures
To breathe the Hollywood air,
Whilst the countryside in blossom-tide
Perfumed the sunset fair.

Well, still there's bloom on the apple;
Don't burrow like a mole,
On foot or bus or cycle
Get out man, air your soul.

Dorcas Mona

The third gene comes through Dorcas Mona, my maternal grand-mother, a Blackett from Wylam, Northumberland, known as 'Darly' to my generation. Everyone loved her; warm, caring and affectionate, she was the perfect partner and antidote to my respected but somewhat domineering grandfather. Darly was also a considerable artist and we still have many of her paintings.

Her family in earlier generations had been unambitious squires with agricultural interests, and royalties from an estate colliery. All that changed in 1800 when Christopher Blackett, Darly's grandfather, inherited the estate. An astute businessman, he ended the system of royalties at Wylam Colliery with its low but easy income and took direct control. In 1805 he appointed the twenty six year old William Hedley as Colliery Engineer, later promoting him to General Manager. Thus began a partnership destined to lead to developments of national and of international significance.

Most of their coal production was taken in horse drawn trucks for some five miles along an undulating track of wooden rails to the jetty at Lemington, outside Newcastle, and then by keels (barges) to ships at the mouth of the Tyne. Times were difficult for the colliery. Landowners along the route skimmed as much profit as they could in 'wayleave charges'. Hauling was costly because each couple of trucks with horse and driver could make only two journeys a day. At this time horses and feed were being diverted on a massive scale to Wellington's army on the continent. The cost of both rose to famine heights and the mine's profit, already weak, was slashed. An experiment using Highland cattle with iron boots was tried in 1811; they ate much less than horses but proved far too slow.

Both Christopher Blackett and William Hedley recognised that survival depended on finding some way to cut their transport costs. They had followed with keen interest various attempts to turn steam engines into locomotives. Back in 1804 Richard Trevithick, the Cornish inventor, had made a steam locomotive which, for a bet, had successfully pulled wagons of coal on the South Wales Pen-y-Daren tramway – once only, for its wheels, probably roughened or serrated, had broken up the track. The major problem was widely recognised, namely that attempting to pull a heavy load with smooth wheels on flat surface rails resulted in wheel spin. By 1812 Blenkinsop at Leeds had a locomotive with wheels which engaged a toothed rail – not surprisingly rails and wheels rapidly (and expensively) wore out.

It was then that William Hedley persuaded Christopher to carry out a series of practical experiments with changing weights to test his theory that there was a crossover point at which the traction power of a locomotive with smooth wheels, held down with the appropriate weight, would provide sufficient adhesion to pull loaded wagons. A track was laid in the grounds of Wylam Hall and experiments carried out in secret to determine the necessary weights for this 'crossover' point.

Christopher was persuaded. In 1813 he took out a patent in William Hedley's name and had instructed him, assisted by Timothy Hackworth,[3] the foreman blacksmith, to build a locomotive in the colliery workshop. The first one failed for lack of sufficient steam. The second locomotive, later known as 'Puffing Billy', and a further engine 'Wylam Dilly' both worked for many years successfully hauling twelve or fourteen, instead of two, loaded 'chauldron' coal trucks the five miles to the jetty in only one hour. This dramatic saving in transport costs saved the colliery, giving it an extended lease of life.

The village still remembers the tale of a seaman, returning one night after a year at sea, being terrified by the sight of one of the locomotives making a huge noise, glowing red with its firebox open and sparks flying out of the funnel. Running breathless across a field to a nearby cottage, the terrified man exclaimed, 'I have seen the devil'!

It was the inventive genius of William Hedley, coupled with the encouragement, investment and determination of old Christopher Blackett that gave the world its first commercially successful steam-hauled coal trains. Later George Stephenson 'the great improver' went on from this to develop the 'Rocket', which ushered in the golden age of steam-hauled passenger trains.

William Hedley's ingenuity was further displayed in 1822. That year a prolonged strike by the keelmen (bargees) held up all coal traffic on the Tyne. Hedley mounted 'Wylam Dilly' on a barge, fitted it with paddle wheels and, using it as a tug, pulled five barges some thirteen miles downriver carrying over twenty tons of coal apiece to waiting ships.[4] Afterwards, 'Wylam Dilly' returned to hauling on the colliery rail track.

Finally, in 1862, 'Puffing Billy' was sold by Christopher's grandson, after protracted negotiations, to the Patent Museum, now the

---

[3] Later a famous locomotive manufacturer.

[4] At one stage, furious strikers stoned these 'blackleg' bargees, and as a result a Marine or member of the Militia was posted on each barge. At that time, the following notice appeared in a Newcastle newspaper: 'The civil authorities regret to find deluded Keelmen still continue to insult His Majesties (*sic*) boats by throwing stones, when protecting those that are willing to work. Finding forbearance any longer will endanger the lives of those so employed. This is to caution the peaceable inhabitants and women and children to keep within their houses during the time the keels pass from Staithes to Shields as the Marines have orders *to fire on the first man that shall dare to throw a stone at them.*'

Puffing Billy: necessity, the mother of invention

Science Museum in South Kensington, for £200, where she can be seen to this day, as can 'Wylam Dilly' in the entrance hall of Edinburgh's National Museum of Scotland.

The first Christopher Blackett died in 1828, to be succeeded by his son, also Christopher. He had chosen the army as his career, serving as a Lieutenant in the 18th Hussars with Wellington in Spain, and was later promoted Captain. Near me, as I write, is the portrait of him in uniform which, his mother wrote, 'delighted her so much'.

Surviving family letters of this period provide some fascination. At one point, his mother wrote to him suggesting he leave the army and marry a certain rich heiress ('due to inherit seventy thousand pounds the day she marries') – 'But what consequence is this to us as she will be snap't up (*sic*) before you return' – 'affluence for the rest of your life'! Somewhat later, at the age of thirty, Christopher married Elizabeth, the highly strung younger daughter and co-heiress of Montagu and Elizabeth Burgoyne. (There are extant portraits by Romney of the bride's parents.)

At age forty one, Christopher inherited the Wylam estate and colliery, only to discover the full extent of a financial disaster which struck the family in his father's latter years. At the time of writing I have not yet been able to uncover the cause. Huge debts had been run up, in particular a loan of £5,000 (now, say, £250,000) due to the late Duke of Northumberland. I have copies of the remarkable correspondence which then ensued between the two sons. In October, 1836, Christopher writes to explain that he can now repay by instalments, and has that day sent a cheque for £500 to the Duke's account at Sir M. Ridley's Bank, a payment he plans to repeat annually. The next day the Duke replies that he is much surprised by this payment, that the loan was a private matter between their fathers and he trusts Christopher Blackett will allow him to return the cheque. Christopher refuses. The Duke writes of his regret and requests that all other debts have precedence over payments to him.

From a motivation which is unclear to me, Christopher had entered the House of Commons in 1830 as the Whig member for the 'Rotten Borough' of Beeralston in Devon. Nomination was within the gift of a Lord Barnsley. Christopher wrote in a letter to his wife, Elizabeth, that his election speech in the market place 'Was no great thing for I was in a horrible fright'. However, later under the influence of much 'burnt brandy' he decided he had spoken 'Damn well' and would be a popular MP. Popular or not, his only recorded contribution in that period was a plea during the debate on the Great Reform Act that Beeralston should remain a constituency on the clearly spurious grounds that it had an electorate of four thousand. Describing that debate in a letter to Elizabeth from Brooks's Club, Christopher writes 'I almost fainted when O'Connel looked towards where I sat and said that he did not address himself to . . . the simpering nominees of peers'!

After the abolition of the Beeralston seat, Christopher sought election for Newcastle, but was defeated by a Tory. In 1837 he was returned unopposed as Member for South Northumberland and served until he retired in 1841 and died six years later, aged fifty nine. During this time he made but two speeches.

Christopher comes across as a bluff, straightforward soldier; a man of great integrity but not particularly bright. His beloved Elizabeth died young in 1833, having borne him three sons and a daughter.

John Blackett

Their elder boy, 'the gifted' John Blackett, was twenty six when his father died in 1847. He had been educated at Harrow and Christchurch, Oxford, and was a Fellow of Merton College. He spent time on the fashionable 'Grand Tour' of Europe. On return, in 1842, he became a student member of Lincoln's Inn (as is this author) but he duly qualified for the Bar. He developed an intense interest in current political issues and wrote regularly for *The Globe* magazine (where he appears to have had a desk and a shareholding), and also for the influential *Edinburgh Review*. On one occasion, having listened to a eulogy by Disraeli following the death of Wellington, he recognised that whole passages had been plagiarised (without giving due credit) from an earlier tribute to Marshal St Cyr. The Editor had the two speeches printed in adjacent columns in *The Globe* – much to the embarrassment of Disraeli!

For some five years after coming into his inheritance, he devoted much of his time to the Wylam estate and its colliery. However, politics was in the genes and, in 1852, Newcastle Liberals saw his candidature as their best prospect of winning the parliamentary seat.

In the ensuing election he defeated the Tory, winning the seat with a larger number of votes than ever previously recorded for a candidate in Newcastle. He must have had double satisfaction in winning where his father had failed fifteen years earlier. There can be little doubt that a hugely successful Parliamentary career lay in prospect as he set up house at 10, Eaton Place, Westminster.

In his maiden speech he gave strong support to Free Trade, deriding those who avowed support but, when it came to the crunch, voted for protection. In scores of speeches in the ensuing four years he campaigned tirelessly for the underdog. This included asylum seekers from Poland and oppressed tenants of the East India Company in Madras amongst others. He supported extending the right to vote in Parliamentary elections. He was particularly incensed by the ban on Dissenters going to Oxford and, indeed, any university. (I have been shocked to discover that, at that time, only members of the Church of England were eligible for entry to universities.)

John was a regular participant in Budget debates and, in one memorable speech (which I enjoyed repeating in the House), he tendered his thanks to Gladstone as Chancellor for admitting that 'if the present income tax was not improvable, it was not endurable in its present shape and that, as it could not be improved, it must be abolished', the only question being one of time.

Alas, whilst four years earlier a glittering career lay in prospect, his health, which had never been particularly robust, deteriorated and, in January 1856, he applied for the Chiltern Hundreds (an MP's way of retiring prematurely) – worn out according to *The Times* by hard work (although, I suspect, more probably, by consumption). He left for the South of France, hoping to restore his health. Sadly it was not to be. He died in Villeneuve, near Chablis, on 25 April and was buried on 3 May at the local church of Ovingham near Wylam. The family erected a stained glass window in his memory, adjoining a similar window for his father. In one of the obituaries, others were urged to follow his example, for he had left 'footprints in the sands of time'. These have long since been blown away, but it seems the genes continue in our family.[5] Later still, a third window was to be added in the church for my grandmother Darly's only brother – killed leading his men in a charge during the Boer War. 'He tried to do his duty' – perhaps a fitting epitaph for the Blacketts of Wylam.

Grandfather Alfred Bower

The fourth gene comes through my maternal grandfather, born Alfred Louis Bower in 1858. The sixth of a large family, an old photograph shows him as tall, slim and alert, surrounded by four burly brothers. The family lived in Highbury where his father was variously described as a wine merchant and as a pub keeper. ALB, as Grandfather was known, traced his ancestry to one of the Norman knights who accompanied William the Conqueror. Part of the family settled near Dundee after participating in the Crusades.

Later the family became merchants and shipowners in Dundee. They owned neighbouring estates of Kinneatles and Kincaldrum near Forfar. Stout Roman Catholics and supporters of the Stuarts, they had been gun running from Spain and storing arms in anticipation of Bonnie Prince Charlie landing in Scotland. Both fought at Culloden. After that defeat, William Bower, my direct forebear, escaped to

---

[5] It is a quirk of genetic family history that the 1800s produced a father and his son following each other as members of Parliament, whilst in the 20th and 21st century this author and his son Andrew in part overlapped their time in the Commons.

England where he bought the small estate of Bowers Hill in Hampshire. His cousin, Alexander of Kincaldrum, was less fortunate. He returned home, living the life of a fugitive, hiding in the woods by day, only returning after dark for supper and sleep. His wife, Margaret (St Clair of Roslin) went on a mission to plead with the Duke of Cumberland for her husband's life, leaving her sister to keep house. Seeing how exhausted Alexander was, she allowed daybreak to come without waking him. Alas, to the dismay of all, a troop of soldiers from Hesse (imported by the Duke from Germany to hunt down rebels) had surrounded the house. He hid in a monk's hole. The soldiers asked his valet-cum-manservant where he was hidden. He denied the Laird was there. A rope over a tree branch round the terrified man's throat, suspending him briefly, had the desired effect. Dragged from his hiding place, Alexander Bower had his hair (grown long in the French fashion) tied to a horse's tail and was then dragged off towards Perth. When they reached Findrik Farm, the tenant offered all the money he could lay his hands on for Alexander to be put on the horse. Alas, he died shortly after being put in his cell in Perth jail. His wife, returning from her audience with Cumberland, learnt he was in prison and came to see him. The shock was such that she died of a seizure in the cell.

They were buried together in their Roman Catholic chapel on a lonely hillside above Easter Meathie Farm. Part of this sad story is recorded on a plaque in the now ruined chapel, also on a plaque in a hotel in Perth. When Easter Meathie was sold in 1760, this chapel was excluded from the sale and the land retained in the family with the right (subject to payment for damage to crops) of 'berying (sic) for the heirs and successors of Alexander Bower'.

Two generations after those events, Grandfather ALB, son of Edward Thomas Bower, was born in Highbury. Little is known of his early upbringing, but it seems he was bullied and had to fight for his corner amongst his brothers. As a young man he had a solid tyred 'penny farthing' boneshaker – the penny wheel being fifty five inches high. Indeed, at first he could barely reach the pedals and fell off many times. Cycling became an important part of his fixation with physical fitness. By the early 1880s he was eleven stone of bone and muscle and had turned to bicycle and tricycle racing. His most remarkable successes were achieved in 1887 on the cinder track at Crystal Palace. Here he broke the world tricycle records for one to fifty miles having covered eighteen miles in the first hour. It is interesting that he took refreshment in the form of sponge cake soaked in champagne!

His business career began as trainee with a firm of stockbrokers but, shortly after he started, they closed. He changed tack and entered the wine trade, becoming apprenticed in 1877 to City vintner Charles Cuff Shireff in his Ludgate Hill business. In 1879, in his early twenties, he started his own firm with a tasting room at 48 Mark Lane, also in the City. Bringing that same determination and energy as he had to cycling, he soon built up Bower and Co. into a highly successful business.

In April 1901 he married Dorcas Mona (Darly), daughter of Captain Edward Algernon Blackett (a younger brother of John Blackett MP). They set up home in 'The Grange', a large family sized house in Chislehurst, Kent. Subsequently they moved half a mile to a larger house named 'Churchill'. However, by that time Winston was out of favour, so ALB changed the name to 'Manor Place', a matter he no doubt regretted, later.

His career prospered in both the civic and business spheres. In 1912 he sought election as one of the two Sheriffs for the City. Taking no chances, he built up the largest set of election supporting committees hitherto known in the City. Indeed, to rub in the message, he attached a list of one thousand one hundred and twenty names to his election address and enclosed a postcard which he requested any further supporters to sign and return. He was duly elected. This single-minded sense of purpose well illustrated his choice of '*Ad Metam*' (To the Mark) as his family motto. In September 1913 as his year as a Sheriff drew to a close (following the usual custom) he was knighted.

1918 saw him elected Alderman for the Langbourn Ward of the City, thus being eligible to become Lord Mayor, but in 1923 the City Fathers let it be known, not if he was trading in the high street in his own name. Out went Bower and Co. and in came El Vino, a private limited company, using his registered sherry trade mark. A sorry commentary on the City's then attitude to trade. In 1924, he was elected Lord Mayor; as such he was made a Baronet, living for his year in the City's Mansion House. The circumstances were unique in that, for the first time since the Reformation, both the two Sheriffs and the Lord Mayor were Roman Catholics. Questions were asked as to whether he would attend services at C of E churches. He chose to have both an RC and a Protestant chaplain. He attended official functions in the 'established' church, but in his private life worshipped as a Roman Catholic.

Happily ALB remembered to invite to the Mansion House fellow old-time cyclists and members of the Amateur Athletes' Assocation of his youth. Interestingly, however generous the hospitality regularly served, he stuck to an evening diet of steamed fish, baked custard, dry toast and grapes. The *Daily Herald* newspaper commented on a 'Topsy turvy world when the Lord Mayor, head of this stronghold of the guzzlers, ate as aforesaid while guests all round him were busy digging their graves with their teeth'. Whenever the evening allowed, he followed a regime of walking from the Mansion House to Westminster Bridge and back, or similarly along the river. One tale of these evening perambulations is worth recalling. Apparently he walked down Martin Lane, off Cannon Street, checking the padlock (to an outsider somewhat suspicious) on the El Vino Old Wine Shades, then climbed up the steps on to Southwark Bridge. Standing there looking at the lights on the water, he was approached by a young constable who had followed him. He tapped Grandfather on the shoulder saying ' 'Ere – ain't you got a 'ome?'

'Yes' replied ALB 'and a nice one.'

The constable produced a notebook and pencil 'Address please . . .'

'The Mansion House.'

'Oh yes,' came the reply, 'and I suppose you are the blooming Lord Mayor – that's why you were thinking about chucking yourself in the river. Come along with me.' The Lord Mayor was led to Cloak Lane Police Station where, happily, the Superintendent recognised him . . .

ALB and his daughter – my mother

So much for ALB's public persona; more relevant to my tale is his relationship with my mother and the schism which kept them at arms' length. Mother, Mona Elizabeth Blackett Bower, born 1903, known as Betty or Betts, grew up in what she described as 'the semi Victorian atmosphere of an over-strict father, a repressed mother and a bevy of frightened servants'. Grandfather, a strict Roman Catholic, ensured his daughter's upbringing included church twice on Sunday (reading nothing but the bible in the morning). Being a high-spirited girl, she rebelled against this excess, starting a long-term rift with ALB which was exacerbated by her marriage – so much so that he never once came to 'Sundials', the house where I was brought up, although Darly came quite often.

Tall and athletic, my mother was a keen swimmer, rider and skier, mad about horses and dogs. Educated at Crofton Grange, Kent, a girls' boarding school, she became one of a group of friends which included my much-loved godmother-to-be, Margaret Spurrell ('Marg').

At age twenty, Betty fell madly in love with a distant cousin, Dick Blenkinsop, some fifteen years older than her, a salesman for Rover cars – to her an exciting man of the world, and definitely not the match her father had in mind. On one occasion when Dick came to lunch at Manor Place, she asked her mother if he could give her a lift to London. 'I can't give you permission; you know that, you must ask your father.' Permission is refused and, later that day, deposited by car at Chislehurst station, Betty goes through the front entrance down the underpass to the back exit where Dick is waiting in his car.

We are now in the year 1924, the year ALB becomes Lord Mayor. Darly agrees that if her daughter does not communicate with Dick for a year and at the end of it they both feel the same about each other, she would pacify an outraged father and support a marriage. Dick, who seems somewhat less committed, agrees. When the year ends, happy anticipation is blasted when her father secures a report from a private detective showing Dick's involvement with another woman. The inevitable dénouement follows, and Betty is taken off to Zermatt for a long holiday to forget it all. Many years later Margaret Spurrell described being in the ski-ing party when by chance Betty met up with Jim Mitchell again. Two years later they were married, in mother's case, on the rebound but how proud my father must have been to have carried off the former Lord Mayor's statuesque daughter whom he idolised. They were married in a registry office and set up home in (I believe) Leeds where Father's work with Simms had taken him.

Sometimes we all spent Christmas at Chislehurst and there were other occasional visits. I have a vivid memory of one such occasion; Mother and Father were in the car, Brother and I saying 'Goodbye' on the doorstep, and Grandfather holding out either a one or five pound note for each of us. I stammered out my thanks . . . 'But we are not allowed to accept money from strange men.' He replied that he was not a strange man, but our grandfather! Alas, I do not recall whether we took the money or not. Many years later, after Darly died, the stiff and formal nature of the relationship with him was again demonstrated in a letter I have by me: 'My dear David B. Mitchell, your grandfather wishes to express many happy returns of the day. Alfred L. Bower'.

I cannot date the occasion when ALB summoned my father to his office in Fleet Street and offered to pay for the entire education of my brother and myself. There was but one condition attached – that he would choose the schools. These would, of course, have been the top Roman Catholic schools in the country. My father thanked him, and refused. I sometimes speculate what difference it would have made if the offer had been accepted. Almost certainly university would have followed, and then what? – maybe ambition dulled in a satisfied feeling that the world owed me a living, instead of having to fight one's corner and prove oneself. Who knows?

In November 1948 Grandfather died from prostate cancer. It was generally understood that his Will provided that his Catholic nephew, Frank Bower (who ran the family business, of which more later) would be the main beneficiary. This expectation had been correct until June of that year. Then, for reasons unknown, Frank was cut out, Mother given a life interest and my brother and I at age twenty five, together with some trusts, came in as remaindermen.

Thereafter Mother divided Manor Place into flats, occupied the ground floor and kept the former cook's bedroom which became my bedsit when I moved there. I had written a pained letter of reproach when she left 'Sundials', taking some of the furniture.

Undoubtedly ALB had risen from humble beginnings to become relatively wealthy. However, Death Duty at 50 per cent halved the value of his estate and, on Mother's death six years later, the 40 per cent rate applied to the remainder. As a result, my brother and I came into an inheritance consisting principally of El Vino Company, weighed down with substantial borrowings. For several years repaying these debts pre-empted resources which would otherwise have been available for expansion.

(See Appendix I – Alfred Bower as Lord Mayor)

CHAPTER 2

Early life

Lack of self confidence leads me to choose market gardening
as career . . . / Member of TGWU / Participate in 1950 and
'51 Conservative election campaigns / Inherit part share in
El Vino, its wartime history, become trainee in 1951 /
Visit Portugal and Spain, learn how Port and Sherry are
made / Marriage to Pam, live in Bloomsbury, St Pancras
Borough Councillor / Parliamentary candidate St Pancras
North 1959 / Death of Father

MY EARLIEST MEMORIES ARE OF my white bearded grandpa Robert Mitchell holding me with one arm and gently swinging his silver pocket watch on its chain in front of me; also the sound of my father, first thing each morning, stropping his safety razor on a leather strap.

Sundials had a sitting room, dining room and nursery on the ground floor, three main bedrooms (one of which my brother Christopher, a year younger, and I shared) and two attic bedrooms. In our early years, the latter belonged to the cook housekeeper and various youngish ladies who looked after us two boys. I do not know if we were particularly difficult, but none of them lasted for long. I recall in particular a Margaret Tee who was particularly nice, and a German Margaret whom we hated – and on one occasion locked in the unlit airing cupboard until she promised not to punish us for so doing!

My parents were very different (the attraction of opposites?) – Father short and stocky, Mother tall and athletic. They played a lot of tennis, Mother rode and walked our two black 'flat coat' retrievers, Soot and Sweep. We played in a sandpit, built a tree house and a sequence of varied little hutments in the acre of garden. Long walks in the surrounding countryside were a regular feature. Mother had a healthy, no nonsense approach to our upbringing, including an early run round the garden and a baked bread rusk before breakfast. In my case, the rusks did not succeed in ensuring good teeth; I hated them and whenever I had the opportunity, hid them behind the sideboard

17

– until the mice drew this to parental attention. I do not recall the, no doubt appropriate, punishment. That must have depended on which parent made the discovery – for their approaches were in sharp contrast – from Mother, a leather dog collar on a bare bottom, from Father it was lines – 'I must not be rude to Ladies' – twenty five times. I still remember that one, and my lack of success in trying to hold two pencils and write two lines at the same time.

I think I was more sensitive than my brother. A cousin reminded me of the house rule that, if we did not eat our first course at lunch, there would be no pudding. She remembers an application of the rule when I burst into tears. Chris, being made of sterner stuff, simply stuck out his chin and said 'Anyway, I didn't want any'. This difference no doubt was also demonstrated when we were learning to swim and Mother, a strong swimmer, took each of us to the deep end of the local swimming pool on her back. I still remember the sheer terror this induced in me. One grows out of such things, but something indelible remains.

Mother had her own mare 'Lady' and we had a hired Welsh cob named 'Kitty'. I enjoyed riding enormously and at this time often went with Mother and a dog for long rides, from which there developed a closeness between us that my brother never really shared.

Our family summer holidays were often spent staying in farm-houses on the North Yorkshire moors around Goathland, near Whitby. This had been a holiday area which Father knew and loved from his younger days in Middlesbrough. Chris and I swam and fished at Whitby, hunted for fossils, dammed up and diverted moorland streams and had such free and happy times, the recollection of which still draws me back there.

We had just returned from Yorkshire, leaving the moors with their miles of purple heather – I was eleven, when Father called us into the sitting room to hear Neville Chamberlain announce that, if Hitler had not complied with an ultimatum by (I think it was) midday, our nation would be at war.

Father joined the LDV (Local Defence Volunteers), later to become the Home Guard, and moved rapidly up to Captain and then Major. Before long a lookout platform had been created up a tree further down the lane on which we lived. This was manned by a roster of Home Guard each night, watching for parachutists. Two rifles and ammo were stored in our locked outside broom cupboard with the key on a string, reachable inside the nearby scullery letterbox.

After a spell at pre-prep school we were sent as weekly boarders to two local schools. For me this was The Beacon at Chesham Bois and, for Chris, Beaumont House near Rickmansworth. At The Beacon, the school dining room occupied the basement. This also acted as an air raid shelter. At night, mattresses lined the floor and boarders slept there. I was supposed to have a weak chest, and Mother insisted I continue to sleep in an upstairs dormitory. One night a bomb fell, close enough to shake the building, some plaster fell and I shot under the bed. Headmaster Mr Fielding (irreverently known as 'Fieldmouse') came up with a torch to check I was OK. I thought little more of it. However, the Fieldmouse was so rattled by this event that Mother was instructed that either I slept with the other boarders, or I be removed.

Shortly after this, in October 1941, I joined Chris at Beaumont House, a larger school with more facilities, including a theatre and a boxing ring. On one occasion I recall that Chris and I were drawn to box each other. The fight was stopped on the grounds that we were not hitting hard enough. Two lasting memories were the joy of Sunday evenings when Mr Veazey, the Headmaster, read Kipling to the boarders. Secondly, the evening before I took the Common Entrance exam, he called me to his study and said that I had not, as yet, learned about decimals and there might be a question in the Maths paper so – then and there – he explained them to me.

It was about this time that Mother, now generally called 'Bear', became increasingly unwell, although no-one seemed to recognise why. Eventually she was diagnosed as having a form of multiple sclerosis, leading to a failure of muscular function. Bear walked with a stick and it helped her to have me lift one foot up each step of the bedroom staircase. One consequence of her illness was that during most school holidays either my brother or I (the least useful at home I suspect), was sent away. I think this applied more often to me than to Chris.

I enjoyed hugely being sent to Margaret Spurrell, my godmother and a friend of Mother since school days. She was unmarried – a bluff, no-nonsense, very capable woman; she had had a pilot's licence (then rare for a woman). She had travelled widely and been a friend, amongst others, of Glubb Pasha, the British officer running the

Jordanian army. When I stayed, she always had time for me; doing things together with her were happy times.

I was also sent as a paying guest to stay with a wonderful scout mistress at Pinkneys Green, near Maidenhead. It was here that I met Charlotte who shared my bed and engendered a life-long love . . . of Siamese cats.

In those days, there was no TV. For entertainment we went to the 'flicks', as the cinema was then known; my favourites were *Dear Octopus, South Riding, My friend Flicka, Keys of the Kingdom, The Master of Bankdam, This Happy Breed* and *Wings of the Morning* – the latter with 'real' actors – Steve Donoghue, the champion jockey, John McCormack, the wonderful Irish tenor and Dame Flora Robson.

At 'Sundials' we rarely met up with other boys. At prep school and then at Aldenham (a good but lesser public school) I tended to be a bit of a loner. Being allowed a small plot of garden at school was an enjoyable escape. As a shy and lanky boy who had outgrown his strength I was, at first, a good target for the house bully. A stop was put to that when, a term or two later Ron Pont, a friend, arrived from my prep school (more of him anon). I was not a particularly bright pupil and was put in a form derisively called 'the Army class' – so everyone, including me, was surprised when (at the second attempt), I passed School Cert. in 1944 with one pass and five credits.

One or two events stick in my memory, such as Hitler's pilotless bombers known as 'doodlebugs' – which had engines with a peculiar and easily recognisable 'rmp, rmp' noise. When the noise stopped, the whole dormitory held its breath as the pilotless plane either dived or, more often, glided some miles further, before hitting the ground and exploding.

On wet days we would be sent out in a long 'crocodile' walk for five or six miles. Sometimes the crocodile elongated so that no-one else was in sight. Another boy and I were in such a position, cold and wet, when the local Carter Paterson carrier stopped and asked if we would like a lift. An impudent impulsiveness in my character jumped to the fore. Alas, we did not stop until the driver (so helpfully!) put us off at the school gates – and into the arms of one of the staff. I forget how many times we had to re-walk that route as punishment. Nor do I recall the various offences for which learning passages of Shakespeare was considered the appropriate punishment so, uncultured though I am, I can still surprise friends with Hamlet's address to his father's ghost, and similar passages.

My school reports were not brilliant; I recall my French one, curiously taught by a Mr English, which read 'His efforts are paralytic, he makes little progress' and in class – 'God moves in mysterious ways, His wonders to perform – and your mind, Mitchell, is one of them'. I saw no point in applying myself to French for I had already decided that market gardening would be my probable career. Not in my wildest dreams did becoming a buyer of French wines nor, needless to say, negotiations with a French Minister on the Channel Tunnel appear on the horizon.

I have no recollection of any careers advice on leaving Aldenham, nor was the idea of me going to University encouraged. For a boy, often accused at home of 'arguing the hind leg off a donkey', becoming a barrister should have been shortlisted. Many years later an announcement that a University Degree would shortly be required of all applicants hastened me to become a Student Member of Lincoln's Inn. I reckon I must be their oldest such member!

I left Aldenham in April 1945, aged sixteen, and promptly started work as one of a number of trainees with F.A. Secrett, one of – if not at that time, *the* leading vegetable supplier to London's Covent Garden Market. The firm was at Hersham, close to Walton-on-Thames. My first pay packet was one pound, six shillings and sevenpence, less threepence for the Hospital Savings Association and, I think, sixpence for some form of National Insurance or Tax. My father's dismal foreboding that I would be 'returned empty' within a fortnight did little for my self confidence.

On 16 August 1945 my diary records the celebrations marking the end of the War (in Europe). En route to Hersham, I travelled by train from home to London and joined the crowds hugging and dancing in Trafalgar Square and then an hour of pushing and shoving in the rain down the Mall to press my face to the railings of Buckingham Palace. Suddenly the balcony doors opened and the mackintoshed figures of King George, Queen Elizabeth and the Princesses Elizabeth and Margaret appeared. Up went a joyous and *deafening* cheer.

I had digs in a small boarding house close to Secrets. Up at 6 a.m. for a seven o'clock start, the four years I spent there were to see many changes in me. I improved my 'digs' three times. Eventually I lodged in a small, two-bedroomed, house with a kind, elderly farmer's

Christopher and David

widow who wanted company. We had gas lighting downstairs and a candle upstairs – she did not need one herself because, she explained, she 'Had the Parish lantern' – i.e. a streetlight which shone into the front bedroom. There was no bathroom, only a tin bath hanging on the kitchen wall, filled from a bucket heated on the gas stove. She was a kind and caring woman who seemed to like mothering this young man.

F.A. Secrett was shrewd and farsighted. He started market gardening at Marsh Farm, Twickenham, which later he sold for building development. At Hersham, Walton-on-Thames, there were three parts to his current market garden – the terreau, the greenhouses and the main fields. On the latter, horses were still used for cultivating, as they impacted the soil less than a tractor. I became reasonably competent at ploughing, harrowing etc.

The most interesting part of this Bell Farm was the Dutch lights (a single pane of glass with wooden frame) over 'terreau'. When the Huguenots fled from religious persecution in France, they brought with them a multitude of skills. Many of those who worked in the Paris gardens settled in the Thames Valley – and had names such as Poupart and Lobjoit. One of the skills they brought was terreau – a system using fresh steaming stable manure under decayed manure from earlier years to heat a frame. This immensely rich soil enabled three crops to grow together at the same time – carrot seeds, cauliflower and lettuce plants. The latter were marketed first, from under the cauliflower which stood well above them – they came next, and finally the carrots. Because of the warmth, we had English spring produce virtually before anyone else. I must try it again myself!

One tale of Secrett's Marsh Farm days is worth recalling. The produce was sent to Covent Garden by horse-drawn wagons with the driver seated in front of the load and half above the horse. The horse knew the way, and drivers habitually went to sleep. Because of the danger of entangled wheels as carts neared central London, the police used to stand at the top of the slope to Hyde Park Corner, with a rope to whack the drivers across the knees to waken them. Alas, one of our drivers, in spite of warnings, went back to sleep once too often; the police quietly turned the horse round so that it arrived back in the yard about 7 a.m. The driver was, understandably, sacked. Some months later he stood at the end of a field morosely watching his former colleagues at work, when FA came over and said 'Stop standing around with your hands in your pockets – get in there and get some work done!'

Horse manure was a vital input to Bell Farm, both for the terreau and, when well rotted, for muck-spreading on the fields. The arrangement was that a lorry driver, accompanied by one of the roster of trainees, would leave at 3.30 a.m. for Covent Garden market. After unloading, there was a fifteen minute break allowed for hot chocolate and a doughnut at a stall in the market. Then away to load with horse manure from stables at an Army barracks, or Windsor Castle or Buckingham Palace. It was to be some twenty two years later that I was privileged to be a lunch guest at the Palace! How that transformation came about inevitably fills many of the ensuing pages.

I vividly remember at about age eighteen, worrying about time spent to little purpose, I then made a resolution that instead of drifting agreeably from day to day, I would programme myself to have some achievement to show at the end of *each* day. I attended evening classes at Woking Technical College on farming and horticulture, and passed the RHS Certificate examinations. Next, much aware of my own ignorance, I undertook a postal study course on Economics which I found hard-going but fascinating. It served me well in later life. It has to be said that the life of a market garden trainee was no doubt healthy, but hardly mentally stimulating. My lack of self confidence had taken me into a career which would never, for me, be all absorbing.

Stirrings of political interest

I have no knowledge of my parents' political persuasion, if any. I joined the Young Conservatives originally for their social programme, but the postwar Labour government disappointed the expectations of a nation which had 'won the war'. Our younger generation expected better than the dull uniformity of utility, austerity, rationing (mainly for financial reasons) of clothing, food – including potatoes – and even soap! Already continental countries were managing with little or no rationing. I admit it must have been an act of faith to believe that a change of government would boost our quality of life. 1946 marks my first diary entry showing a direct interest in current affairs. During that January I listened to a debate in the Commons on food with Jennie Lee (Aneurin Bevan's wife) speaking. I began to have letters published in the local paper, critical of Labour government policies. Before long our YC branch published its own five page magazine *The Realist*; the title page pompously read 'The Official Journal of the Hersham Young Conservatives' – Editor, Mr Barron Terry, the two Sub Editors, and then 'General Factotum and Slave-driver' Mr David B. Mitchell. Hmph! I organised a recruiting drive for our Branch. We had a thousand leaflets printed for £4.50 and secured three new members: Pam Haward, her sister Ann, and a friend of theirs. It was to be seven years later that Pam and I married.

Our YC branch had a varied programme. One entertainer, Dave Stewart, was a hypnotist. Nearly half of those who volunteered were successfully hypnotised – I was not (it was explained that the more intelligent with good concentration were the most susceptible!). The hypnotist, holding a silver coin, told the subjects to concentrate deeply on it; as he talked they gradually became hypnotised. Then he told them it was hot and they could remove their jackets if they wished. The hypnotist turned these jackets inside out, and invited his subjects to put them on again, saying that they would only become aware their jackets were awry when he ended their post hypnotic trance by making a particular tapping noise. The subjects were then 'counted out' – returned to seeming normality – only to feel rather silly after hearing the tapping and realising they were wearing their jackets inside out.

The next day, in the greenhouse, I invited a volunteer for me to hypnotise. Peter White, a younger trainee offered. I followed the exact routine of the previous night. To my surprise it worked; then I became terrified I would be unable to 'count him out'. Fortunately all was well, but the following day he told me his parents had forbidden him to be involved ever again, and had suggested neither should I; an unnecessary warning, such had been my fright.

In 1946 I had joined the Walton-on-Thames Sea Cadets and, on registering for National Service, opted for the Navy – only to be failed for my eyesight. Not long after this disappointment, F.A. Secrett applied en bloc for deferment of his trainees since Agri/ Horticulture were classed as an essential occupation. At the time I saw no reason to regret this. Subsequently I have realised that I should have objected. The services would have made a man of me much earlier and hugely broadened my horizons.

In 1947 I represented Hersham YCs on the Constituency governing council and (since I still have a typed-up draft of the resolution) I must have played some part in a younger members' drive to force the sitting MP (Commander Marsden) to announce his intention to retire at the following election and, 'if he did not do so, a special meeting be called before the following February (1948)'.

1948 saw the Croydon by-election, a three cornered fight in a Labour held seat. The YCs turned out in strength, with a march in support of the Tory candidate. Winning back this seat was to be the first step towards recovery after the defeat of 1945. The Liberals put up the charismatic 'Pathfinder' Bennett, famous for dropping the flares to guide our bombers to their targets deep into Germany. My most vivid recollection was attending one of Bennett's meetings, addressed by Dingle Foot, then a Liberal (later Labour's Solicitor General). He came to the front of the platform, rubbing his hands together as if washing them, waited for the applause to die down, then 'My friends, what has the Liberal Party to offer?' – a YC voice rang out '£150 deposit' – a piquant moment! How I wish I had been present at another meeting where the speaker started 'I ask myself this question . . .' . . . Heckler 'and a damn fool answer you'll get!' Alas, such cut and thrust at meetings is now rare.

That summer I had become Chairman of Hersham YCs. Pam joined the Committee which sometimes met at her home. (I recall her doing cartwheels on the lawn before a meeting.) There was a YC weekend conference at Bognor, followed by a dance, and later Pam and I walked miles along the beach in the moonlight. 'Perfect peace and happiness' my diary records although, a week later, I was worrying whether I was unfairly 'leading her on'.

Our YC branch must have made something of a splash, for the local paper records us joining with the Walton-on-Thames branch to run a 'Country Fair' which attracted 'more than a thousand people'. Perhaps the reporter had double vision. I was just beginning to learn how to enthuse others and organise a team of support.

Later that year, I secured a job as a trainee with a mushroom grower near Faversham in Kent; it was an interesting specialisation. I lodged in a council house with kindly Mrs James and her husband, Dowie. While there I applied to join the Agricultural Workers' Union (as a Conservative, I believed every employee should join their appropriate union, not least to keep it out of the hands of militant minorities). I received a reply that, under a zoning agreement, I would instead become a member of the T&GWU. Soon after, I applied for and secured a short course scholarship to the union summer school held near Carlisle. It was a riveting experience. I can still remember Tim O'Leary, the National Docks Officer (I think that was his correct title) lamming into the group, particularly the docker Shop Stewards, for undermining agreements made through the union, for example by calling lightning strikes for extra money just when only the tail end of a ship's cargo remained to be unloaded. On our last evening we were invited to try our hand at a short speech, fairly light hearted, on a subject of our choice. For reasons I cannot now imagine, I did my four minutes on the ridiculous subject of 'The case for the banishment of bus stops'! Do not dismiss too lightly – see section on Bus Deregulation, Department of Transport. [page 203] Later, I received payment for the cost of a train ticket to Carlisle. I replied that since I had gone on my motorcycle I was due considerably less, but was told that it was a standard arrangement and I should keep the money. Surely this makes me the only Tory MP to have made a profit out of the T&GWU!

1949 saw me apply successfully to the NFU for a place as an exchange student in Holland.

An exchange student in the Netherlands and an attack of election fever

In December I took ship from Harwich to the Hook, then train to Tiel and thence to Ophemert after a little local difficulty, since no-one had heard of 'Offemert' as I had pronounced my destination. The village is dominated by its moated castle. I was to work on its extensive fruit orchards. My accommodation was over the former coach house and I was to eat with the castle gardener and his family. My welcoming supper was a large soup plate of potato and red cabbage, hollowed out in the middle and filled with hot liquid fat – Ugh!! In the village, only the Burgomaster's wife spoke English. Van Lith, the estate manager, had as little school French as I had, but it sufficed. It was the pruning season, pretty tedious, but I learned the language and how to walk in clogs – an essential skill since the icy cold of the ground went straight through the leather soles of my Mother's ski boots. Christmas was lonely and I felt sorry for myself, particularly about no letter from Pam, although I had a clutch of presents from her, including knitted mittens.

The Dutch were then a deeply religious society. Many villages were either Catholic or Protestant, distinguishable because the Catholic village church displayed a cross whilst the Protestant one did not. A Catholic village businessman rarely employed a Protestant, and vice versa. For the first time I became aware of religious hostility. I had not encountered this divisive culture before, and did not do so again until I served in Northern Ireland.

During 1950 I was moved to work on a market garden at Barendrecht near Rotterdam. Fortunately I was able to time and space the change to coincide with the 1950 General Election. I went to Rotterdam docks and bought a passage on the *Greenfinch* – a cargo boat which docked at St Katharine's dock below Tower Bridge. I had asked the South East area of Conservative Central Office where I could be of most use. Good fortune followed, for they sent me to Merton and Morden. The former Wimbledon constituency had been divided in two; the sitting Member, Arthur Palmer, had chosen this southern, for him, safer, part – to which had been added the St Helier council housing estate, making it secure for Labour. Our candidate was Bob Ryder, the agent Ernie Sorrie. I lodged with a branch Chairman and his wife, and joined the candidate's 'circus' – i.e. the team which went canvassing with him until late afternoon. One evening I went to help with a street-corner meeting, and took a turn on the 'soapbox'. I think our audience numbers peaked at eleven — however it was reported back that I could cope.

Two or three of us were then let loose with a loud hailer on a pub forecourt opposite Morden's terminal tube station. This was the spot where huge numbers of commuters queued nightly for buses to complete their journeys to St Helier and neighbouring areas. Our job was to collect an audience which Bob would address at about 6.30 p.m. Provided one was sufficiently provocative, the odd heckler would turn up, and the ensuing shouting match soon collected a crowd on our side of the street. Nightly audiences of fifty plus were delivered to the candidate, building up as we neared polling day. Two evenings before Polling Day (21 February 1950) the Labour Party 'pinched' our site so, at 9.30 next morning, David Williams and I occupied the forecourt, starting a meeting at 11 a.m. and taking it in turns, finishing at 9 p.m. I spoke last, introducing Bob when (according to the Police) we had a crowd of six hundred and fifty. Bob Ryder was well pleased with these meetings, except once, early on, when I introduced him as 'Red Ryder, VC — the hero of the St Nazaire raid'.[1] At next morning's briefing I was given a thunderous rocket! Bob won the seat after an exciting count. I have a super handwritten letter from him (1950) with an accompanying copy of his book about the raid.

Later that year I applied to join the Central Office candidates' list, only to be told that with seven hundred already on the list, I could not be interviewed until after the next (1951) General Election.

---

[1] St Nazaire near the mouth of the Loire had the only dry dock big enough to service the German battleships sinking Allied shipping in the Atlantic. Knocking it out would (if it could be done) be a serious blow to the German ability to keep these raiders at sea. Ryder was given the job of sabotaging it. The *Campbelltown*, her bows below the waterline stuffed with explosives, with an escort of smaller vessels, set off up the Loire. Ryder and his crew with some deceptive flag signals got close to St Nazaire before discovery. The lock gates were duly rammed, by which time all hell was let loose, mainly from a machine gun nest on the jetty from which a shore-going group were due to evacuate. (They were captured next morning.) The boats in which Ryder and his crew were to escape were raked with fire, but at least they got away.

Alas, all this was seemingly to no avail. The *Campbelltown* had not blown up! The dock gates were repairable. German propagandists flooded Europe and the neutral countries with photographs of this débâcle. They even held a celebratory reception on board two days later, in the middle of which, with devastating effect, the *Campbelltown* did indeed blow up.

I returned to the Netherlands, taking my motorbike with me. I then had a lot of enjoyment taking a tent and exploring round the country at weekends, sometimes with a Dutch colleague. Once we visited the 'Kinderdyk' at Ablassadam on a bend in the Rhine. There was still a string of working windmills there. Many, many years before, an upstream flood had washed a cradle containing a baby and a cat into the fast running river, as the cradle tipped perilously one way and then the other, the cat moved swiftly back and forth to redress the balance until, happily, it drifted safely ashore on this bend, giving it the name.

Another weekend we hoped to pitch our tent in a field alongside a house overlooking the Rhine. On asking the occupant if we could camp the night, I was somewhat embarrassed to receive not only consent but also an invitation to join them for supper. The time was some five years after British forces had liberated the Netherlands, this was a bit more than typical of the generous welcome I received everywhere. Supper over, we were invited to stay the night. They had already been generous enough to two strangers, so I thanked them and politely declined. I have never forgotten (nor heard since) the telling response 'You have watered the wine of our hospitality'.

I returned to England at the end of my stint in the Netherlands with a huge respect for the hard working and kindly Dutch people. At times I had found it very lonely, for I am a gregarious animal. At first it had been difficult making friends because of the language barrier but by the end I was reasonably fluent. With plenty of time for reading, I had taken in a lot of history (the *History Today* magazine was a favourite) and the *Economist* from time to time, also revisiting my economics course. I reckoned I had learnt a lot about Dutch methods which would put me ahead in seeking a management job. So it did, for I secured a job as Deputy Manager of a north London market garden and worked there for some months.

With time to myself I learned eagerly some of the modern history I had missed at school, needless to say including the differing strands inherent in the Conservative Party. Disraeli with the one nation concept, deploring the gulf between rich and poor, along with Shaftesbury protecting workers' safety in the Factory Acts. I was intrigued by Joe Chamberlain as he campaigned for Free Trade within the British Empire. The same theme recurred in Stanley Baldwin's election campaign of 1923. Indeed, it played no small part in the Party's defeat that year which ushered in the first minority Labour government (sustained by the Liberals). The manifesto for the Election of 1924 played down that concept and Baldwin returned to office. The one nation theme originating with Disraeli reappeared in Baldwin's healing influence and conciliatory approach to the General Strike of 1926.

In 1929 there followed the second Labour government (again led by Ramsay Macdonald and sustained by the Liberals). This was the depths of the Depression; by 1931 unemployment had doubled, the government dithered unable to decide what to do. The Liberals withdrew their support, precipitating the 1931 General Election with employment, or rather unemployment, being the dominant theme. The Tories campaigned with a poster showing a queue of unemployed men with the slogan 'Vote Tory and get him a job'. There followed a landslide Conservative victory (only fifty two Labour MPs returned).

Although Baldwin preferred to support Ramsay Macdonald leading a National Government, it was clear that he (Baldwin) steered the ship of state. The opportunity was seized to implement his strategy on Empire Trade, resulting in the 1932 Ottawa Trade Agreement for Imperial Preference. The ensuing recovery in both trade and jobs enabled the Conservatives to fight and win the 1935 election – interestingly using the same poster, but with the slogan changed to 'Vote Tory and help him keep his job'.

All of this impacted on my own political thinking and I came back to Britain a keen supporter of Empire Free Trade with this a frequent theme when speaking to Young Conservative branches (it might now be described as an Empire Common Market). Of course, other political issues were taken up as the caravan of politics rolled on; before long, it was defence, particularly the dangers posed by CND (Campaign for Nuclear Disarmament). Central Office Speakers' Department put me in to bat at a CND public debate in Clapham. With about a hundred present, it became clear that the odds were stacked against me by a hundred to one. Closing a rowdy meeting, the Chairman thanked me, adding that it had not been the intention to use me as a punch bag! Politics, however varied, was becoming a consuming passion.

For the 1951 General Election I helped mainly in support of Pat Hornsby-Smith, the charismatic redhead Tory candidate and MP for

Chislehurst. One Saturday afternoon I was to work up an audience for her in the Sidcup car park. To collect a crowd and to bring on the genuine hecklers, I asked a Chislehurst YC, Tom Watkins, to start the heckling. At the time Tom had a red scar on his forehead. This, combined with a dirty old mac, gave him a thoroughly down-market appearance. In addition, his heckling was pretty aggressive. I passed the meeting on to another speaker and left. On my way to my car an elderly man stopped me and said wearily 'You know we'll never have any real peace and quietude in this country as long as there are jaundiced chaps around like that fellow with the scar'. I just managed to keep a straight face!

I was also drafted in as a support speaker one evening in Dartford. Our candidate was Margaret Roberts. After the meeting, her fiancé, Denis Thatcher, took the organiser and speakers off for refreshment. I recall him saying 'If you can hear the woman you love making the same speech twenty one times and you still love her, it's going to be all right.' (I am not certain of these final words). All right it certainly was!

El Vino: watering hole of the press

In 1952 after some months in the north London market garden, my father suggested that, since my brother and I would eventually become the majority shareholders in El Vino Co. Ltd, my late grandfather's wine firm, I, as the elder, should now work in the business for a year to learn what it was all about. This was arranged with a directive that I was to be treated the same as any other trainee. I moved from lodgings to live with my now severely disabled mother in Chislehurst, Kent, and became a commuter.

I found myself in a remarkable and, in many ways unique, wine business. It had been started by ALB in 1879 with a tasting room in Mark Lane in the City, supplying City institutions and 'gentlemen of substance'. It was largely financed on borrowed money in the form of Promissory Notes which had to be repaid within six months, with severe penalties if not. ALB had a superb palate; he imported wine from France and Germany, but the main turnover in those days was Sherry. After a time he found that customers tended to cluster in the late afternoon and gossip, instead of serious tasting. He then charged for sampling after half past three in the afternoon. So started the concept of a tasting house cum wine bar. The business prospered with branches opening in Martin Lane in 1900, in Fleet Street, near where the *Telegraph* subsequently had offices, moving in 1913 to its present site at 47 Fleet Street. Other branches followed in Gutter Lane in the City and a much bigger operation in Piccadilly Place in the West End.

In Fleet Street, ALB exercised his right as a member of the Vintners' Livery Company to sell wine (only) without holding a relatively expensive Justices' Licence. This ancient 'Vinters' Privilege' had been granted under Royal Charter by James I in 1611. Alas, this harmless but time-hallowed custom was largely abolished by the Labour government of 2003, with iconoclastic disregard for the preservation of history and tradition.

In 1951 the scars of wartime bombing were ever present; we stacked our empty bottles on a derelict plot adjacent to our back wall. I have in my hand a photo taken in October 1940 showing 47 Fleet Street boarded up and roped off, with a couple of large notices 'Danger unexploded bomb'. Time bombs had fallen in Crane Court and Serjeants Inn behind us on the 18 October and were defused by the 25th.

History records that early that November saw the first night not interrupted by air raids for fifty seven days. However, the last Sunday of 1940 saw the Luftwaffe's threat to create a second 'Great Fire of London'. Literally hundreds of incendiary bombs were dropped in the Fleet Street area. Sadly, St Bride's Church, spiritual home of so many journalists and their memorials, was gutted.[2] January 1941 saw a direct hit high explosive bomb blow up Mitre Court immediately behind No. 47 and, in May, the lovely Georgian houses of Serjeants Inn were wiped out.

Frank Bower, my grandfather's nephew, by then MD of the Company, had been one of the City ARP fire watch. He recalled for me standing on the outer gallery of the dome of St Paul's, seeing incendiaries bounce off the concrete roof of Vintners' Hall where many years later I was to become Master.

He did not see the incendiaries which destroyed all the buildings between El Vino's Old Wine Shades in Martin Lane off Cannon

---

[2] The official list of bomb-damaged London newspaper offices included those of *The Times*, *Sketch*, *Herald*, *Mail*, *Mirror*, *Daily Worker* and *Evening Standard*.

Street and the Thames. However the Manager there recalled for me that for three days fire burnt in the coal cellar adjacent to our party wall 'hot enough to boil an egg' on our side. It was a near miracle that this building survived. We were less fortunate with our largest branch in the West End's Piccadilly Place. This was so severely damaged, it never re-opened. Likewise, our branch in Gutter Lane changed overnight from active trading to a deep hole in the ground. Later its licence was transferred to Fleet Street, enabling the sale there of spirits as well as wine. With the war, the importing business died away and the company concentrated on the wine bar operations. 'The Old Wine Shades' is a uniquely interesting building, being the oldest wine house in the City. However, it was in 47 Fleet Street that the Company was to become famous under the direction of Frank Bower.

My training started with working in these two surviving branches; the hours were 9 a.m. to 8 p.m. two or three nights a week, with a 5 p.m. finish the other nights, and Saturdays finishing at 3 p.m. I have always had an unsteady hand. As I nervously poured a whisky the first time, the customer commented 'I think you need this more than me'.

The Wine Trade lectures at Vintners' Hall were particularly useful in teaching me about wine and how it was produced and shipped. This aspect gradually resumed its prewar prominence in the firm's activity. In September 1952 I was sent to visit suppliers in Portugal and Spain and to learn about the making of Port and Sherry. It was an interesting journey: train and ferry to Paris, then through Bordeaux to Irun on the frontier, arriving somewhere north of Madrid in the early hours of the morning. The train was late. I just made the connection for Portugal, only because a fellow passenger told me to follow him. As the train stopped he jumped out on to the track, not the platform, and climbed into the neighbouring train, which promptly started. A very worried me breathed a sigh of relief when a fellow passenger assured me it was, indeed, bound for Portugal.

It was a strange journey. There were soldiers with rifles mounting guard on the tail coach. We stopped for breakfast and lunch. The eventual arrival at the Portuguese frontier was a shambles. The through coach was uncoupled and, having missed the 'rapide' was finally attached to the water train which stopped to water the flowers on every halt, arriving six hours late at 1 a.m. in Oporto. No hotel booked, but a kindly priest led me to one. Next morning I crossed the Douro on the two deck harbour bridge to Vila Nova de Gaia, and met up with Gilbert Eastaugh of Martinez Port who took me up the Douro and explained how interestingly different Port is from other fortified wines. This, I discovered, is because the fermentation of the grape (the process of turning sugar into alcohol) is stopped by adding brandy. This provides most of the alcohol, leaving the natural sugar still in the wine; truly bottled sunshine! I also visited Cockburn, El Vino's oldest Port supplier.[3]

After four hectic days I left by train for Lisbon. The route passed along the famous Wellington defensive lines of Torres Vedras. After crossing Lisbon harbour, and a lengthy journey via Seville, I arrived in Jerez de la Frontera (so named from its historic position on the border between the warring Christian and Moorish occupiers of Southern Spain). The Hotel du Commerce proved adequate and I identified Los Cignes for the future, when I hoped to be better off.

Now I was in the heart of the Sherry trade. Our two suppliers were Garvey and Cuvillo, both old and respected Houses, the former run by charming upper-crust gentlemen, and the latter by working family directors. I was well entertained and taken to the Fiesta by the first, and learned the basics of Sherry making from the second. On each visit I was struck by the cathedral-like bodegas with their tall, slender arches, each filled with row upon row of casks piled four or five high, the bottom layer 'Solera' (or soil) casks giving their name to the (almost) unique system for making Sherry.

In contrast to Port, Sherry is fully fermented so there is virtually no sugar left. After the wine making comes the real skill when gifted and experienced tasters[4] determine, mainly on the nose, whether this raw material is to become an Oloroso, Fino or Amontillado.

Although all three types start out as a pale, white wine, a cask filled to the bung will gradually become darker in colour, almost

---

[3] Oldest they were, but not continuous. On one occasion in ALB's time a hogshead (a cask) was damaged whilst being unloaded from the horse drawn delivery van. A gallon was lost. Cockburn refused to reduce the bill. ALB closed the account. Some years later, Wyndham Fletcher, then an enthusiastic young salesman for Cockburn called, and was told we did not do business with his firm, and why. Having discovered from ALB that three shillings was the amount involved, he fished in his pocket, put it on the desk and asked if he could have the account back – and got it. Many years later I learned the story from Wyndham, a senior and much respected figure in the wine trade.

[4] These often come from succeeding generations in a family who have inherited a palate sensitive enough to detect minor variations of flavour.

mahogany, with a powerful aroma and a tremendous depth of flavour. This is *Oloroso*, dry in its natural state, but coming from it there are sweeter variations, including Cream Sherries which are made by adding wine from grapes dried on rush mats in the sun until they resemble sultanas.

By contrast if the cask is not filled completely, but left with a significant air space, the wine develops in a dramatically different way. Gradually a layer two to three centimetres thick of living yeast (flor) forms and floats across the top of the wine. This prevents the normal ageing process with the wine remaining pale, crisp and dry. There you have a *Fino*. A *Manzanilla* is simply a Fino from grapes grown near the sea where the wind ensures the vines ingest enough salt to produce the characteristic slight tang of this Sherry. If, having produced a Fino, the flor is removed and the cask filled up, it will start to develop as does an Oloroso. This cask-aged Fino is *Amontillado*.

When ready for bottling, only a third is drawn out from each Solera cask, annually. This is then replenished from the cask above and so it continues, in turn, until the casks of new wine are reached to begin their 'education'. This system produces a uniformity of age and style, eliminating the variation of each harvest. Hence Sherry, unlike much Port, does not have a vintage. Inevitably the summer heat causes high evaporation to rise from the casks, approximately 2 per cent – this is known as 'the angels' share'. The workers' share used to be a free half bottle a day.

Down from the hilltops of Jerez to the sea at Puerto de Santa Maria, I spent time with the Osborne business, learning and tasting. Later I was taken along the coast to Fuente Bravia to a wonderful open fronted restaurant looking out across the bay[5] to Cadiz. A lot of ground covered in just over a fortnight, enormously worthwhile for me and, I hope, interesting to my readers.

Local politics

It was about this time I acquired 'Bessie', a 1932 Austin 'beetleback', a two-seater semi sports car, a great joy, later replaced with 'Boanergees' a 1935 Rover with that engineering triumph known as

---

[5] The bay where Drake 'singed the King of Spain's beard' with a west wind sending his fire ships in to destroy the Spanish fleet.

a ratchet freewheel.[6] My free time was now increasingly given over to Young Conservative activities. Chislehurst's prominent water tower on the road to the station had accommodation below it. Putting up a poster one night, I fell with a loud clatter; a window opened and an elderly lady wearing a nightcap enquired what was I doing –

'Putting up a poster . . .'

'Why not do it in daylight young man?' she asked.

' 'Cos I would look ridiculous climbing up here.'

'And what do you think you look now?' she said, shutting the window. My pocket diaries reveal a frenetic round of meetings partly for the Central Office Area Speakers' Panel, and in part in places where I was known through my earlier membership of Amersham YCs, my spell in North London and, now, my time in Chislehurst. In 1952 Chislehurst Constituency entered a team for the Conservative Party Debating Competition with Raymond Pope as Chairman and me as speaker. On 6 December we won the national final at Church House, Westminster. The celebrated A.P. Herbert and Edward Boyle were the competition judges who awarded us this fine Christmas present! Four years later the same team beat seventy others to win the party public speaking cup. In retrospect, I never made enough of it.

The Chislehurst constituency included the ward of Mottingham South, a large solidly Labour LCC (London County Council) estate, with a small private sector estate alongside. The latter provided most of the branch committee, which selected me as candidate for the Council election in May 1952.

The idea of a handwritten photo-printed letter from the candidate appealed to me. To make it appear more genuine, I included a couple of crossed out words, had it printed off and brought copies to the next campaign committee meeting. Imagine my horror when the committee rejected it as illiterate and its distribution was refused. Meeting my protests part way, it was eventually agreed it could go out, but only on the LCC estate.

---

[6] Most cars operated as today, i.e. if you take your foot off the accelerator, the engine slows the car. With this Rover, the engine disconnected and the car ran along until it slowed of its own accord; a great saving in petrol on every downward hill or slope. (Why do they not re-introduce it now in this more pollution conscious era?)

I campaigned tirelessly, well supported by the Chislehurst branch YCs. My little car had a poster on the front 'Here comes Mitchell' and, on the back, 'There goes Mitchell – Vote for him'. Council elections do not often have open-air street corner meetings, but this one did. I parked in the service road at the end of the shops, standing precariously across the driver's seat, with my loud hailer beamed on the Saturday shoppers. Not many paid any attention, but the noise attracted a number of youngsters. Alas, they discovered the handbrake was only half effective and proceeded to push Bessie and me ignominiously back down the service road to the dustbins! The result of all my efforts came with the declaration of the poll. I had attracted the largest ever Conservative vote, the largest ever Labour vote and Labour's largest recorded majority! The following year, I stood again; we contacted only our supporters and had a respectable result. In 1954 I became the candidate for the larger St Pauls Cray ward. With the YCs' and Pam's help, we polled close on a thousand votes, losing by a narrow margin. The Association Chairman wrote that we had exceeded his wildest dreams.

This was in May 1954, and not a bad note on which to leave Chislehurst politics and focus on the search for a matrimonial flat in London. In February 1954 I had proposed to Pam and been accepted, but I was to ask her father, Dr Clifford Haward, for his consent. He listened to what I had to say and replied 'Well, I suppose you know what you are doing' and, after a pause, 'I must go and stoke the boiler'.

Pam's parents were divorced and her mother lived in a cottage at Peacehaven, near Telscombe – an attractive village buried in the downs between Brighton and Newhaven. We were married there in September with the reception at the Ship Hotel in Brighton. Boanergees carried me safely from Chislehurst to Lewes where my godmother, Margaret Spurrell, laid on a small lunch party which included my best man, Roland Beecher-Bryant. The church was decorated with heather from Goathland, the sun shone as we came out and, after the usual photographs, moved to the car. Horror, Boanergees had a puncture; we ignored any implied omen and after the reception shot back to Chislehurst to see my mother, now bedridden, and then away to London for the night. Next day we were off to Gibraltar, a night in Algeciras, a coach journey to Cadiz and ferry across the bay to Puerto de Santa Maria. Then a blissful time in one of the thatched chalets in the garden of the restaurant to which I had been introduced by the capable and charming Gabriel Osborne.

In the 1950s, the ground and basement floors of Gordon House, 12 Guilford Street, Bloomsbury, were occupied by a minor drug manufacturer, distilling Valerian with its strange smell. The three upper floors were let off as flats. The caretaker had one of the smaller ones on the top floor with, alongside it, the one we had seen advertised by the sitting tenant.

This was the era of strict rent control, a system endowing a sitting tenant with a valuable asset – encashable by demanding 'key money' from his (or her) successor. The landlord was outside this profitable loop, although in this case his consent to assignment was required. Shocked to learn the sum demanded from us, the landlord said he would refuse consent for any newcomer introduced by the sitting tenant. I do not recall exactly the compromise eventually reached, but this became our happy first home.

Andrew was to be born whilst we were there in 1957 (with a taste of champagne before Mother's milk, as befits a wine merchant's son). Later, with Suki on the way, we moved round the corner to 21 Mecklenburgh Square, the upper of two family sized maisonettes. Below us lived the charming, elderly R.H. Tawney, Professor of Economic History at the LSE, and intellectual powerhouse of the Fabian Society.[7] Alas, my schooling had failed to introduce me to the career of my brilliant and no doubt stimulating neighbour so, regrettably, we never talked on these matters.

A key to the square provided a safe locked garden for the children to play in, whilst easily observed from above. At this point and for the next nineteen years a great treasure, Minka, an affectionate Siamese cat joined the family.

Guilford Street lay at a convenient walking distance from my work at El Vino in Fleet Street and, by chance, just in the Borough of St Pancras (now part of Camden). In parliamentary terms, the largest part of the Borough formed the safe Labour seat of St Pancras North, the smaller southern end joined with Holborn as the marginal constituency of Holborn & St Pancras South.

---

[7] By 1931 he had become so disillusioned with Ramsay Macdonald, the outgoing Labour Prime Minister, that on receipt of a letter from the PM saying he was minded to recommend the King to grant him a peerage, he returned the letter, writing across it 'What have I done to betray the Labour Party?'

The Borough and its Council had, I was to learn, a long history of political vitality. Karl Marx lived there, in a house provided with staff by his mentor, Engels. Krishna Menon, later India's Foreign Minister, had been a Councillor (reputedly the most efficient Chairman of the Libraries' Committee ever). George Bernard Shaw had served on the Council (that must have been an invigorating time!).[8] Later the two of them became the only Freemen in the history of the Borough.

Politically, the Borough had swung between Conservative and Labour. Indeed, I was told that in 1937 Conservative control had been retained by the election of one Councillor in one ward by one vote! The liveliness of the Borough's political past was soon to be eclipsed by coming events. *Mon dieu et mon droit* ('My God, I'm right' as my children once translated it). It all began quietly I am told, in a poorly attended meeting of Camden Ward Labour Party. Those present were delighted at the prospect of recruiting fresh blood when a number of newcomers joined. It was not long before the local Party had been hijacked by neo-communists, led by one John Lawrence, the organising Shop Steward at Briggs strike prone motor works.

I was elected in 1956 to a Borough Council which became virtually a Communist soap box. It was led by Lawrence and his Chief Whip Jock (now Lord) Stallard. They had overthrown the established leadership at the first Party meeting after the election. Within a year they voted to abandon their Statutory Civil Defence duties. Rab Butler, as Home Secretary, put in a Civil Defence Commissioner, whose costs fell on the Borough. Lawrence chained himself across the iron-gated entrance to the Borough's civil defence HQ. (The police cut him free just before the Commissioner arrived.)

There could hardly have been a more exciting moment in the Council's history in which to become involved, not least in the heated debates in the Town Hall. Boiling point was reached on 1 May 1958. Just before 7.30 a.m. the Red Flag went up to replace the Union Jack on the Town Hall flagpole. The debate that proposed this in March had produced such uproar in the Chamber and public gallery (where eggs were thrown) that the Mayor suspended the sitting while the galleries were cleared and the police called. Huge

---

[8] It is said that GBS once sent Winston Churchill two tickets for the opening night of one of his plays – accompanying them with a note 'am sending a second ticket for you to bring a friend, if you have one'. Winston returned them, saying he was not free that week, but could he have tickets for the second week – if there was one.

protests rolled round the Borough. I must have been somewhat of a firebrand at the time, for I was usually in the thick of it, sometimes provoking uproar in the gallery and frequently clashing with Welsh Councillor Clive Jenkins, General Secretary of the Union of Scientific and Technical Staff.

Later that year, Transport House had had enough. Morgan Phillips, Labour's General Secretary, wrote suspending John Lawrence's membership and then, in an unprecedented move, suspended the whole of Holborn & St Pancras South Labour Party. Lawrence and fourteen of his fellow travellers formed a breakaway group on the Council along with Jock Stallard. The official Labour Councillors now agreed to restore civil defence and to reconsider their disastrous rent policy which pegged tenants' heavily subsidised rents, regardless of ability to pay moderate increases, so leaving insufficient funds for maintenance. In May 1959 Conservative candidates for the Council were swept into office. I had stood down to free myself for the coming General Election.

Besides my Council Committee work on General Purposes, Planning with Housing Development, and increasing responsibility at El Vino, I served on the Margaret Day Nursery Trust for the benefit of unmarried mothers of St Pancras, on the local Almshouse Management Committee and as Vicar's Warden at St Bartholomew the Less in Grays Inn Road. The church, bombed during the war, carried on its services in the Church Hall. The land was later sold by the Church Commissioners to the *Sunday Times* for car parking, amidst strong objections from the Parish. As one of the protestors, I had my first BBC interview.

In February 1958 I went to Holborn Town Hall to hear the Minister of Housing and Local Government, Henry Brooke, defend the controversial Rent Act devised by his predecessor, Duncan Sandys, for partial deregulation of rent control. It was a rowdy and exciting meeting. Towards its close, an attempt was made to rush the platform. I was one of a number who jumped up on it, stamped on the hands of those trying to climb up and helped to push others back. The police escorted Henry out of a back door.

It was about a year before this time that the Conservative Agent for Holborn & St Pancras South, Pat Blakemore (later first wife of Ted Bowman MEP until her premature death) told me that St Pancras North Conservatives were selecting a new prospective

Pam with Andew and Suki, 1959

Parliamentary candidate. She recommended me to put my name in. I did, and was selected. There then arose the little matter that I was not on the Central Office list of approved candidates. I went back to Donald Kaberry, the Vice Chairman of the Party responsible. I reminded him that, at an earlier interview, he had advised me to go away and gain experience in local government before reapplying. He smiled and said 'Yes, I did, but you have not come back empty handed.' It was September 1957. I was now aged twenty nine and the way was open for my official adoption as prospective candidate. My father came to that meeting; I think he was quite proud of his sometimes wayward son.

So I came to St Pancras North ready to make all the mistakes an eager and energetic newcomer makes before the sharp edges have been rubbed off. The seat had been Conservative until 1945. The Association had five active branches and some smaller committees. We were lucky in having Jim Hankey, an experienced, full time agent. Generally he and I worked happily together, but I recall one sharp clash. I led regular canvass teams and, in my enthusiasm, pushed others to join, complaining to Jim that he was not rounding them up. He said he assumed I thought he just sat around making friends (which I did). He then showed how those pushed too far gave up, but when an election came he had a very large body of friends who, as my supporters, would give their all for the limited time of an election campaign, and would I please not allow my enthusiasm to alienate them.

Later I invited my regular canvassers to a drinks party in the Commons. Ted Heath, Chief Whip, had agreed to put in an appearance. Amazingly he turned up with the Prime Minister, Harold Macmillan, who made a surprisingly emotional little speech 'in support of this young man starting out on a political career'.

The Central Women's Group of supporters met on Wednesday afternoons in a hall adjacent to the Constituency office. They were led by the redoubtable Miss Boughton and Miss Bull, I guess both approaching their seventies. The first time Pam and I attended their meetings we were taken aback when proceedings started with Miss Bull at the piano hammering out 'Land of Hope and Glory'; the piano was off-key and it was difficult to keep a straight face. I was competently introduced and said my bit. They had an excellent

At a drinks party in the House of Commons with Harold Macmillan

system for limiting visitors' and candidates' speeches. As the speech began, the gas was lit under the hot water urn for tea and, when it whistled, the speaker was expected to sit down. Pam was popular with her talks on the lives of famous musicians, illustrated on the (now retuned) piano. Jim Hankey was always there for the tea and it must be recorded that when an election, local or general, came round these were the people – many too frail to canvass – who addressed circulars, stuffed envelopes and did more than their share of the work without which a successful campaign cannot be mounted.

Of course Branch Committees were younger and here we made a number of new friends. I recall particularly Bob and Edith Bell. He was Chairman of the YCs when I arrived, and of the senior Association when I left in 1963. Later he was President when John Major became candidate for both elections in 1974. Amongst others were Johnnie and Daphne Green in the Highgate ward; she became our son Graham's godmother. Another friend was Roland Walker, later a very successful Chairman of the Borough's Finance Committee. His lawn sloped to the road making it an eye-catching poster site. It was regularly vandalised. Going to bed one evening, Roland heard rustling below his bedroom window, quietly filled a handy potty with water and tipped it all over the offender (as he thought). Unfortunately it turned out to be his mother tidying up a flowerbed.

I remember years later being astonished when, during a meal with Enoch and Pam Powell (also friends), Enoch said to me in a tone of surprise, 'But David you don't have friends in the Constituency'. We certainly did, and a great many more were collected when later we moved on from one constituency, through revised borders, to the next.

Having nursed the seat until selected for a safer constituency, I offer one piece of advice for Constituency Associations and would-be MPs alike. This is the benefit of having first fought an opposition-held seat. It is useful to do this in a hopeless seat with only a handful of supporters. Much better is the experience of working with an active Conservative Association. This is where you learn an enormous and justified respect for the voluntary side of the Party. This becomes built into your relations with your supporters. There have been a number of MPs who have come unstuck because they have taken party workers for granted. I have at times been horrified by the arrogant way in which a few MPs (certainly not confined to the Tory party) regard their supporters.

I started a regular advice bureau, at first once a month, but the deplorable housing situation with over six thousand on the Borough waiting list coupled with black propaganda against the Rent Act, created such demand that it became a weekly feature with a generous barrister (including John Newey and Howard Aplin) or a solicitor giving free legal advice once a month.

For an opposing candidate, 'baiting' the sitting MP is always good fun. Challenges to debate an issue are invariably ignored or refused on the grounds that the Member is not going to provide an audience for his opponent. Such pinpricks are brushed off and forgotten. St Pancras North was different. The issue was not differences between Government and Opposition, but within the ranks of MP Kenneth Robinson's own Labour Party. The MP was a moderate with a local party now taken over by the extreme left – who also controlled the council. He could have defended his moderate views robustly, but to do so would disillusion the core of his party workers. A trappist silence now enshrouded him. This, of course, provided an excellent excuse for a string of letters and speeches for the local papers. Themes such as – don't be shy, tell us your opinion on unilateral nuclear disarmament – the electors are entitled to know. 'Come, sir, silence will convert no-one – I'll pay the cost of the hall to debate your views' etc.

Up and down the country the 1959 election was fought on the great issues of the day, defence, pensions, education, health etc. – but not in St Pancras. The newly elected Tory council's scheme of differential rents dependent on income for council tenants was almost the only issue – no matter that seven other Labour controlled councils had similar systems. Street corner meetings were lively. I used to stand on a platform made by the flat, opened boot of an old Rover car. In Mornington Crescent, thunderflash fireworks were thrown past me (and, more worryingly, under the car's petrol tank). That stopped when one just missed an elderly lady and the crowd turned on the villain of the piece. On the Saturday before polling day I set up in Kentish Town opposite the street market, collecting only a handful until Oswald Mosley finished his meeting on the edge of the market, then a good sized crowd came over to heckle. They were a lively bunch!

One unusual aspect of the constituency was the large number of Greek Cypriot residents. Accordingly I had a Greek version of my election address printed. This was quite complicated because there were only three printers capable of producing Greek script and two were Communist supporters and one, The Aegean Press of E1, royalist. Jim Hankey found the right one, we visited, drank quantities of Greek brandy and just hoped the translation was correct. Maybe I set a precedent ... The response was mixed. One back street shopkeeper filled his window with an enthusiastic home-made poster, but the office received a number of abusive calls from English widows with Greek surnames assuming we thought them to be Greek (a friendly estate agent having shown Jim how to tell a Greek from a Turkish name on the electoral register; there were several hundred to be circulated). Well done Miss Boughton, Miss Bull and co.

Another precedent concerned Lord Rowton, a benefactor in the 1800s who raised capital on the basis of 'charity plus 5 per cent'. He built hostels to provide low cost overnight accommodation for otherwise homeless men. The Rowton House in a rundown part of Kentish Town was full with something like two hundred workmen, mainly off building sites. At a general election all candidates were invited to visit, accompanied by a Chairman, some twenty minutes being allotted to each of us. It would be a pretty rough all male audience and Jim Hankey advised me to take a strong, experienced Chairman. Naturally the candidates listened to each other. I liked Jock Nicolson, the Communist, but not the National Socialist (ironically Licensee of the Black Horse pub). Robinson remained reserved and left directly he finished. I drew last, bringing Pam as my Chairman(!). I was told they had never had a woman within the place. We were met with astonished wolf whistles but, when eventually they died down, Pam explained that if they did not interrupt I would make only a short speech and take as many questions as possible. She was brilliant and had them 'eating out of her hand'. I had the best hearing that evening.

Pam played a full part in the campaign; baby sitters were invaluable, not least Gillian Morris (now Lady Rees-Mogg). Pam's canvassing was enlivened by an elderly lady who patted her on the cheek and said 'Bless you dearie, I do hope your father gets in'. Our result was a seven hundred reduction in the Labour majority, which was not bad.

The General Election was over, but the controversy over the Council's new rent policy continued. The time came when increases in rents (albeit modest ones) were notified to council tenants. The Labour Group on the Council organised tenant opposition and backed the United Tenants Association in support of those who refused to pay. Arrears inevitably led to tenants facing summonses to court. Two tenants, Cook and Rowe, still refused to pay and the court instructed bailiffs to constrain or evict. They both barricaded themselves in.

Eventually, at 6.30 on the morning of 22 September 1960 the bailiffs started to remove the tiles on the roof of Mr Cook's house, preparatory to entering. (The staircase had been blocked off and covered with slippery oil.) Cook fired rockets from his balcony to summon some multi-dozens of supporters; a group of them clashed with the police who were in attendance, both on foot and mounted. One demonstrator, a bicycle held above his head, charged a mounted policeman; the horse shied, throwing its rider. Another had a fish tank dropped on him from another flat. Similar scenes occurred at the other tenancy involved. That evening a procession several hundred strong set out to march on the Town Hall. In the ensuing Euston Road riot, there were eleven arrests for obstructing and assaulting the police, having an offensive weapon etc. The Chairman of the Housing Committee, Paul Prior, had a police guard on his house for several months. The fact remained that if Messrs Cook and Rowe did not want tenancies on the terms offered, there were plenty of the six thousand on the waiting list who did. All this provided the backdrop to the spring London County Council elections. Our three candidates were George Dare, Geoffrey Tucker and myself. (Geoffrey, an advertising executive, was credited with having thought up the Macmillan slogan 'You've never had it so good', and possibly the crude pub joke about the girl who only knew the man was a Conservative.)

Our result was a very respectable reduction of more than five thousand in the Labour majority. Candidates' valedictory speeches at the count can usually be heard. Mine was 'drowned by jeers, the Red Flag and the St Pancras Tenants' Rents Song sung lustily from the packed gallery of the town hall' (*report in local newspaper*). The El Vino customer who had bet me a barrel of wine to a cigar that I would not get in, had (as anticipated) won his bet.

I was readopted as the Parliamentary candidate, with the understanding that I could apply for winnable seats elsewhere. The

Chairman commented 'we are a training ground, we like seeing our candidates in the Commons', but it was clearly understood that, as a General Election drew near, I would have to commit myself to them. My eventual letter resigning, accurately portrayed my feelings: 'Wherever politics may now carry me, we shall never forget St Pancras, the sore feet and friendly faces that canvassing has brought us, and the many friends we have made throughout the constituency.'

Back to 1959. Soon after the elation of a successful General Election campaign, gloomy events followed.

On Tuesday, 27 October, Father had chaired an El Vino Board Meeting. Nothing amiss, but early that Thursday evening he died suddenly aged seventy of a massive stroke. I do not suppose I am alone in having regarded my father as a permanent and indestructible part of (my) life. I hurried to 'Sundials': I had never seen the effect of death on a human face before this – complete relaxation, wrinkles gone, and so much more gone for ever from our lives, as Tennyson put it

> Break, break, break,
> On thy cold gray stones, O Sea,
> And I would that my tongue could utter
> The thoughts that arise in me.
> . . .
> But O for the touch of a vanished hand.
> And the sound of a voice that is still. . . .

It was to be the Sunday after this that Grannie came to realise that her much loved son had died – three months later she joined him. She could remember Queen Victoria being proclaimed Empress of India; so much of imperial history in the lifetime of one elderly lady.

As he had instructed, Father was cremated and my brother Chris and I scattered his ashes beside a rock on a remote part of the North Yorkshire moors – a spot he had indicated to us some years previously, where he had proposed to my mother, the correct rock being confirmed by my brother who had presciently slipped a coin into a crack all those years before.

CHAPTER 3

Old Fleet Street

Old Fleet Street, Frank Bower, nephew of Grandfather makes
El Vino a Press and Fleet Street institution / Alan Watkins and
other interesting customers, including the original Eric Barker,
'Stroller' of the 'Evening News' / Tale of a debt collection

THERE ARE STILL CUSTOMERS WHO recall my cousin, Frank Bower, the Pickwickian figure who for forty years presided over El Vino's Fleet Street Branch. His Edwardian dress of long black jacket, striped trousers, wing collar and flowered waistcoat marked him as a character. Before the doors opened at 11.30 he would add a fresh rose or red carnation (or sometimes a green one, courtesy of Quink ink). Favoured suppliers and overseas representatives with an appointment would be received in the back smoking room at 11.00 and invited to share the contents of Frank's chipped teapot and to report on their latest vintage. If few customers came in, Frank would don his bowler hat and walk down Fleet Street, greeting those he knew with a smile and 'see you later', and to departing customers in the evening 'see you tomorrow' – both inspiring a subliminal commitment.

The row of standing casks behind the counter were no façades; they contained Ports and Sherries which arrived from the docks in similar casks of some fifty four to fifty seven gallons (often per Murray Laker's pair horse van). They were slid down from the van on a wetted skid, head first and adroitly turned sideways before they hit the tarmac, rolling harmlessly a few yards according to speed. The *Manchester Guardian* of 15 January 1957 (whose London office was close by El Vino) records a cask which had sprung a leak. Frank was to be seen, bowler-hatted, with the craftsman's tools of coopering iron and mallet, carrying out a hasty repair – a spectacle enjoyed by curious passers-by and the London correspondent of that paper.

Part of Frank's success came from following the doings of his customers. For example, if one of them appeared in *The Times* Law Reports, he would mention it to them (or the powerful Chambers

48

Clerk) when next they came in, not forgetting the evening group with C.J. Crespi, John Marriage, Roger Gray and other barristers at their table inside the back door.

Likewise he kept up with the activities of editors, journalists, commentators and cartoonists. Philip Hope-Wallace, doyen of opera and drama critics, had his regular chair (now embossed with his name). Along with him would often be Alan Watkins who was, and still is, a shrewd observer of the body politic, having progressed from the *Sunday Express* crossbencher to *Spectator*, *New Statesman*, *Observer* and *Independent on Sunday*. Also Paul Johnson who once remarked to Watkins, 'D'you know, one of the waiters here is a Tory MP!' Standing at the front would be Derek Marks, the formidable Editor of the *Express* (Patrick Catling once described him as having a pen sometimes resembling a stiletto and sometimes a pick-axe). He was in Keith Waterhouse's phrase 'a legend in his own lunchtime'. Together with him would often be Victor Patrick, Roly Hurmer and Henry Fairlie.

The latter, a leading political columnist and a charmer with many admirers, was so absorbed in the arguments and personalities of the political world that betimes he forgot the mundane matter of paying bills, including one of reasonable size owed to El Vino. Frank, knowing Pam and I were weekending near Brighton where Henry lived, instructed me to call and collect the debt. Never having been so outwardly bold before, I asked Frank what to do if he said he had no money: 'There'll be a clock or something on the mantelpiece, move towards it and say you'll take it in lieu of payment'. Considerably disconcerted, I called the following Saturday morning. Lisette, his enchanting wife, let me in and called Henry who came down in his pyjamas – and did indeed say he had no money in the house. I said I'd take the clock. Henry beat me to it and pulled out from behind the clock nearly a dozen cheques he had not paid into the bank. I drove him to the bank, collected the money and delivered him home.

No account of the customers in the Fifties should omit Hugh Cudlipp, the abrasive, thrusting Editor of the *Mirror* whose book *Publish and be Damned*[1] makes compelling reading.

Saturdays would often see John Junor, formidable Editor of the *Sunday Express*, along with Arthur Brittenden, Foreign Editor, and

[1] A phrase originally used by Wellington in response to threats of exposure from a courtesan.

Terence Kilmartin, one of the great literary Editors of the *Observer*. From time to time Denis Compton, one of England's finest cricketers and John Arlott, the leading commentator, would come in – the latter had built up a fine cellar of our wines. Charles Wintour was once summoned to the phone by Lord Beaverbrook and told in the thin accent of Scots Canadian rectitude 'You will not find stories in the bars of Fleet Street.'

One well remembered regular was Eric Barker (the original; beware of imitations!). Before his day, news of glittering social events was collected by reporters hanging around outside the doors. Handsome, bearded and, he told me, once married to a beautiful Russian Princess, Eric broke the mould by being an invited guest. His column 'The Stroller' was a huge success for the *London Evening*

Making the news in El Vino

News. (In those days, the *News* and the *Standard* were the two leading evening papers in London.) Naturally West End restaurateurs and society hostesses, hoping for a mention, welcomed him. Alas Eric, by now retired, started to imbibe more than was good for him or his reputation. That was until one day Frank sat him down in a corner and talked with him for over an hour, after which Eric never drank anything stronger than ginger wine.[2]

A cartoon can often convey in a flash the whole purport of a long article; Jak of the *Evening Standard* was unfortunately barred from no 47 a number of times during the 1970s on account of bad language. However, a rich collection of his work hangs in the basement lunch room at El Vino, whilst I have the original of another which Jak gave to Pam across which is written: 'To young Pam from old Uncle Jak '81', then listing the years in which he had been barred! Vicky, the wee cartoonist, incurred much wrath for putting on Frank's bowler hat (which rested on his ears). Our Fleet Street branch had become a Press institution, an exchange for gossip, rumour and even facts. Part of the rôle then played by El Vino is well illustrated in Maddocks' cartoon.

John Mortimer's glorious 'Rumpole of the Bailey' stories frequently refer to 'Pomeroys' – modelled on El Vino. (Thanks again, Sir John, for the inscription in my copy.)

On Frank's retirement The *Guardian* of 8 December 1965 referred to his forty years in Fleet Street's most written about wine shop, adding 'No book or novel or magazine article in the last twenty years touched on Fleet Street without mentioning El Vino. The character of the place was almost entirely imposed by Bower, strict about manners and dress . . . nobody allowed in shirt sleeves or without a tie'.

Management of El Vino Fleet Street was then taken on by my brother, Christopher. He brought a less flamboyant style, but considerably greater efficiency behind the scenes. The business continued to prosper, for customers and friends (they can be both) like the feeling that they are dealing with one of the family.

---

[2] As a wedding present, he gave us a superb Victorian Sheffield Plate wine funnel which remains in regular use.

CHAPTER 4

Basingstoke

Profumo announces retirement, shortlisted for his Stratford on
Avon seat, runner up / Chosen Parliamentary candidate for
Basingstoke constituency / Value of local newspapers /
Drama at birth of son, Graham / 1964 General Election
campaign (a carthorse canter)

I WAS NOW ON THE CENTRAL OFFICE approved list for parliamentary
candidates. I had, it seems, 'won my spurs' by putting up a
creditable performance in St Pancras. I arranged for my name to be
submitted to both safe and winnable seats. Nothing happened!
Four years later, by 1963, I was ruefully coming to the conclusion
that my face did not fit and I should do something else. Then, one
day I was in our Fleet Street Wine Bar when Mavis, my wonderful
secretary, transferred a call from the Conservative Agent for
Stratford-on-Avon. He said 'Following Mr Profumo's decision to
retire, this Association is seeking a successor. Would you like to
come up next Monday for interview? We hope your wife can
accompany you.' He went on to explain this was to be held at X . . .
Manor, the home of the Association Chairman. We were to arrive at
2.25 p.m., using the left hand of the two drives. As we drove up, the
car of the previous interviewee was leaving by the right hand drive.

I had been told by friends that I looked too young to be a
Parliamentary Candidate – and by others that I looked older in a bow
tie; accordingly I wore one. Pam was given tea by the selectors' wives
and soon cottoned on that she also was being assessed. I was taken to
another room for interview. It seemed to go reasonably well in a
low-key fashion. However, as we walked back, the Association
President drew me aside and said quietly, 'If we were to ask you back
for a further interview, would you mind wearing a more ordinary
tie?' We drove back to London, saying that it had been a useful
experience, although personally I had no high expectations. As we
climbed the stairs to our flat, I was surprised that someone was
phoning after 10 p.m. It was the Agent instructed to invite me to
attend as one of their final shortlist of four.

This time the interview was in the Association offices. The Agent showed us to a small, carpetless, upstairs room containing only two chairs and a card table. He explained that I had the third interview. We listened intently as, through the floorboards, we heard the footsteps of the first entrant followed by polite applause, the drone of a distant voice, more light applause, questions followed by more polite applause, and the returning footsteps. The second interview followed a similar pattern. Then it was my turn; about thirty to forty people crammed into the room. I said my well-practised piece and received the same polite applause. First question – a man holding up my c.v. asked in a voice of utmost disdain, 'What possible benefit could it be to the Conservative cause if Mr Mitchell were to remove himself from St Pancras North to, ah, Stratford-on-Avon?' Clearly I had nothing to lose, so I went for him with the sharpness normally in play on a Kentish Town street corner. The meeting woke up, other more reasonable questions followed, and I left to a clap slightly warmer than that received on my arrival.

We returned to our eyrie, to hear the footsteps of the last of us four hopefuls, followed by loud applause, speech – applause, questions and, in conclusion, wild applause. Ten minutes later the Agent came to thank us for coming and to announce that Angus Maude, Suez rebel and darling of the Tory shires, had been chosen. Why had we bothered to come? – but then the Agent helpfully added as a comforting throw-away 'but you were the runner up'.

There were normally a couple of hundred or so applicants for every safe seat. No Selection Committee aspires to see them all and heretofore none asked me for interview. I now wrote to the Chairmen of each of the four subsequent constituencies to be engaged in the selection process, saying I understood well that they could not interview all applicants, but I was the runner-up to Angus Maude. Three invited me to interview, the last of which was Basingstoke. I was initially interviewed in the 'White Hart' at Whitchurch – a small town in the centre of the constituency. I sensed interest in me arose because of my experience as a candidate in St Pancras. Thousands of new voters were due to move into the two planned London 'overspill' towns of Andover and Basingstoke, both within the constituency, with potentially worrying political conse-quences. The interview seemed to go well and I was shortlisted. Interestingly, one member of the panel told me years later that the only note he wrote on his interview pad was 'Dark suit, brown shoes'. On such major considerations as bow ties and brown shoes can prospective parliamentary careers be founded or founder! The final selection was a week later in front of the hundred and twenty strong constituency executive. It would be a full hall on what was to be one of the most formative days of my life, for more than one reason. If a horoscope does influence our lives, Gemini must have been going all out in my direction on that day.

I had long hoped to become a Liveryman of the Vintners, 'The Worshipful Company of Vintners of the City of London' to give its full title. On this same day, I was due to be interviewed at 3 p.m. seeking admission to the Livery – for me a coveted situation. Unfortunately I was ineligible for the normal entry by Patrimony (for my father was not a Vintner), nor by Apprenticeship. Thus I hoped to join by the less certain route of Redemption. No doubt helped by grandfather having been Master in 1927, the interview was considerably more harmonious and less difficult than Stratford-on-Avon and happily I entered a brotherhood of wine lovers which deserves a chapter on its own.

The fates then turned less kind. The car had broken down; Pam had to rush out and hire another. Fortunately she was able to meet me off the train in Hampshire. We drove to Whitchurch as I put the finishing touches to my notes, and then met the other three finalists – Malcolm St Clair, the former MP for Bristol, Patrick Medd, the Vice-Chairman of the Constituency Association, and there was a leading County Councillor. The Agent, Major George Farquharson, explained the procedure: fifteen minute speech, ten minutes of questions, followed by a series of eliminating votes until one candidate polled over 50 per cent.

I was last to be called to the Church Hall, which was across the road and packed with members. It was certainly one of my better speeches, helped enormously by having the responsiveness of a large audience. Then came questions, but the last of them – in a total break with precedent – came from the retiring MP, Denzil Freeth, a former Junior Minister and a formidable debater. 'Would the candidate tell the meeting how he would respond to a situation in which the interests of many constituents were directly contrary to a decision of his own Government?' If Exocet missiles had been invented, this was it . . . I replied that, for me, the issue would rest not on constituents versus a Tory administration, but on which course accorded with Conservative principles.

We retired to the 'White Hart' and, five minutes later, George Farquharson re-appeared. He went straight to Malcolm St Clair and expressed appreciation for his coming (surely an obvious introduction for the winner) and then turned and said 'Mr Mitchell, please come with me'. I was totally unprepared, and had given no thought to what a successful candidate should say in a short acceptance speech. Happily I was sufficiently fired up to rise to that occasion!

My constituency pre-election

My only previous knowledge of the constituency came from passing through Basingstoke, and the traffic jam at the railway level crossing in the middle of Andover, on our way to holidays in the West Country.

The constituency seemed enormous, stretching some forty miles from Newnham village near Hook, west to Tidworth on the Wiltshire border, and from the villages of Kingsclere, Burghclere and Highclere on the impressive and beautiful North Hampshire Downs to the chalk streams on their southern edge – the Anton, the Bourne, the Dever and the Wallop Brook, feeding into the Test, one of the finest trout rivers in the British Isles. There were main towns of Andover and Basingstoke, shortly to expand explosively as London overspill towns. Just as interesting were the smaller towns of Overton with its papermill, Whitchurch with its silk-weaving mill (water powered from the Test), Old Basing with its ruined castle, relic of the Cromwell siege (Septimus Burton, the local farmer, still dug up cannon balls) and, not least, the Roman town, but now village, of Silchester. In short, the constituency held glorious countryside, fascinating towns, over a hundred lovely villages and hamlets, as well as the bustling change overtaking the two main towns.

What a contrast with my old four by three miles St Pancras! Well, yes, but there was also the common thread of an active Conservative Association linking supporters throughout the constituency. Pam and I arrived as strangers but soon found ourselves at home with the start of many new friendships. It would not be easy to follow Denzil Freeth, retiring member, ex Minister and a brilliant university-style speaker. I listened to him at the Mayor's banquet, thinking 'next year, none of those clever and amusing phrases'. I confided my fears to the Constituency Agent, George Farquharson. He was an impressive figure of a man,[1] a former major in the Black Watch with firm ideas on when and where his new candidate should appear. He partially reassured me with the comment that, since I was more down to earth, people would find it easier to identify with me . . . I could only hope so.

The next few months were taken up with the season of Branch Annual General Meetings, often two an evening, and arranged so as to fall weekly within the catchment area of each of the main local papers. These play an important role in any community, keeping readers in touch with what is going on in their locality. Indeed, they are often the only way people hear of developments which will have a direct bearing on their lives, such as planning or the many activities of the Borough or County Councils. Perhaps, most valuable of all, a good local paper provides a sense of inclusiveness that leads on to wider participation in community activities. Good examples are a campaign by Joe Scicluna, editor of the *Andover Advertiser* in 2007 spearheading recognition for the unsung heroes whose volunteer efforts keep so many worthwhile charities functioning. Likewise, Mark Jones, editor of the *Basingstoke Gazette*, with his campaign for pride in Hampshire's most thrusting town. His logo, 'Basingstoke – a place to be proud of'.

The County has indeed been fortunate over the years in the editors of the *Andover Advertiser* and the old *Hants and Berks Gazette*, now *Basingstoke Gazette*. Back in 1964 the *Baz Gaz* was still in Church Street above a pub, the editor Ted Tillen approachable, firm but fair, and always ensured each Parliamentary candidate at a General Election had exactly the same coverage (as did the *Andover Advertiser*). The *Gazette*'s last issue before polling day always featured the candidates all standing round a metal table, still called 'the stone', on which lead printers' type was set. Alan Jones, businessman and managing editor, moved the *Gazette* to its out of town site. Subsequently Andrew Renshaw computerised the technology, took the paper tabloid and introduced midweek freebies.

When I came, the *Andover Advertiser* and a large stationery shop in the High Street were owned and managed by Francis Holmes and his wife. It was very much a 'hands on' family business, with offices and

[1] For evening dress events, he turned up in full kilted tartan rig and, at least once, was mistaken for the candidate and I for his Agent.

printing works over and behind the shop. Later they were joined by a daughter, Alison, who married a subsequent editor. In 1964 Cyril Berry[2] was editor; fortunately for me he regarded the MP's activities and speeches as legitimate news worth publishing. Hence cuttings filed by Pam over the years conveniently fix many dates and events for this book. Although the *Hampshire Chronicle*, based in Winchester, and the *Newbury Weekly News* both covered parts of the constituency, it was understandably more difficult to secure coverage in them, but they, and even the *Reading Evening Post*, were fair in covering stories within their spheres of readership.

Then there were visits to the main employers – memorably the thrusting, successful and rather formidable Emmanuel Kaye of Lansing Bagnall, fork-lift truck manufacturers in Basingstoke, and Portals' mill (making banknote paper) at Overton, also Taskers of Andover. The Association Chairman, Brigadier Ben Brittorous, took us to lunch with the fascinating Lord Caernarvon at Highclere Castle (son of the discoverer of Tutankhamen's tomb). He pressed Pam (who was six months pregnant with Graham) to an enormous sloe gin with which I secretly watered an aspidistra.

Any constituency with a few blades of grass then had an active NFU branch; we had two – Basingstoke and Andover, the latter chaired very capably by Michael Colvin,[3] later to become MP for Romsey. Soon after selection, a new Parliamentary candidate would be invited to a meeting, asked to say a few words and answer some (as it turned out, searching) questions. Do not be deceived by the affability of the occasion; if you do not know your stuff, the Association Chairman will be phoned to say what a pity the new candidate is not interested in farming and does he (the Chairman) really think he is up to representing a farming constituency. My earlier career saved me.

Commuting in reverse after a full day in El Vino was no great joy so, in the early months of 1964, house hunting also became a

---

[2] Berry was also an enthusiastic maker of various fruit and herbal 'wines'. As a sideline he wrote and published a home made 'wine' and beer newsletter, then a magazine and, by 1967, the sideline took over his career and he left the *Advertiser*. One of his books on home-made beer sold over a million copies.

[3] Michael, alas, was to perish very sadly with his charming wife, Nichola, when their house burnt down – an appalling tragedy which shocked me and so many in his and my constituencies.

preoccupation. At the Selection Committee I had been asked whether I would live in the constituency. In response I gave an undertaking to have a home in, or near. Eventually we found the ideal. A couple of miles out of Odiham village and four from the nearest elector, was Berry Horn Cottage (if the children raided the neighbours' apples it would not be a political incident!). We still had our maisonette in Mecklenburg Square, later moving to a house in Eaton Terrace, but for me, this cottage has really always been home. And Mother came too or, to be precise, Jennie – a middle-aged donkey – more of her later.

Before the war, this cottage had been the local road mender's home, later abandoned. In 1944 it was bought by a Thames conservancy engineer, restored and extended to have two and a half bedrooms. He personally dug and barrowed away the soil to create a reinforced concrete swimming pool with a depth of eighteen inches to six feet and ideal for children. Two years before we bought, he had sold to a 'moderniser' who changed the layout, put in central heating and lifted the price to £12,500. Fortunately he left the glorious open log fireplace intact. It was probably the latter aspect which dominated the decision to buy on my part; more likely the central heating for Pam. Forty years later it is still home, and the grandson donkey and partner trumpet their welcome when my car draws up.

4 March 1964 was another red letter day, with the birth in London of Graham, our youngest. Both Andrew and Suki had been born in hospital. Pam's sister, a nurse, recommended a home birth on the grounds that a midwife did nothing else and was bound to be more experienced. Everything started conveniently after supper; I phoned 'our' Scots midwife who was out on another case and her much younger deputy came. Not long after, she became concerned all was not well and asked me to phone the doctor. A recorded announcement – he was out on another call. The midwife became more agitated. The door bell rang; thanks be to God, it was 'our' very capable Scots girl who immediately phoned for the UCH (University College Hospital) flying squad. In an amazingly short time the room was filled by a Registrar, an anaesthetist and two stretcher bearers. I followed the ambulance with its blue lights flashing, then paced up and down outside the delivery room. The cord was round the babe's neck starving him of oxygen. Apparently the flying squad had arrived in the nick of time. It was not to be Graham's only 'dice with death' . . .

Lord Caernarvon with Sir Alec Douglas-Home

The Election 1964

Looking back to 1964, it might be another world. *The Times* still had its front page dedicated to advertisements ranging through Births, Deaths, Marriages and Personal to Kennel, Farm and Aviary and dancing lessons from Miss Gem Mouflet, not forgetting Miss Ollivier who regularly advertised colonic irrigation. This was the year when Khruschev fell from power, the year Dr Erhard, the German Chancellor, suggested the six Common Market countries should 'begin formal negotiations for organised political collaboration'. Repeated demands for autonomy by Kurdish rebels in Northern Iraq provoked another crisis in that strife torn country. Corals, the bookmakers, took £200,000 in bets on the General Election. This came on 15 October. Prime Minister Alec Douglas-Home always appeared diffident but his short tenure after succeeding Harold Macmillan had shown him to be capable and shrewd. It is difficult to fault decisions he made – indeed with a more united Party behind him, he could well have won.[4]

---

[4] Both Iain Macleod and Enoch Powell declined to serve in his Cabinet.

It is history that Labour won by the narrow margin of only four seats, with Harold Wilson Prime Minister. Kenneth Robinson (whom I opposed in St Pancras North) took over the Department of Health; a *Times* editorial commented that his task would have been easier if he were not following Enoch Powell, adding that Enoch 'might justly claim to be the most influential Minister of Health since Bevan'.

Locally our campaign had gone well; virtually every village had a day-time visit from Pam or me. I imported from St Pancras my running canvass. This consisted of three or four helpers moving down a road, fetching the householder to the door, saying 'David Mitchell wants to meet you'. I arrived, said my piece, offered to answer any questions, then ran to the next house in which someone had been found to be at home. One journalist described me as arriving 'at a carthorse canter' – a not unfair description! Surprisingly, I gained weight during elections. Fortunately the longstanding tradition of ducking the Tory candidate in the North Waltham village pond had been, at least temporarily, forgotten.

I recall a canvassing incident involving a Service Officers' estate near Andover. I started early before the team arrived. Knock . . . door opened by an attractive young officer's wife. My standard patter went 'I'm David Mitchell, your Conservative candidate. I am getting around because I think people like to see the man they are asked to vote for. Have you thought about it yet?' At this point a red setter appeared; I stroked the dog and said 'Aren't you beautiful, aren't you gorgeous; I'd like to take you home with me'. Suddenly the husband, who had not seen I was addressing the dog, appeared with a clenched fist. I fled.

One Saturday, to George Farquharson's disapproval, 'we don't do that sort of thing here', I held an open air pavement meeting in Andover market standing on a doorstep near the Guildhall with a loud hailer (something I repeated at each ensuing election). A friend from Whitchurch came over to heckle; the ensuing noise attracted a small crowd and drew in the genuine opposition. All was proceeding normally until a young man suddenly rushed forward, jabbing my loud hailer into my face. With incredible speed my Whitchurch friend (I believe ex-SAS) sprang forward, grabbed the youth by the collar and dragged him off shouting 'Apologise, apologise, apologise!' Had 'my' heckler not done this, I fear I would probably have had my teeth knocked in.

Further down the market, I was approached very respectfully by a schoolboy asking for my autograph – (rather good for my ego). However, he then asked if I would mind doing five more. Yes, if he wished, I said, rather puzzled and, as I signed the last one, he explained that with six of them he could do a swap for someone important (not so good for the ego).

Evenings followed the traditional lines of that period with fifty eight public meetings (three and even four a night) covering all the larger villages and a number of wards in the two major towns. I shall always be grateful to my predecessor for, at some thirty of these, Denzil Freeth acted as 'warm up speaker', coming to an enthusiastic peroration in my support at a signal indicating my arrival.

In general, these meetings were successful, but with one huge misjudgement when it came to Faccombe village. My theme for that week was the property owning democracy. The Chairman, The Hon. Mrs Butler Henderson, introduced me. I said my piece to an audience which showed little interest and no enthusiasm. The meeting over, the Chairman led me swiftly to the exit door explaining that it was the tradition for her to introduce each of the audience as they departed. It went something like this: 'This is my housekeeper . . . meet my gamekeeper . . . here is my woodman, my chauffeur, my head gardener, my tractor driver, my bailiff, farm manager . . . etc. My memory recalls there were only three present who were not on the estate payroll. The property owning democracy had not reached Faccombe! Fortunately, the eve of poll meetings in Andover and Basingstoke were crowded and enthusiastic.[5]

The Count took place in a Basingstoke school, with the formal declaration by the Returning Officer from the balcony of the Town Hall, overlooking the town square. This was packed with vociferous supporters of the three candidates. The traditional thanks to the Returning Officer, to his staff and to the police, falls to the winning candidate, seconded by the runner up. I had my speaking note to propose in my left hand pocket, and to second in my right – and did so at every election except 1979. Happily I was in by a healthy majority of 7,976.

What followed took me by surprise. I was to go down the hill to the Conservative Club, then in Church Street, but on reaching the

---

[5] Crowded because George Farquharson, agent, insisted each branch produce a car full, the packed meeting giving a great send-off to polling day.

Declaration of the poll, Town Hall balcony, 1964

street I was hoisted shoulder high and carried to cries of 'For he's a jolly good fellow,' to the Club. Great stuff – it does not happen these days! Then, after drinks all round and a snack, off to Andover and the main villages with a loudspeaker car to announce the result and to thank supporters for all their efforts.

In the aftermath of the Tory government defeat, most of our Party reckoned that Harold Wilson's wafer thin majority would be eroded by by-election losses and we would soon be back in government. Contrariwise, Denzil's predecessor (1935–55) Patrick Donner made the shrewd assessment that we were 'in the anteroom of a major defeat', and so it proved at the election of 1966. I had worked hard over those two years to serve the constituency and to make myself better known; I was then returned with a majority reduced from 7,976 to 3,659.

CHAPTER 5

In the House

Pressures of working at El Vino and as backbencher / Maiden
speech, unexpected consequences / Progression of legislation
for lay reader / An industrial relations Bill / Justice for
Mr Miles courtesy *Daily Telegraph* / Constituency surgeries,
some cases make me angry / Unknown tale of young
Margaret Thatcher

THE FIRST OF MANY SURPRISES for a new MP arriving at
Westminster is the speed with which the police already know
your name and constituency – so you get in hassle free. The Palace
of Westminster is a vast building with hundreds of rooms, green
carpet for the Commons, red for the Lords. One entrance is through
the Great Hall of Westminster with its magnificent hammer-beam
ceiling. I remember my sense of awe as I walked in; only the most
prosaic new Member can do so without that feeling as one passes the
brass plates set in the floor recalling great historic events. Here stood
Sir Thomas More, Speaker of the House and author of *Utopia*, on his
condemnation to death July 1535; another where stood Charles
Stuart, King of England, for his trial and sentence to death in 1649
and, more happily, where Warren Hastings was acquitted on trumped
up charges 1788–95. Also recalled are the Lying in State before their
funerals of kings and queens, of Gladstone in 1898 and Winston
Churchill in 1965, and a happier time when our Queen Elizabeth II
replied to a Loyal Address on the occasion of her Silver Jubilee.
Whatever one goes on to contribute to public life, one will remain
a very small part actor on the great stage of England's history.

On then to watch and participate for the first time in the
Ceremony of Taking the Oath, without which no-one can serve as
an MP.[1] I pinch myself that I am really here, but soon fall to

---

[1] Ask an American who was the first woman elected to the Commons and they will proudly
respond 'Nancy Astor'. Wrong; it was the Countess of Markiovitz the Irish wife of a Polish
Count, elected in 1918. Being Sinn Fein she refused to swear the Oath of Loyalty to the
Crown. Hence, although elected, she could not take her seat and serve as a Member. A year
later, Nancy was indeed elected for Plymouth Sutton, took her seat and served until 1945.

wondering how on earth some others got there. Taking the Oath one subsequent year, an older Member behind me provided a running commentary. I recall him on barrister Nicky Fairbairn (Conservative, Kinross) 'If you got caught in M & S by the store detective with your hand actually in the till, he could get you off', and of one lady member 'a woman of easy virtue' (how did he know, I wondered).

On Wednesday, 3 November, 1964 came the colourful ceremony of the Queen's State Opening of the new session – central to it, the Queen's Speech written for her by the Government, setting out their plans for the ensuing year. No-one knows her Majesty's own views, but another time I saw a flickering smile when she spoke of legislation on equal rights for women. Next, to debate 'Her Majesty's Most Gracious Speech' on a motion moved and seconded by two backbench Government supporters. I cannot resist jumping forward a generation to give you the description of this event provided by my son, Andrew, when seconding the motion in 1992:

> As you will understand, Madam Speaker, I do not usually have the pleasure of being joined by so many of my colleagues on both sides when I address the House. Faced with this task today, I took myself to the Smoking Room to seek the advice of a distinguished and senior member of my party. He said 'Don't worry, you will be fine. The motion is nearly always proposed by some genial old codger on the way out and seconded by an oily young man on the make.'
>
> I decided to take some further advice and went to another distinguished member of my party – an ex Minister. I asked him what I should do. He said 'You will be fine. You come from a political family and follow in immensely distinguished parental footsteps.' I said, 'Thank you for your advice – Father.'
>
> I decided not to take any further advice because, as I walked down the Library Corridor I met another immensely senior and distinguished grandee of our party. He put out his hand to me and welcomed me to the House of Commons. He said that if I needed any advice in my first few days, he hoped that I would come to him. Such is the mark that I have made in the House during the past five years.

One tale survives of canvassing in the red light district in her first election when escorted by a naval officer in full uniform. Knock on door, opened by small boy. 'Is your mother or father in?' 'No.' 'Don't worry, we'll come back later.' 'No, no, you're expected. Mother said when a naval officer arrived with a blonde lady I'm to show them into the third bedroom on the right.'

Father and son

The Parliamentary day starts with the Speaker's Procession, down the long corridor past the Library and on through the Central Lobby. Here the public form a packed crowd, anxious to get a glimpse of the Sergeant-at-Arms carrying the Mace on his shoulder, the magnificently robed and bewigged Speaker, then his train bearer, and finally the Chaplain and Speaker's Secretary together. Everyone must stand back silently to give free passage. Members bow their heads. The procession having passed on to the Chamber, conversation resumes and everyone disperses. For some years I shared a double desk facing Neil Marten MP in the former members' cloakroom. Once, anxious to catch him, I called out 'Neil' just as the procession had passed; a small group of American visitors dropped to their knees.

It has been said that MPs are like swans, calm on the surface, but madly paddling underneath. In reality it is largely up to the individual Member how much work he does and the time spent in the precincts. However those who freewheel will avoid the cares of promotion and eventually be caught out by their constituents.

People, indeed Members, have differing ideas on the rôle of an MP at Westminster. Mine is to judge those in power using the criteria of the policies and principles on which I had sought election. To do this effectively it is necessary to familiarise oneself with current issues before Parliament and be ready to explain them to constituents in report-back meetings. In addition, in my view, it is important to develop an expertise on a limited number of subjects (preferably linked, such as Defence and Foreign Affairs, or Finance and Employment etc.) and to keep abreast as they evolve. However, there is no better way of gaining the respect of the House than to arrive there bringing genuine personal expertise in some useful niche – after all, party political enthusiasts are two a penny.

This is one reason I deplore the fall in number, in all parts of the House, of those who have an ongoing occupation outside the Commons. Solicitors and barristers have a particular contribution to make, exposing and interpreting the law of unintended consequences in draft legislation. Farmers are uniquely able to enlighten and inform on agricultural matters; likewise those from professional and business environments bring their own expertise. I know that my own continuing rôle at El Vino made me a better and more effective MP than would have otherwise been the case. Later I will illustrate this in relation to the work I did on Small Business policy. I do not disguise that for me running parallel careers became more difficult and more onerous as the years went by. Many Members would put in six or eight hours a day and more at weekends in their constituency. This left them with the leisure time to follow their hobby or otherwise as they pleased. For those in business or the professions, much of their leisure time was pre-empted.

True, I was fortunate in having a London-based family business to which, if I was not on a Standing Committee, I could go for three to four hours in the morning. It was much more difficult for Members whose business or profession was based out of London. I remember one of the most level-headed Northern Ireland Members, a retailer who got up early to dress his shop windows before catching the plane for Westminster. Indeed, one of the, if not *the* most valuable contributor to debates on proposed government control of prices and incomes was Sir Tatton Brinton, a carpet manufacturer from Kidderminster. It is, I know, an unfashionable view, but I am not persuaded that the House did a poorer job when many MPs openly represented vested interests in our commercial life – the textile industry, the coal mining Trade Unionists, the farming lobby, the T&GW Union MPs. Nor do I say we do not need the full time professional politician, but a good dose of mundane reality and experience can bring great benefit to the work of the House.

It is still possible forty years later to remember the excitement of that (for me) first Parliament. I would be working at my desk or in the library when the monitor clanked out the name of the next speaker – perhaps someone I wanted to hear – and I would rush off to the Chamber.[2]

There are many Committees in the Commons, some to which one is appointed, others to which one can attach oneself. Before the setting up of All Party Select Committees with the powers to monitor Government, the most interesting of these were meetings of the Party Committees. Chaired by the Shadow Minister, when in opposition, elected when in power, they met regularly to discuss anything affecting their department of government ranging from recent events to questions worth posing to Ministers and the evolving of our future Party policy. Frequently a visiting speaker would lead the discussion, for example the controversial Dr Beeching on rail transport. I found these meetings thought provoking, stimulating and intensely interesting. Accordingly I attached myself to the Labour (Employment), Finance, Industry and, to a lesser extent, Agriculture Committees. There was always a member of the Whips' Office in attendance; little did I realise the significance of this during that first year. The Party Committee system was suspended in 1997 as a result of reduced back bencher numbers to cover them.

A maiden speech is special in a number of ways. Firstly it is virtually the only time a backbencher can arrange with the Speaker that he will be called at an agreed time. By tradition you start by painting for the House a verbal picture of your constituency. It is entirely up to you to decide how soon or long to wait after entering the House. In the Smoking Room some years earlier, over an after dinner whisky or two, a Scots Member was teased for not having made his maiden speech after three years. He responded that it was

---

[2] I had inherited an excellent secretary from my predecessor, but she looked after two other members; each of us fitted to a timetable. Alas, too frequently I was late, held by the magnet of events in the Chamber and reluctant to miss the conclusion of a speech. Her exasperation was justified and we parted by mutual consent.

nothing special, and that we'd all made hundreds of speeches before coming here. As Scottish business was being debated at the time, his 'friends' urged him to go for it. He downed another Scotch, went into the Chamber, was called, and started 'My Lord Provost, Ladies and Gentlemen'. It was his first, and last, speech in the House! I decided it was better to take the plunge relatively early. On this first occasion, there is something unnerving about the wide open space between you and the Speaker, over the heads of seated colleagues. I decided the subject should cover familiar ground. Since Defence and the British nuclear deterrent had been a regular theme of mine both before and during the election, a debate five weeks into the session on this subject suited my purpose.

I now digress, intentionally, to the eating arrangements in the House. The first choice is between Cafeteria and Members' Dining Room. In the latter, Members eat alongside their party colleagues (Tories one end, Labour the other and then a table for the Liberals in the middle). The only precedence is the Chief Whips' reserved table – otherwise you sit wherever there is a space. So it was that a few days before the debate I found myself next to Sir Alec Douglas-Home, by then Leader of the Opposition. His advice to seek out some really new aspect on defence was indeed a valuable steer. I phoned a friend, John Gay, who worked in the nuclear power industry, and asked if there was anything new since the election which could be relevant. John's response was an eye opener. The Chinese had just tested an atomic bomb much sooner than anticipated, but to the astonishment of those in the know, had used a technology five years in advance of France, and capable of being developed into the manufacture of a hydrogen bomb.

A maiden speech should not be too controversial but I guess it was unnecessary to be impartial, so I mentioned that the appointment of Frank Cousins as the Minister responsible for AWRE, the Atomic Weapons Research Establishment at Aldermaston, on the edge of my constituency, had aroused some surprise since he was already well known there as a leader of the annual CND (Campaign for Nuclear Disarmament) protest march to its gates! The speech went on to display John Gay's inside knowledge on nuclear matters and to express concern at the danger for Britain of unilateral disarmament with its inherent risk of being blackmailed by a nuclear power. The Committee of Selection, having noted my spuriously intimate knowledge of nuclear matters, put me on the Standing Committee[3] for the Nuclear Installations Bill, much of which seemed concerned as to whether an unborn infant could sue in the event of a nuclear accident. I had nothing useful to contribute.

By contrast I welcomed the opportunity to serve on the Committee stage of the 1965 Trades Dispute Bill. This had been introduced following a legal ruling which put in doubt the immunity from prosecution (for intimidation) of a Trade Union negotiator when threatening a strike. The Bill sought to 'Put the law back to where it had previously been thought to be'. I moved an amendment to withdraw this immunity 'if done for the purpose of compelling another person to join or remain a member of a Trade Union' against his will. There was a lively debate which takes up thirteen pages of Hansard. Now I encapsulate the discussion in one paragraph.

I was then, and still am, much in favour of 100 per cent voluntary Trade Union membership but dead against the compulsion inherent in the 'closed shop'. I saw the Bill as potentially a flagrant attack on the liberty of the individual. From Magna Carta on there has been a right to join or not to join an organisation. Moreover, compulsory membership of a Trade Union or any organisation is against Article 20 of the UN Declaration of Human Rights signed by the Attlee Government in 1948. Worse still, if my amendment were not passed, someone (I had a constituency example) would risk losing their job if they fell out with their Union and decided to leave a closed shop. The amendment was lost by ten votes to twelve.

There was an interesting sequel to this, for in May 1971 Mr Miles, a constituent and member of the Boiler Makers' Union, came to see

---

[3] The procedure for legislation is a First Reading, which is no more than publication of the Bill. The Second Reading is the major debate, after which the main principle of the Bill is entrenched. Next, the Standing Committee of, say, fifteen members according to Party strengths, meets in a Committee Room upstairs (and open to the public) to consider the measure clause by clause and line by line. Committee members can move any amendments they wish, vested interests offer ammunition, worried constituents seek clarification so a 'probing amendment' is useful to secure detailed explanation from the Minister. The Report Stage comes next, back in the Commons Chamber. Here all Members can seek amendments provided these were not discussed in Committee. Then, the Third Reading – a debate only on whether to accept or reject the amended Bill as it stands. Next to the House of Lords and on to the Queen for signature.

me in some distress. He had refused to join the one-day strike against the Conservative Government's Industrial Relations Bill. In consequence he had been fined £5 by his Union which on principle he refused to pay. The strike was political and not in furtherance of an industrial dispute and, therefore, unlawful. This was a particularly unpleasant case since Taskers, the employer, had a closed shop agreement with this Union. If Mr Miles did not pay, he would have his Union card withdrawn, not be allowed to work there and hence lose his job. My constituent had already seen a solicitor and been advised that, since the Union was adamant, a High Court writ (or the threat of one) was the best way forward. However, the cost of this could be prohibitive. I concluded that the most effective way of supporting my constituent would be to secure financial backing for this writ. The result would either be a probable (but who could be sure?) win in the High Court, or, better, that on seeing that Mr Miles had the guts, resolution and finance to proceed, the Union would back down.

Accordingly I had a letter published in the *Daily Telegraph* explaining this situation and inviting readers to write to me that week if prepared to help fight this mean, spiteful and unlawful penalty. The result was heart-warming as well as a great relief. Nearly £1,000 came in, a few readers sending £20, more £10, over eighty people sending £5, many elderly pensioners £1 or £2, and some a lesser amount as all they could afford. Others wrote, offering to share in the costs when known. Covering letters spoke of 'opposing tyranny', praise for 'those with the guts to make a stand', 'courage, freedom and justice', 'malicious use of Union power', 'dictatorial and undemocratic power', etc. Most interesting was a letter enclosing a donation from a branch of the Transport & General Workers' Union! Faced with this determination and knowing funds were available to see it through, the Union backed down. Fees were modest. One of two Counsel waived his fee, the solicitors kept the costs down, and I was able to write to all contributors saying I had decided not to take up the smaller contributions (including many from OAPs) but to draw £2 from those sending £10, and £3 from the £20 donations, and to return the rest.

During 1965 Eddie Wainwright, a kindly mining Trade Union MP, offered to take some of us new Tory MPs down a coal mine. It was an unforgettable experience going to the coal face where a line of self-advancing pit props moved forward, followed by an earsplitting crash as the rock crashed down behind to refill the space where the coal had been taken out. Our group included George Younger, Patrick Jenkin and Patrick McNair Wilson and me. In the Opposition reshuffle in the Autumn of 1965, Patrick Jenkin was made junior spokesman on Treasury and Trade matters (under Iain Macleod and Margaret Thatcher), the other Patrick on Energy, whilst George and I joined the Whips' Office. Eddie claimed he subsequently had a queue of young hopefuls wanting to join his next pit visit!

Constituency surgeries

Much of my constituency work came in through the post, visits to businesses etc. and my regular advice 'surgeries'. The latter were advertised in the local newspapers and on Basingstoke station. I'll never know whether it was by chance or not that the poster above mine read 'Pregnancy Testing', and below that 'If you need help contact David Mitchell – Advice Sessions at . . .'

There were two unexpected features of my 'surgeries'. First, the failure of our education system to teach the rudiments of who does what in organising the society in which we live; for example that Education is a County responsibility whilst Housing falls to the Borough and District Councils. I recall a young man of about twenty with a pregnant girlfriend telling me that it was my job to provide a house when the baby became due. The UK is incredibly fortunate in the number and dedication of so many who serve as Councillors in local government – the unsung heroes of our society. For many years I took up with the appropriate authority all the problems brought to me. Then I came to realise that in too many cases I was shielding Councillors from the vagaries of local officialdom. After that, I announced that if people had come about such matters as Housing etc. they were fortunate because Councillor so and so, who was responsible for such things, was also present.

The second surprise was the time it took for many people to come to the point of their visit; this was more true of personal problems. I recall vividly a middle-aged man who described his bungalow, the fruit trees, the hens etc. etc. Eventually out it came; all this was on offer, but how could he find a wife to share it?

Matters raised by constituents divided into national or local issues and personal problems. Of course, the national items were continually changing over my thirty three years in the House. Early on, there was much on CND seeking unilateral disarmament, and later the Greenham Common women, protesting against Cruise missiles. Per contra many of those who worked for AWRE lived in my constituency in Baughurst and Tadley. They believed, rightly, in the preservation of peace through an effective nuclear deterrent.

Then there were hard fought issues such as abolition of the death penalty, abortion, and the gradual but significant change in attitudes to homosexuals, immigration, inadequacies in the NHS, abolition of grammar schools, and the plight of UK pensioners now overseas and denied indexation of their pensions. Other national issues included perennials such as excessive taxation, council tax, education, defence, the EU etc. Also regular Conservative complaints of BBC bias.[4]

My postbag was generally larger than that of most constituencies, not least from the many retired service officers in the west of the constituency. They had time on their hands and were highly literate! In spite of that, back in part of the 1960s, dictation and typing were coped with by our au pair, Judy – now Mrs Peter Abbott, who did the secretarial work after taking the children to school and before their 4 p.m. collection. A competent and conscientious secretary is vital in providing a high quality service for constituents. By the time I left the House, we were doing just on ten thousand letters a year and needed a full time secretary – computerised, plus a clerical assistant and a part time researcher. I had several secretaries over my thirty three years in Parliament; I was fortunate to have the wonderful support of, among a number of others, Judy early on, Annabel Kirk (née Linney) for eleven years, Karen Grieve for nine years, and Vivienne Davies until her husband's posting to Paris. All became good friends as well as working colleagues. Mavis Hazell, a real

---

[4] This is unsurprising. Surveys show that overall, contrary to popular belief, those at university do not overall greatly differ in their political colouring from the general public. *But*, – and it is a big but! – those reading engineering, medicine and law etc. are predominantly Conservative, whilst those studying arts and social sciences are left wing. Understandably the BBC, much of the media and, alas, parts of government seek to recruit only from this left-inclined pool. When like-minded people work together, they assume that their commonly held views are free of prejudice and thus group bias becomes built in and increasingly pernicious.

treasure, was with me at El Vino for fifteen years. Now, once or twice a year we all have a reunion.

One reason the post increased so much was because of big changes in our national newspapers. Apart from the *Financial Times*, the days are gone when opinion was confined to the editorial columns and reporting was pretty factual. First came the massaging of news to reflect editorial opinion. Subsequently newspaper editors realised that sales increased when running a campaign, preferably on an issue with emotional appeal. This had the side effect that, aided by photocopiers, people wrote in droves to their MPs asking for support and representations to be made on the media's current cause. So, in would come dozens of letters a day on protecting the whales, numbers of illegal immigrants, the slaughter of seals, export of live animals etc. Believe me, when the then government banned raw dog meat from slaughter houses (known as 'knackers' meat'), it seemed every pet owner wrote in, indeed for over a month the knackers' meat post exceeded all other topics!

Fluoridation of water supplies is an interesting example of a national issue which had strong constituency connotations. The Department of Health supported it as a cost effective means of reducing tooth decay, particularly in children. Opponents claimed that some people were allergic to it, and that mass medication is wrong in principle. Also that there are examples (thalidomide etc.) where yesterday's recommendation has become today's prohibition. No doubt those against were a relatively small minority, but they held and expressed their views vehemently!

When the then Government invited Andover to become one of five towns to be used for a pilot scheme, the Borough Council agreed. Shortly afterwards a lady complained that it made her ill. Happily she had a garden well, drew water from it and recovered. The story featured in the *Andover Advertiser* and other people joined the bandwagon. Before long, the lady was bottling and selling her 'pure' well water. The Environmental Health Officer obtained a sample and, after analysis, condemned it as unfit for human consumption. I am told that at the ensuing Borough Council Election, all the Councillors who had voted to accept the Government's invitation were defeated. Basingstoke Borough Council discussed the issue and resolved to hold a debate before voting. They invited an official from the Department of Health to propose the motion, with the opposing view put by a barrister (I understand provided by industrialist Emmanuel Kaye). The Department's representative used his twenty minutes to explain the benefits and the risk-free nature of what is involved. The barrister took less than five. He produced two glasses of water and put in the first a teaspoon of calcium fluoride, explaining that this occurs naturally in some waters of the UK. In the second glass he put a teaspoon of sodium fluoride, the chemical used in the fluoridation process. He then announced he would drink the first glass and invited the Department's representative to drink the second. The hapless official refused, saying it would poison him. The Council voted unanimously to reject fluoridation of the local water supply. (The explanation is that a teaspoonful in a glass is very different from x parts per million gallons.) Constituents' opposition surfaced from time to time, but less frequently as fluoridation became the general practice in more of the national water supply.

Surgery visits brought mainly local issues and personal problems. These included making representations on 30 mph limits, car parking, tree preservation orders, against helicopter noise and motorcycle scrambles, provision of footpaths, layout of town centre redevelopment (Andover) bus services and stops, planning both in favour and against proposed developments (alas you do not buy the view when you buy a house), against double yellow lines in a village shopping centre (Whitchurch), sewage flowing down St Mary Bourne main street, the need for a number of bypasses (in many places), and calls for the moving-on of gypsies and new age travellers. A number of the latter came to my surgery and I became quite well acquainted with one small group – two men and a woman with a daughter, plus three vehicles. They set up camp near Chilbolton where they expected to be little nuisance. Inevitably the nearby householders complained and, in due course, they were moved on . . . but to where? What was needed was not an expensive well fitted-out site, but simply a piece of flat ground away from other habitation, with cinder or gravel surface, a WC, a cold water tap and a large rubbish bin, nothing more; the cost would be minimal. This was not on offer, so they moved a couple of miles to a much less suitable site, causing far more nuisance, and before long they were moved on once more. It is said that 'perfection is the enemy of improvement'. This was certainly true of the provision, or lack of it, for gypsies and new age travellers.

The Andover surgery was advertised from 10–12.00 on a Saturday. Often it over-ran, occasionally as late at 2.30, but on a sunny spring morning the queue might finish well before 12.00. On one such morning the last 'challenger' to sign in was an elderly ex-wartime fighter pilot with a service pension problem. Having concluded this, he stayed and chatted. He described how he had been shot down off the Dover coast and fished out by Air Sea Rescue with burns to one leg and arm. After treatment at Basingstoke Hospital with its major skin graft unit, he was sent to Newcastle for some specialist work. It was a slow train journey with many stops, including Grantham where, following an air raid warning, passengers were told it would not continue until next morning. Everyone organised themselves as best they could. Later he was accosted by an ARP (Air Raid Precaution) Warden who asked him where he was spending the night. My constituent replied that he was OK as he had a space on the ticket office floor. 'No you haven't,' came the disturbing reply, then, 'you are coming home with me'. So, a total stranger, he spent the night in a comfortable bed. Breakfast was cooked by the pig-tailed daughter of the house. Having eaten, she picked up her satchel, kissed her parents and left for school. His breakfast had been cooked by a future Prime Minister. Doesn't that tell us all something about the home and its values from which sprang The Rt. Hon. Margaret Thatcher?

A Nigerian man came to my Basingstoke surgery asking me to make representations to the Home Office for his nephew to join him. Having completed my notes, I said that I would write to him as soon as I heard [the format with every 'surgery' case]. Whereupon he produced a stuffed and bejewelled model baby elephant as a present. I explained that I was not allowed to accept gifts etc. but no need to worry, he would hear from me. Oh dear, at my next surgery there he was again, accompanied this time by his wife. He explained he now understood he could not give me a present but he was sure his wife could give my wife a gift . . . No!

The only time I recall accepting a gift (a box of Black Magic chocolates) was after months of representation on behalf of an ex service constituent who had, over time, lost bowel control as a result of an infection caught while in the Army in Egypt. His claim for a disability service pension had been disallowed on the grounds that it was a disease a civilian could equally well have caught. Eventually the authorities accepted my argument that no way would a man with his pre-war occupation have gone to Egypt, and consequently that he would never have caught this infection unless in the forces. Better still, he was awarded not only the disability pension he was due, but it was backdated for a number of years.

Another much more recent Andover case arose while I was in the Department of Transport. I had the previous evening been dealing with papers regarding the Lifeboat Service. My constituent sat down and, as he finished giving me his name and address, he added 'I have to tell you I am a lifer'. My mind switched back to lifeboats. Then the penny dropped. He went on to explain that he had murdered his wife, had served his 'life' prison sentence and been discharged a number of years. His initial problem had been finding a job. Eventually he had been taken on by a firm providing agricultural relief workers. One job as a shepherd had become virtually permanent. Clearly he had put in a big effort, which greatly pleased his manager. One day he said a new ram was needed and, happily, he had heard from his brother in Gloucestershire of an appropriate animal. 'That's fine' says the manager. 'I'm going up there for a wedding and I'll check and bring it back on Sunday'. That morning at a drinks party someone says to him, 'Hey, are you the chap employing Mr X? You know he's been in prison for murder.' Shock, horror and as soon as convenient my constituent was sacked. I shared his distress – indeed, I was angry on his behalf, and I advised he bring a case of wrongful dismissal. I do not remember the exact context but the case ended up in Winchester Court where the judge expressed considerable censure.

Another case which incensed me involved refusal of planning consent for the re-erection of a house in Jacks Bush, a hamlet on the Salisbury Road. It had some years before been condemned and then demolished by the Council, except for the fireplace and part of the chimney. Nelson Day had been born there. His father had been a gypsy who came to rest on this smallholding. After following a nomadic life, the son and his wife had returned and erected a semi mobile home on the site without planning consent. Understandably the Council took enforcement action. I looked at the site and recommended he apply for planning permission for a permanent dwelling. This was refused on the grounds that the exit on to the main road was dangerous, and the site outside the boundary of the

Jacks Bush settlement. I recommended him to appeal. He could not afford a solicitor nor a planning specialist, so I represented him at the Appeal Hearing. For an MP to act in this way caused a local stir and is probably unique. (In the light of the preparation time involved, I do not recommend other MPs to follow in my footsteps!) We won on the access question, but lost on the 'envelope' of the hamlet. No doubt technically the Appeal Inspector was correct but the site cried out that, even though the last house in a semi contiguous settlement had been demolished, it did not make the site other than a natural for inclusion in the hamlet. Happily, all was not lost. Common sense prevailed over bureaucracy when, shortly after, the Test Valley Borough wrote giving him consent to stay *in situ* for his lifetime.

No account of constituency surgeries can be completed without mention of Alfie Cole. He had inherited land on the outskirts of Basingstoke which became subject to Compulsory Purchase. Dissatisfied with the price and with my efforts on his behalf, he decided on direct action. He drew attention to his plight by dropping a load of manure to block the main street in Basingstoke, and another outside the Mayor's house. He followed this up by riding to London in a pony and trap, demanding to see the Prime Minister. He told me he was going to chain himself to his seat in the public gallery of the House, while he launched a verbal assault on the District Valuer. I warned the Sergeant at Arms of this prospect. I understand a pair of heavy duty wire cutters were on hand, but Alfie let that idea drop. He was only one of many who complained that the local District Valuer was acting more as a bargaining agent on behalf of the purchasing authorities, rather than fulfilling his proper rôle as an impartial valuer.

In 1966 the Chamber of Commerce had called a public meeting with a considerable attendance of dissatisfied people. Following this, and my own detailed assessment of some of the cases, I raised the matter by letter and questions in the House, to no avail. Each time the Treasury Minister responding suggested appeals to the independent Lands Tribunal, something beyond the purse of many of those involved. Eventually I secured an Adjournment Debate at 1.15 in the morning.[5]

---

[5] Adjournment debates occur for half an hour at the end of official business, generally only the MP raising the question and the responsible Minister are present, but it does ensure that the Minister becomes personally and fully aware of the problem.

I pointed out that no complaints had arisen in Andover, which was served by a different Valuer. More importantly, Emmanuel Kaye of Lansing Bagnall (with a deeper pocket than most) had taken an appeal to the Lands Tribunal. This had overturned the District Valuer's figures, substituting £220,000 for the District Valuer's figure of £100,000, and £115,000 instead of £37,000. Harold Lever, recently appointed Financial Secretary to the Treasury, responded that he could not accept any imputation of any kind on this District Valuer, merely because there was a sense of grievance. Etiquette demanded this Ministerial defence of an official in his department – but shortly afterwards the said District Valuer was moved on.

These real life examples of the work of an MP involved both failure and success; the latter made all the time and effort worthwhile.

CHAPTER 6

In the Whips' Office – 1965–67

*I am made a Whip, Willie Whitelaw Chief Whip – what they
do, the stuffed owl, pairing, Whips' integrity / Inside story
behind Labour government's defeat on 29 March 1979 and the
MP 'who came to abstain in person' / Three line and a four line
Whip / The power to delay government legislation / Locked
out of Prices and Incomes Committee / I whip on Labour's
Leasehold Reform Bill, Committee stage, an ill-considered
vote / I am no longer a Whip, cards marked 'unreliable'*

THE CONSERVATIVE WHIPS' OFFICE OF 1965 consisted of the Chief
Whip, the redoubtable Willie Whitelaw, the deputy chief Brian
Batsford, the Pairing Whip – Bill Elliott, and nine others (including
me). The Whips met briefly at 2.15 daily under Brian Batsford and
on Wednesdays at 12.00 when there would be an hour-long meeting
led by the Chief, ending with a glass of something.

The job of Whips is the management of their Party in the
Commons (and similarly in the Lords). All but the Chief and Deputy
are responsible for the MPs of their geographical area – South East,
London, North West, Scotland etc. As a Whip, it is your job to get
close enough to 'your' Members, to know their general political
stance (left, right, sturdy loyalist or potential rebel and, if so, on
which matters). This is so that when an issue arises on which any of
your flock are sensitive, you know which ones to sound out.

The Chief Whip, although not a member of it, attends the
Cabinet. His advice is sought when an issue arises with conflicting
views in the parliamentary party, particularly if there are potential
rebels. He is equipped to do this through the Wednesday feedback
from the area Whips plus any similar entry in the, then so called, 'dirt
book' between meetings, with, of course, any soundings of his own.

My appointment as a Whip after less than a year as a backbencher
came as a surprise in the reshuffle before the Party Conference of
October 1965. I had seen myself as a businessman in politics rather
than a career politician, and was still sufficiently new not fully to
appreciate its fast streaming potential. In fact, Willie believed 'in

getting the best people into the Whips' Office and while there would never be any commitment as to the future' he did not regard 'service in the Whips' Office as an end in itself but as a valuable training'. Amongst their several duties, a Whip attended every Party Committee Meeting. I then discovered they reported both whether anything important had transpired and on talent shown by any new Members.

I enjoyed my time in the Whips' Office; a useful job to do with tremendous camaraderie and team spirit. Looking back to those Wednesday meetings, I have in mind Willie's fascinating, wonderfully indiscreet and confidential briefings on Shadow Cabinet deliberations etc. and the discussions which followed. The Whips form an ongoing two-way channel of communication, that is to say, they are often approached by back bench colleagues seeking to ensure their views are known by the Front Bench, and vice versa.

Those Wednesday meetings invariably involved Willie inviting our individual opinions on current issues. I gained a healthy respect for George Younger's judgment (subsequently Secretary of State for Defence and, later still, Chairman of the Royal Bank of Scotland). Long after our time in the Whips' Office we exchanged views on financial and economic questions. Francis Pym was interesting to watch. He seemed to assess Willie's view, concurred and normally commented last. Too often I was the first contributor. Had I been both more politically aware and career ambitious, I would have listened more and followed Francis's lead.

Back in 1951 Lt Col Walter Bromley-Davenport, later Sir Walter, had been a Whip when 'an all doors operation' occurred. This happens when there is uncertainty as to whether there will be more than one vote at the end of business. As a result some Members might, in error, leave before the final vote. To forestall this, the Whips vote first and then move to their allotted exit door to warn of further votes. Walter had been allotted the doors at the top of the steps leading to the Members' Cloakroom. An older Member arrived – there was a minor altercation which went something like this:

'Goodnight Walter.'

'You can't go, there's another vote.'

'I've had enough of this place for today.'

'You mustn't go, I'm here to stop you.'

'I said I've had enough, I'm off!'

'If you go through those doors I'll knock you down the steps!'

He did go. Walter, a former Army boxing champion, did knock him down the steps. Shortly afterwards, a brief announcement appeared in *The Times*: 'Lt Col Walter Bromley-Davenport has retired as a Whip in order to devote more time to his constituency, Knutsford, majority 16,930, and in his place Mr Churchill has appointed Mr Edward Heath, Bexley, majority 133.' Fast streamed, Ted never looked back (until Margaret handbagged him!).

The public has an image of Whips as arm-twisting political thugs, devoid of integrity and humanity. True, it may be pointed out to someone that, if they hope for preferment, a particular course of action may not endear them to the current powers that be. There was one occasion during the time of John Major's narrow majorities when one of our lady Members, hesitating as to whether to vote, stood just outside our Division Lobby door. A bluff Whip said, 'Come on, stop standing around like a silly old tart, get in there and vote.' She did, and later complained to the Chief Whip but only on the grounds that she had been called 'old'.

The arm-twisting power of the Whips is much exaggerated, particularly when there are significant issues involved – for example, the votes on sanctions against the régime of Ian Smith, the Southern Rhodesia rebel Prime Minister. Feelings within the Tory Party ran high. On one important vote, although whipped to abstain, a considerable number voted with the government in favour of sanctions, and an even larger number against.

As for Whips' integrity, there is no more shining example of this than the little known Whipping events of 29 March, 1979, which brought down Jim Callaghan's Labour government. The opposition leader, Margaret Thatcher, had tabled the classic motion 'That this House has no confidence in her Majesty's Government'. That morning, the government and opposition Deputy Chief Whips met to 'touch base' and ensure there were no misunderstandings on who was paired,[1] and who was not.

Walter Harrison (Labour) arrived, confident that the government would have a majority of one. Bernard 'Jack' Weatherill (Conservative) indicated dissent. Walter pointed out that he would be able to poll his full strength, except for Dr Sir Alfred Broughton, the seventy seven year old MP for Batley and Morley, who was too ill to be

---

[1] Explanation of pairing arrangements, see page 84.

brought to Westminster.[2] He confirmed his majority of one, relying on another long-established convention, namely to pair the sick. Clearly Broughton came in this category and accordingly should, he claimed, be paired with a sick Conservative. Weatherill responded that this could not happen for the simple reason that he had no sick Member to offer (and in any case by tradition the sick were not paired for full dress debates on a motion of No Confidence in the government of the day). Harrison complained that this refusal amounted to bad faith. Stung by this attack on his integrity and realising that Harrison was genuine in his expectation that a pair would be forthcoming, Weatherill resolved the moral dilemma by himself offering not to vote. Harrison, recognising that by acting in this way, Weatherill would wreck his career, responded that he was not prepared to accept such a sacrifice.[3] So it was that the Labour government fell, the '79 General Election followed and Margaret Thatcher became Prime Minister.

I think it is worth recording that Jim Molyneux's (Leader of the Ulster Unionist MPs) last minute offer to support the government in return for some restoration of local government in Northern Ireland was honourably spurned by Jim Callaghan. Likewise an earlier offer by Enoch Powell of support in return for an undertaking to provide a gas pipeline link between Northern Ireland and the mainland.

One other curious event that evening has long stuck in my mind. When the votes were recorded Frank McGuire, an SDLP (Northern Ireland Social Democrat and Labour) Member, had not voted although he was known to be in the House. Frank, a pub keeper from Fermanagh and South Tyrone, subsequently claimed that he had come over 'to abstain in person' – a lovely, if somewhat unlikely, phrase. It is known that his wife came with him; she was seen in the Members' families' room and later in the Gallery during the SDLP Leader Gerry Fitt's speech at 6.30. Gerry, a regular supporter of Labour in the Division Lobby announced then that because of government policies in Northern Ireland, he had to support the No Confidence motion. He added that there was a rumour that McGuire

---

[2] There existed a convention that those too disabled or ill to walk through the lobby would be 'nodded through' if they were seen to be in the precincts.

[3] Unlike other Deputy Chief Whips, Walter Harrison never received the normal recognition in the Honours List, but he can take greater pride in having put integrity before Party advantage.

was in discussion with government Whips (I am told they were actually trying to fill him with drink) but he (Gerry) 'would be watching very carefully how McGuire voted and if he goes into the government (Labour) lobby tonight . . .' It may be that Mrs McGuire saw this as a threat and hastened her husband away. Be that as it may, this doubly ensured the government's loss of the vote. Curiously Gerry Fitt himself does not appear in Hansard as having voted.

Anyone watching Parliament on TV will notice that there is someone sitting on each Front Bench with a large folder on his lap. He is the 'Whip on Duty'. Each of the nine of us would be on a roster whenever the House sat. This involved noting the time, who spoke and whether any surprising contributions were made – an unexpected hint of rebellion, a powerful new argument or niche knowledge etc. Occasionally Parliamentary business gave an opportunity throughout the night for a Member, lucky in the ballot, to raise a subject of their choice. There ensued a sequence of half-hour debates for which a Minister had to be there to reply. Normally there would be only a handful of Members present, frequently only Member and Minister. It seemed to me unlikely anything would be worth recording in the Whips' folder. At the 2.15 Whips' meeting on the day concerned, I questioned whether a Whip needed to be present; Brian Batsford said 'Yes' and I asked 'What do I do, just sit there like a stuffed owl?' He said 'Yes David, you sit there like a stuffed owl'. Next day when I arrived for the meeting, Brian said 'Here comes the stuffed owl.' For some years after, I was known as 'The Owl'. When he retired, Brian Batsford presented the Conservative Whips' Office with a white-faced stuffed owl in a glass case as a leaving memento. He called it 'Opposition Whip 1965–67'. It went to No 12 Downing Street, the Government Whips' Office in 1970, and back and forth as we moved in and out of office.

There is an altogether different Whip – this is the sheet of paper which sets out the business for the ensuing week. This is important in itself, but also for pairing and is a mystery to those not familiar with the House. Typically this would refer to the House meeting at 2.30 – Questions to the Secretary of State for, say, Transport, then at 3.30 perhaps a Ministerial Statement, or a PNQ (Private notice question, probably a Member raising some ghastly incident in his constituency seeking a Ministerial Statement). Then the main business, say the Second Reading of the Channel Tunnel Bill with a

10 o'clock vote, followed by the words 'Your attendance is *essential*' underlined with three thick black lines. This meant you were expected to be there, however inconvenient. I recall one Member interrupting a business trip to New York to be present and furious when he discovered the Government majority was nearly a hundred! The lesser imperative read: 'your attendance is essential unless you have registered a "firm pair"' underlined with two black lines and, finally 'your attendance is requested' underscored once.

I have framed near me that which may be, as far as I know, the only *four-line* Whip ever promulgated. See illustration on page 85.

I presented a copy to the Conservative Whips' Office but this was mistakenly left at 12 Downing Street in 1997; I understand there has been a reluctance to return it.

To pair, a Member and someone on the opposite benches agree that both will be away, leaving the Government majority unaltered. Pairing is a personal matter; it can be done on an *ad hoc* basis, but far better to have a regular pair. For many years mine was the late Harold Walker, the Labour Member for Doncaster. We were both to become junior and successively more senior Ministers in our Governments. When Harold was a Minister needing to be absent, I would pair him even though I remained in the House that evening. When I was a Minister he reciprocated, an arrangement with which we were both content. That was, until one day – alas for me – he was made Deputy Speaker. Neither Speaker nor Deputy can show any political partiality[4] so neither vote nor pair. I could not find a regular pair for that whole year. The *Sunday Express* reported that I had the best voting record of any Minister in the Government – little did anyone know it was *force majeure*.

We Junior Whips each had a desk in the Lower Whips' Office; after a while I was invited to share an office with Bill Elliott, the

---

[4] This is well illustrated by an exchange between Michael Foot and Mr Speaker Thomas (later Lord Tonypandy). Foot complained of the Speaker's ruling that the Aircraft and Shipbuilding Industries Bill was *prima facie* Hybrid and this ruling was no way to treat an old colleague, to which he received the rebuff 'Mr Speaker has no old colleagues'. He then turned from Michael Foot to Robin Maxwell-Hyslop standing the other side of his Chair who thanked him for his ruling.

Perhaps not the rhetorical flourish proclaiming the independence of the Chair by Mr Speaker Lenthall's famous statement that 'he had no eyes to see, no ears to hear and no lips to speak save as this House is pleased to direct me'. Nevertheless it is an up to date and robust affirmation of the impartiality of the Speaker.

Important.

On Friday July 7th the House will meet at 2 o'clock.

The "Prevention of Crime" Bill will be taken on Report.

Amendments of Great Importance, will be moved.

The Government Concession on Clause 13 restricting Night Search will be opposed.

Mr Gibson will propose his Amendment making Boycotting the subject of Compensation.

On both of these, Divisions of the greatest Importance will be taken.

Your attendance throughout the 2 o'clock Sitting is most earnestly & particularly requested.

RowWinn

House of Commons 11 July 1882

This is a specially interesting 'Whip' because on the 7th July 1882 in the afternoon sitting, the 'Gladstone' Government received its first defeat on a question affecting its Irish Policy

Charles C. Ross.

Four Line Whip

pairing Whip. The Whips' staff keep a register of members who have paired, and give the 'Pairing Whip' the list of those absent but not paired. If they have not appeared, they are then invited to come in and explain.

Most members are pretty conscientious. Nevertheless, I recall one absentee (I'll call him 'the old lag') whom Bill had to deal with more than once, but this time it was different. A week or so earlier X, a senior former Minister, had asked Bill if he could have leave of absence on a three line whip (pairing not allowed) in order that he could attend his Association AGM. It was known he had some difficulty with his constituency Association because he was not around as much as they expected. Having this in mind, Bill reluctantly consented. Next morning, 'the old lag' came in to apologise for his absence and to explain he had been at Annabel's (night club) and there was this gorgeous girl . . . 'Well, you know me Bill, I just couldn't tear myself away.'

Bill responded, 'Not the first time . . .' etc, 'it was a three liner, you are letting the side down.' etc.

The old lag interrupted. 'But Bill, I wasn't the only one – X was there too.'

Later that day by pure chance, Bill was crossing the Members' Lobby when X came in; seeing Bill he came over and thanked him for the previous evening. Bill asked how the AGM had gone and received a suitable response – then 'But yours must be the only Association to hold its AGM in Annabel's.'

X's briefcase crashed to the floor, his mouth dropped open, and he said 'Bill, how on earth did you know?'

To Bill's eternal credit, he said 'But the Whips' office would never be able to function if we did not have the doorman at Annabel's on our payroll!'

Each Whip would cover two or three Party Committees. When there was pending legislation, he would stick with the subject through the Committee Stage of the Bill. This might run for several weeks, meeting twice a week from 10.30 a.m. to 1 p.m. with extra afternoons and, sometimes, evening sittings on long and controversial legislation. The only real power Opposition Members had was that of delay, so sometimes evening sittings would then run the whole night.

Members are not allowed to filibuster by constant repetition. If they do, the Chairman will interrupt, calling them to order. I recall one such all-night sitting. Speeches from our side often starting 'I do not want to delay the Committee (!!) but this amendment is important, it gets to the heart of XYZ'; perhaps a colleague would then rise and ask him to 'give way' and then ask if he would elaborate on a point he claimed he could not fully understand. It may sound childish; certainly it was good fun but importantly could cause serious delay to the Government legislative programme. Cumulatively this would result in squeezing out some Bills through lack of time to complete before the ensuing General Election. For example, in the spring of 1997 Labour's Whips succeeded in losing John Major's government four important Bills.

An interesting and rare example of one member, on his own, seriously delaying the government's programme was provided by my friend, Robin Maxwell-Hyslop MP.

He knew, or certainly understood, the Parliamentary procedure as well as, and betimes better than, the Clerks of the House whose duty is to advise on such matters. Normal Government 'Public Bills' go through the House relatively quickly. By contrast, a Bill affecting an individual interest involves a lengthy, time-consuming process. In 1976, the Labour Government introduced a 'Public Bill' to national-ise five industries. Robin spotted that it was a 'hybrid' and so subject to both processes. A lengthy wrangle ensued. Eventually Robin was proved right. As a result of his efforts alone, Labour's Aircraft & Shipbuilding Industries Bill was held up for some eighteen months.

Robin was a man of integrity and courage who would speak up for what he believed to be right, regardless of whether his view was generally acceptable or not. In 1972 just after Ted Heath's famous – or rather, infamous, U-Turn, the Prime Minister came to address the 1922 Committee (a group to which all non-ministerial Tory Members automatically belong). He explained his reason for this reversal of a central theme on which his Government had been elected.

The Chairman said 'Any Questions to the Prime Minister?' Robin rose. 'Chairman, it is an accepted part of our Parliamentary traditions exemplified in the Crichel Down case that, when a Minister makes a serious error, he should resign. Is there any reason why this should not apply at the top?'

There was a sudden, deathly silence. For a few moments the colour drained from Ted's face. Then, after a pause, he said 'That may be what Robin thinks, but others do not share his view.' The tension broke and Ted had got away with it. Robin, despite his many qualities, never saw ministerial office . . .

On another occasion Robin mounted a campaign against the easy availability of long-barrelled pistols, a dangerous weapon too easily bought, at that time, off the shelf in a variety of shops. He had raised the matter in correspondence, all to no avail. Finally came an appointment with Monty Woodhouse, the Minister of State (No 2) in the Home Office. In those days this department was in the old Georgian buildings on the East side of Whitehall.

Spot on the appointed time, Robin arrived, complete with the offending .410 pistol and ammunition, and was ushered into the Minister's room to find him behind his desk signing letters, his legs tipping his chair back on to its two back legs. Monty said he would only be a minute and Robin sat by the empty fireplace. After a few minutes he said 'Minister, I had an appointment.' 'OK, I won't be long.' Robin's fuse can be a short one and several minutes later, it blew. Picking up the pistol and loading it, he pointed it up the chimney and pulled the trigger. The noise echoed through the old building, soot came pouring down the chimney and the Minister's chair went over backwards. Civil servants rushed in to a scene forever imprinted on their memories, and in the annals of the Whips' Office – the Minister still flat on his back, Robin, smoking pistol in hand surrounded by a haze of soot. Eventually, his campaign was indeed successful.

Locked out!

I whipped George Brown's 1965 Prices & Incomes Bill. This sought to control both of them, but was largely impracticable. I became enormously impressed by Shirley Williams, one of the Junior Ministers handling the Bill when George Brown was, not infrequently, absent. Her responses to questions and probing amendments were uniformly logical and succinct. The last Committee sitting on this Bill was an all-nighter with the final debate on a Government new clause providing 'authority for employers to disregard pay increases in *existing* contracts' of employment. John Biffen raised the case of workers whose contract of employment provided pay increases tied to the cost of living index. Sir Tatton Brinton, the carpet manufacturer, raised the forty-five-year-old RPI pay agreement in his company, putting him personally in the hot seat as a manufacturer either breaking his word to his employees or deliberately defying the Government. This pay increase was, he explained, due to be implemented that very day. After a lot of heart searching 'we decided we could not and should not defy the Government. We have broken our word and we are ashamed'. I pointed out that the sanctity of contract is central to the organisation of our society. Then I instanced constituents in the expanded towns of Basingstoke and Andover who were buying houses and taking out hire purchase contracts in the knowledge they had salary increases coming to them. What uproar if a Tory Government had done this! It was, I said, the most disreputable and disgraceful piece of legislation introduced by any Government this century and I hoped that if 'Hon. Members opposite vote for this . . . they will go back to their constituencies and that their constituents will tell them what they think of them. They serve ill their Trade Unions, they serve ill their constituents and they serve ill the House of Commons in which they sit.' In retrospect, if I was somewhat overheated, it could be forgiven since it was 9.35 on Friday morning and the Committee had sat (after its morning sitting) with limited breaks from 4 o'clock the previous afternoon (having already sat through Tuesday night until 7 a.m.).[5]

During this stage of the Bill I made twenty nine speeches. When one Division was called, I looked round to find Kenneth Lewis, one of my flock, was absent. I hurried down the corridor to the loos to alert him; he was not there. I ran back to the bank of telephones, no luck. As I pushed the door to re-enter the Committee Room there was a click as the door was locked. I hammered on the door, but it was not opened. The sitting was in Committee Room 12, the only one with two glass-panelled doors. Standing there fuming, I could hear the count taking place, so when my name was called I shouted 'No!', causing considerable laughter, it being the Whip who was locked out. The doors re-opened and I resumed my place, to some hilarity. On a point of order, Tatton Brinton raised whether my vote would be included. It turned out that Kenneth Lewis had re-entered the Committee by the other door at the precise moment I left to look for him. I explained this to the Chairman and asked for my vote to

---

[5] This was, in fact, the longest Committee stage for any Bill since 1947, including two all-night sittings, one lasting over 24 hours.

be recorded. He said that when my 'anguished poundings came to his ears' and he observed that the missing Member was a Whip, he had both enquired of the Clerk whether there were grounds to unlock the doors and then whether my vote could be recorded, but it was not within his power, adding 'the Hon. Member's vote will be recorded more permanently in the memories of other Hon. Members than a vote ever has been in the Official Report'.[6]

Subsequently, from time to time, George Brown would enquire of me whether I had been locked out of anywhere recently. He was a nice man, often wrong-headed but sincere (a charge rarely laid at Harold Wilson's door). Also he was, from time to time, wonderfully indiscreet. For example attending a reception at the Norwegian Embassy at a time when backless dresses were all the rage, George apparently told the Ambassador's wife that she looked stunning in this dress, however adding that it would look even better the other way round. She was furious and when officials remonstrated, George simply responded that he had only said what everyone else was thinking.

I cannot resist another tale told to George's embarrassment. At a big civic dinner in Leningrad he noticed, during the social break before speeches, the gentlemen streamed out through one labelled door and the ladies through another. So, carefully noting the Russian for 'Ladies and Gentlemen' he started his speech accordingly. On sitting down, he turned to our Ambassador and said he hoped his speech would help improve relations, only to be taken aback by the response 'Foreign Secretary, it may be some while before the good citizens of Leningrad recover from being addressed as Ladies' washbasins and Gentlemen's urinals'!

Leasehold Reform Bill

I also whipped the Leasehold Reform Bill. Long leases, often for ninety nine years, had been a big feature in Victorian times. By 1966 many of these leases were running out, causing an outcry from tenants who had either to move elsewhere or negotiate new leases at rents very much higher than the, often nominal, level to which they were accustomed. The National Union of Mineworkers weighed in,

---

[6] Erskine May, the official guide to Parliamentary Procedure, states that a member sought to vote from outside the Committee. The Chairman, Harold Lever, ruled that disembodied voices do not count.

and enfranchisement for tenants featured in Labour's election manifesto. Hence they introduced their Reform Bill in 1967, giving lessee tenants the right to buy out their lessor's freehold. Much of the Committee stage was taken up with two issues: what price the tenant would pay and whether all long leaseholders would have this right or, as the government proposed, only those with properties up to a rateable value of £400 in London (£200 elsewhere).

The Minister, Fred Willey, established a so-called principle that the ground belonged to the landlord and the house to the tenant, so on enfranchisement the tenant paid only for the land and received the house for nothing. The first Conservative amendment moved by the rather dry solicitor, Graham Page, leading for us, sought to insert that the tenant could acquire 'for fair compensation'. I spoke in support of the concept of spreading owner occupation, but at a fair price. I pointed out that many of these long leases were created on the basis that the original tenant was required to build a house to a certain standard and, in return for so doing, he paid an almost nominal rent – I instanced £8 a year for ninety nine years. The Minister accepted the amendment, but stuck to his so-called 'principle' claiming it to be fair. Next there followed a lengthy debate as to whether the proposed upper limits of £200 and £400 should be swept away for, if it was right in principle to enfranchise some tenants, then logically that principle should stand for all.

In practical terms there were many unfairnesses in these arbitrary upper limits – erecting a garage, installing central heating and other improvements could put enfranchisement out of reach. There were houses sub-divided for multiple occupation, some valued as a single unit and others per apartment. Those above shops were often valued with the shop, etc. There was almost cross-party unanimity in supporting the amendment. The Minister agreed that the Bill as drafted was too restrictive and he undertook to bring forward a government amendment at the next stage in the Bill's progress. Graham Page, our Shadow Minister, provided the only opposition on the grounds that, although we had succeeded in inserting 'fair compensation' into the Bill, he did not follow his colleagues 'and hide my head in the sand, disregarding later provisions in the Bill and the intention to confiscate the lessor's interest in his property.'

In the ensuing vote virtually the whole Committee, Labour and Conservative alike, supported the abolition of the limits, so enfranchising all tenants. However, one (Graham Page) voted against; the Whip, that's me, abstained. My failure to vote in support of our Shadow Minister was taken on the spur of the moment, not a carefully thought-through plan. I recall my decision was influenced by it being both the honourable thing to do when the rest of our members on the Committee knew that I agreed with them, and also the thought that if the rich and powerful landlords were included there was a real chance that the resources for a successful campaign against the Government terms of compensation would be forthcoming.

I understand that later that day Ted Heath was not best pleased to receive a deputation representing the ranks of high value freeholders now to be brought within the compass of the Bill. Furthermore the Chief Whip was not amused. The Committee's near unanimous decision was subsequently reversed at the Report stage in the Chamber of the Commons.[7] Later, called by Willie Whitelaw to account for my misdeeds, I was reminded that Whips are responsible for the management of the party in the Commons, that since I was more interested in the politics of issues this was best pursued from the back benches. He added in a more kindly tone that he was not going to sack me from the Whips' Office, but that if I remained I would make no further progress there. To leave in the anonymity of the long summer recess seemed the best way forward and was agreed.

But the fact was, I had blown it, my cards must have been marked as unreliable. It was to be twelve years before I became a Minister, happily earning the reputation in the then Whips' Office for being a 'safe pair of hands'.

---

[7] During this latter debate John Boyd-Carpenter MP was accused of giggling, and replied 'When a Minister in charge of a major government Bill votes one way in Committee and within a matter of weeks moves an amendment to reverse his own vote, a little merriment is surely permitted'.

CHAPTER 7

Er and Um

A pot pourri of family and personal anecdotes

POLITICS SHOULD NEVER BECOME such an obsession that it excludes everything else. This could not be the case with me, for my time was split between the demands of a family business on one side and the great Parliamentary issues along with constituency work on the other. With so much to do, it was inevitable that I became a workaholic, but a happy one. However, I am now more aware of the two chronic mistakes I can so easily slip into, the first being to put the urgent before the important.[1]

Looking back now, I recognise more than ever how precious are the memories of Pam, the children in their formative years, our country cottage with its productive organic garden, my bee-keeping efforts, donkeys, horses and holidays. Of course there are many other indelible memories.

For example, MPs and their wives receive an invitation to one of the summer Garden Parties at Buckingham Palace. I still remember the particular thrill of the first time: the discovery that the entrance opens out into a large courtyard, steps up on the far side, and indoors a stunning display of priceless porcelain. Then steps down into the garden, tea tent on the left and flamingos on the lake beyond. My uncertainty as to whether to wear, with my grandfather's morning coat, his black or grey waistcoat and top hat? Standing on the inner steps surveying a sea of grey toppers, I found Harold Macmillan beside me in black murmuring 'You and I appear to be the only ones properly dressed'. Then iced coffee, cucumber sandwiches and cakes, the band playing, a wander along the flowerbeds and bumping into old friends – all one lasting and happy memory. Another year, hatless and using a side entrance to go in (no queue) we crossed with Enoch and Pam Powell coming out: 'David, where is your hat?' demanded Enoch and then, 'You cannot go in without one – take mine'.

---

[1] For the second, see the Chapter 'Travels with a Wallaby'.

Later came the great red letter day in February 1968 when I was a guest for lunch; no reason given for this wholly unexpected privilege. I suspect that Willie Whitelaw as Chief Whip had a hand in it. My most lasting impression of that day is the thorough briefing Her Majesty had mastered on each guest, her comments on Basingstoke's expansion, together with her enquiry whether I had been to the new town of Cumbernauld to see what lessons should be learned; I had not.

Andrew and Suki started at the Play and Learn Montessori School run by the Vicar's wife. Andrew played, Suki learned. We decided a more traditional school was needed and found it in Kensington, not too many rules but these were firmly enforced. The only problem was the twice daily battle through the rush hour. This led us to house hunting in the Sloane Square area, mid way between school and the Commons. I bought the last twenty years of the lease on 46 Eaton Terrace; it had been empty for eighteen months and the vendor was anxious to sell.

A constituency visit to North Foreland Lodge School near Basingstoke decided us that Suki should go there, rather than any of the three others we had seen, the intention being that she should go on to Benenden for sixth form work. When that time approached we paid a visit there, together with her school books. We met the redoubtable Head Mistress, Miss Clarke. Her response was that 'Suki's work is fine, she can come here provided she wants to and commits herself'. Suki's response, when we returned to the car was 'Dad, if you send me here, I'll run away.' Talk of daughter having father over a barrel! No matter, for she later became PA to the Editor of *The Times*.

I think Andrew was seven, not long after he could write, when we had a drinks party. Andrew was allotted the task of taking round a tray of food. Later I heard Walter Khan, gliding enthusiast and cigar importer, guffaw with laughter. No Andrew in sight, but in childish handwriting a note 'help yourselves'. Walter said, 'When he grows up I'll give that boy a job', which he did – for at least one holiday.

Another day, Graham aged three decided to have a second brush with death and toddled down the garden, through the 'child proof' railings and into the swimming pool. Judy, then a new secretary-cum-mother's help, suddenly said, 'There is something in the pool'. Pam rushed out, saw only two hands above the water, jumped in, held Graham upside down while water poured from his every orifice.

Thank God, he started to scream. After a hot bath, all was well. Needless to say Judy, now Mrs Peter Abbott, is, and always will be, a very special person to our family.

About five years later I was gardening when Graham asked me if I remembered when he was small and got through the pool railings. I said, 'Of course'.

'Do you think I could still do it?' he asked. I said decidedly not. Next it was, would I have a bet? I agreed at half a crown. To my surprise, the little blighter did it. A few minutes later I heard a voice down by the house say 'Mum, do you remember when I was small . . .?'

As mentioned previously, we had bought a donkey to give the children the feel of riding, prior to getting a pony. Unfortunately she bucked them off and when I said, 'I'll show you,' she bucked me off. When we moved from our weekend farm cottage in Kent to Odiham, Jennie came too. Before long she was in foal to the local blacksmith's jack producing Topsy, an enchanting and easy to handle chocolate brown youngster from whom in turn we bred three foals; the last one is still with me.

After one thoroughly enjoyable holiday pony trekking on Dartmoor, we returned with April, a grey mare for Suki. Later, when Suki became a boarder at school, Pam or I had to exercise the animal. We each became bored with doing this on our own. We bought a second horse I had ridden on a previous holiday, and rode together. Alas, there is a lively difference between a hard-worked horse on poor Dartmoor hay and one with only weekend exercise on rich Hampshire grass. My own enthusiasm waned after a fall which produced two broken ribs. We put both horses in foal and subsequently sold all four, retaining our much loved Topsy whom we counted as one of the family. She ensured we had the best compost heap and the richest garden soil for miles.

I had inherited two beehives from my father. They were put to good use, but our bees provided a number of surprises. One afternoon I was extracting honey from combs (slice the top off the comb, clip it in a drum, briskly turn the handle and the honey spins out). I had not finished before I had to go to a meeting. I left everything in the kitchen ready to complete later. On my return I found, to my consternation, the bees had come in through a small window and taken back to the hive all the honey left in the extractor – indeed they had been so thorough that its inside was not even sticky!

Graham survived!

Family pets are quite capable of causing embarrassment. One evening Pam and I were watching TV and enjoying a smoked trout supper on our laps. I had cut off the head of mine, then when I looked down, only the head was left on my plate. Minka, our slinky Siamese, had removed the rest without disturbing me. We had a drinks party the next evening. In the middle of arrivals, Minka strolled in. I pointed to her and said to those around me, 'Meet the most accomplished thief in London' – at which moment Patrick McNair-Wilson, a fellow MP, hove into sight; he blushed and asked what on earth I was talking about.

Another embarrassment came when a pet hamster, invited by Suki for a short stay, escaped from its box and, only after a long search, was found amidst some Common Market regulations after quietly chewing the corners off a number of letters ready for posting to constituents.

As with every other parent, I worried about the children when they first started driving. Andrew distinguished himself by crashing into the stone retaining wall of the river bridge at Egton near

Whitby. Such was the force of impact (allegedly at 25 mph!) that the wall collapsed, the car went over it and down the river bank. Fortunately it was stopped by a small tree just above the thirty-foot precipitous drop into the water.

What is it about bridges? Some years later Graham, his younger brother, spent an agreeable evening in the Forest Inn on Dartmoor with, among others, Suey, the local farmer's daughter. I had foolishly lent him my camper van. He was due to camp by the river below the farmhouse. Offered a lift, Suey declined since she had arrived on her pony. Yes, you've guessed it, Graham crashed the passenger side of the camper into the parapet of the bridge. I have no recollection of Suey accepting any future lift from him.

The last word in this short chapter belongs to Suki, then aged ten. I had to take her with me to a meeting on the Common Market, a subject I feared would bore her as much as it would any other little girl of her age. To my pleasant surprise she sat at the back, listening with rapt attention. Afterwards on the way back to the car she said 'Daddy, did you know you said 'er' or 'um' twenty three times'!

CHAPTER 8

Small business – the seedcorn of prosperity

Potential of small firms unrecognised / I find myself a
niche / New Parliamentary group to champion small
businesses / Andrew Rowe, later an MP, and I create the
Small Business Bureau, launched by Margaret Thatcher / Our
Parliamentary Committee and SBB play a crucial part in
changing the business culture of our time

AT THE TIME I ENTERED PARLIAMENT, and for more than a decade after, the conventional wisdom of the nation's opinion formers was all about the economies of scale and the perceived benefits of mass production. By contrast the rôle and potential of small businesses was ignored and largely unknown. It was against this background that in 1969 Bernard Weatherill MP and John Cope had written their pioneering pamphlet 'Acorns to Oaks'. This had focused mainly on manufacturing. Mr Speaker Weatherill, as he is widely remembered, ran a successful tailoring business whilst John, now Lord, Cope – a Chartered Accountant from Leicester – subsequently with Conservative Central Office Research Department and later an MP, brought that special insight which Chartered Accountants possess on the internal affairs of their clients. Their publication put the case for a more balanced approach, homing in on the alert small firm, able to run rings round the giants, but needing a level playing field.

Between 1964 and 1972 I had intermittently spoken to defend the interests of small business, usually as a result of constituents' representations against the impact of legislation. For example, the Labour Government's Budget of 1965 had introduced Capital Gains Tax. Apart from other damage, this meant that anyone ploughing their profits back to build up their business would face a tax of 30 per cent or 40 per cent of the gain from their efforts when they sold out on retirement. Worse still, increased value resulting purely from inflation would also be included in their tax demand. I moved an amendment to the Finance Bill, without success, to exempt these illusory profits from taxation. The next Budget in 1966 brought in SET (Selective Employment Tax) designed to benefit employment by manufacturers and disadvantage the services sector. This was ill thought through and full of anomalies; for example, a baker who made bread on his shop premises paid the tax, whereas his competitor who baked in a workshop across the street did not. In another anomaly, the direct labour departments of nationalised industries and local government did not pay this 'jobs tax' whilst the private sector, tendering in competition for contracts, had to pay. I moved an amendment designed to ensure a level playing field; alas, this was also defeated.

There was a rowdy scene when the Deputy Speaker, judging the main debate on the SET clause had gone on long enough, 'put the question', i.e. terminated the debate by calling a Division. I was one of those seeking to raise a 'point of order', which gave rise to an amusing incident. The rules of the House then sensibly provided that, in the mêlée of Members moving around the Chamber on their way to vote, anyone raising a point of order had to be seated and wearing a hat. This naturally caught the Speaker's attention. I was seated next to the formidable Dame Irene Ward who must have been going to a Buckingham Palace Garden Party, since she was wearing a large flowered hat. She took it off and passed it to me. Unfortunately this was before sittings were televised![1]

A parliamentary group for small business

With the change of government in 1970 Ted Heath became Prime Minister and Nick Ridley the first ever Minister directly responsible for small business policy, followed by Tony Grant. In spite of being pretty busy with both my tasks as Keith Joseph's PPS and my work at El Vino, I started to become a one-man pressure group on behalf of small firms. Whilst welcoming the progress being made by our Ministers, particularly in implementing the important Bolton Committee's recommendations on small companies, I constantly urged them to go further. Indeed, in some quarters I started to be seen as

---

[1] Dame Irene, a widely respected older Member, was disturbed in 1941 that factories were turning out thousands of sailors' uniforms but, alas, few for the Wrens. She tabled a PQ (Parliamentary Question); the Minister's answer spoke of priority for sailors. Irene's supplementary question ran 'Is my Rt. Hon. Friend telling me that Wrens' skirts have to be held up until the needs of every sailor in the Navy have been satisfied'!

a bit of a nut case, forever banging on about small businesses. Regardless of party loyalties, I would frequently badger our government on their behalf. Joel Barnett, later Labour's Chief Secretary to the Treasury, once commented that in 1972 he was in the strange and unusual position of having willingly to support the Member for Basingstoke, saying that he would not be quite as fierce with the Conservative government as I was, adding, 'I am staggered. I should not have dreamt of using such strong language.'

Many MPs come into the House hoping or often misguidedly believing that they will, single handedly, change the course of history. It is not like that; if you really want to achieve change you are much more likely to succeed if you join with like-minded colleagues and form a small pressure group. This started to happen, probably through chatting in the Members' tearoom. By 1973, together with John Loveridge, John Hannam, Eric Cockeram, Peter Rost and Richard Luce and others, we formed an unofficial Conservative Small Business Committee with varying support growing to between twenty and thirty members. I was elected Chairman with John Loveridge as the Secretary. It was an enormous help that he could call on the facilities of his own secretarial college. At the time we said we would study in depth the contribution small businesses made to the national economy, together with their potential and the problems which held them back.

Even our limited research revealed that almost all UK major companies had, in fact, started as small ones. Taylor Woodrow, a worldwide construction company, was started by Frank Taylor with £30 and a bank loan of £400. He built a pair of semi-detached houses in Blackpool and then won the contract to build a public loo for £1,000. Similarly Laings, another construction giant, started as the village builder fifteen miles outside Carlisle. The great Cornish china clay industry owed its existence to the experiments of a local doctor in Fowey; Morphy Richards, back in 1973 an electrical appliance giant, started in a barn in 1936; Plessey in a shed next to a print works. Glaxo, Beecham, Marks & Spencer and Unilever all trace their start-up to a small business. 'From acorns can grow mighty oaks', we said over and over again.

It is true that, like people, some businesses will have a lifecycle starting small, growing, but with the passage of time, becoming jaded, their products out of date, only to be overtaken by a competitor and

Speaking in the House of Commons

die. As one generation of businesses went, traditionally another would spring up to take their place with new ideas, new vigour and new products. At that time, it was estimated that within ten years, half the products in our shops (apart from food) would be ones not then available, many of them new inventions. Further research uncovered the alarming fact that Britain had 40 per cent fewer small firms than the continental equivalent; nor was it irrelevant that in West Germany the proportion of family owned firms, the majority of which would be small, was twice as large as in the UK. Since small firms were clearly the seed corn of large ones, this was an ominous and chilling statistic in terms of Britain's future economic prospects.

Our committee established a continuing 'working relationship' with virtually all the bodies representing both the self-employed and small firms, among others the Small Business Association, later the Association of Independent Businesses, The National Federation of Self Employed, the National Chamber of Trade, the Small Firms Council of the CBI, the Association of British Chambers of Commerce, together with many local Chambers, the Forum for Private Business and others.

1974, with its two general elections, restored a Labour Government led by Harold Wilson. It also brought into the House a number of welcome additions to our band of small business enthusiasts. Some did not come empty handed; in particular John Cope introduced the concept of the 'Proprietary Company', a category of smaller business which could then be recognised as different from the large public company. This would offer the opportunity to relieve them of costly compliance with a huge amount of regulation, most of it appropriate only to much larger businesses. They could also be taxed differently. Peter Morrison, a good ideas man, joined us, as did Richard Page, who like me was an active small businessman and later a capable minister for small firms. Also John MacGregor fresh from the hustings came, keenly aware of the hardship caused by rocketing rate demands on small shops and similar businesses. For householders, the problem had been partially mitigated by a measure of domestic rate relief and the opportunity to pay by instalments. In 1975, John introduced a Bill to extend these benefits to small firms. News of his proposals had resulted in a huge postbag of support. Drawing on these letters, John's well researched speech gave some shocking examples including increases between 1972/3 and 1974/5 for a village post office from £153 to £513, a small grocer from £65 to £229, another shop from £157 to £866 and a tiny florists from £352 to £1,114. The Bill foundered because of the Government's opposition to it, but it had successfully highlighted yet another small business problem.

Small firm motivation

In 1974 I wrote a booklet 'SEED CORN' subtitled the 'Problems and Potential of Smaller Businesses', published in August that year by Aims of Industry. This stated at the beginning that it was a booklet with a purpose. I wanted to show what makes small businesses tick and to illustrate their collective contribution to our national prosperity. In addition to point up how a government minded to encourage and exploit the potential of this sector would benefit all our people through the resultant surge in the creation of additional wealth, also importantly, the extra yield for Government from a wider tax base. First I identified the obvious, and then the interestingly different motivations of those who start and build up a business, or expand an existing one.

There is the so-called 'selfish motive' of an improved standard of living for oneself, one's own family and older dependants. Selfish it may be, but without the prospect that success will satisfy this motivation, significantly fewer people would undertake the risks and worries inherent in running their own firm. A related motive is the desire to give one's children a better start in life than one had oneself. That this is a forceful motivation is well illustrated by the tremendous sacrifices many parents make to pay school fees.

One powerful desire in many men and women is to preserve something they have created and built up, also, related to this, the dynastic urge to build something which will go on to future generations. In the case of those who inherit such enterprises, there is often a feeling of trusteeship; a sense of responsibility to pass on to the next generation at least as successful a business as they inherited and, hopefully, add another storey to the house. A different but widespread motivation can be summed up in one word: 'challenge', whether it is climbing a mountain, entering a competition, or running a race. Challenge and its co-partner, a sense of achievement and the satisfaction from success, are often the spur. I recall it was Bertram Mills who, whilst watching an uninspiring circus perform-ance, commented 'I'll eat my hat if I cannot do better than that'. On being taken up on this challenge he started up his own highly successful circus. As a boy I had a holiday job in their stables.

One satisfaction, it is probably fair to call it a motivation, is the opportunity of self expression, which is more than simply backing your own judgment; each part of the business is a part of you, an expression of your personality, your own decisions on product, service and style etc. I had been constantly impressed by the infectious enthusiasm and the determination of so many of those starting up on their own. Never overlook the feeling of indepen-dence, nor 'status', being respected in your local community, the exhilaration of being your own master, nor, for that matter, the demands on oneself. My father used to say 'the only person more demanding to work for than your own father is working for yourself'. Whatever the proprietor's motivation, you can be certain that love of the Chancellor of the Exchequer motivates only a handful of entrepreneurs – if any. As I write, I hear snide remarks from time to time, suggesting that Margaret Thatcher was responsible for develop-ing a 'selfish society'; actually it was a motivated and self-reliant

With Margaret Thatcher on a visit to Basingstoke constituency

society. Her critics overlook that the renewal of the private sector creates the future wealth and taxes needed for the expenditure we all, including said critics, want for our public services. Those who vilify her now, choose to forget that her popularity was so widespread she became the first Prime Minister to secure three successive election victories since the 1820s!

Back in 1974, the cumulative contribution of small business to the national economy was much greater than generally recognised. John Bolton, the then accepted 'guru' on the subject, referred to seven million working in small firms who were about a third of all working people outside the public sector, and collectively producing a quarter of the whole GNP (Gross National Product). In grasping the small firm's contribution, one has to remember that many industries dominated by large firms, – aircraft, cars, shipbuilding etc. are assemblers of bought in components, a large percentage of which are produced by small specialist suppliers. Not only that, but the small firms are considerably more inventive, innovative and flexible than larger ones. This is increasingly important now the pace of technological change is so great.[2] Nor should one overlook their contribution to the quality of life by providing wider choice and variety for consumers.

New and growing firms provide competition to established operators, particularly valuable when linked to a new product. Be in no doubt that competition does more to increase efficiency and lower prices than can any amount of legislation, official board or appointed regulator.

For me, there has always been another and deeper reason for wanting to be involved in and, as it turned out, to lead a Parliamentary pressure group seeking to increase the number of small and growing firms; simply that the dispersed economic power of each new business is one more brick in the edifice of creating and spreading wealth more and more widely throughout our society.

Alas, the incoming Labour governments of 1974–79 had no comprehension of the financial needs of small firms. In particular they did not understand the dependence of both the self employed and almost all owner-managed businesses on retained profits to finance growth and development. The reason for this is that the high street banks do not invest in their customers' business, but lend, invariably with a proviso that they can demand repayment at will. Moreover, they lend against tangible assets, not the amount necessary to assure success of a project. If a business has property, they will lend against that. In most start-up situations, there will be no business property, so the entrepreneur has to mortgage his house, his pension etc. Keith Joseph sent on to me a letter from a businessman commenting that there is no English word for 'entrepreneur', but the best interpretation would be 'an undertaker of risk'. The high street banks were in the business of holding clients' money, not taking risks.

Many, if not most, new businesses start as self employed or sole traders, either alone or with a small number of employees. I found even MPs amazed when they discovered such businesses paid income tax not only on the money they took out of the firm, but also on the profits they retained in the business. For this reason, the higher rates of income tax had a disproportionate impact on such firms, both in destroying the entrepreneur's motivation and taking out of the business the cash it needed for its expansion.

---

[2] See T. Eiloart and P.G. Peterson, *Fanning the Flames of Innovation*.

Denis Healey, Labour's Chancellor, famously vowed to tax the rich until the pips squeaked. He raised the top marginal rate of income tax to 83 per cent, hugely above any other major country in the world. His 'making the pips squeak' also imposed a tax surcharge on income from savings and investment, taking that marginal rate up to 98 per cent, but who in their right mind would take the downside risk of investing in a small firm with the upside benefit of 2 per cent left after tax? Just £20 left out of £1,000! Swept up in this penal tax net along with wealthy high earners were countless struggling smaller firms who desperately needed to retain this cash in the business for working capital. One of the under-recognised sources of start-up finance was to borrow from relatives, mainly uncles, aunts, parents and also, not infrequently, a wealthy acquaintance. In the latter case, this could bring the added benefit of financial advice from someone older and more experienced. (For example my paternal grandfather put up part of the money to enable Stakesby's Garage on the outskirts of Whitby to get started.) Alas, thanks to Healey, there became little or no incentive for individuals to back small businesses.

Faced with the tax penalties of being a sole trader, the more successful moved on to become limited companies. This eased the tax burden on the working proprietor but still left his business largely dependent on retained profit for expansion. Unhappily, Healey then increased corporation tax!

Inflation and unemployment

Worse still, by 1976, all businesses large and small were suffering from a more insidious attack – inflation. This had gone up from just under 13 per cent when Labour took office to peak at 27 per cent in August 1975. As inflation accelerated, every business needed to retain more money within it to carry on the same volume of trade. For example, to put it at its simplest, a corner shop with £5,000 worth of stock on its shelves would, with inflation at 20 per cent, need one year later £6,000 for that same volume of stock. This inflationary effect hit every manufacturer or trading business through-out the country. Whilst the large public company could borrow or raise more working capital on the stock market, it was the smaller firm which was most at risk. Undoubtedly this, coupled with the Chancellor's tax take, played a large part in the record number of small firms choosing to close down, and the highest number of bankruptcies since records began in 1914. Investment behind each worker, the key to productivity, was in British manufacturing already less than half[3] that in France, Japan or the US and well below that in Germany or Italy.

Unemployment was edging towards one and a half million, an increase of nearly nine hundred thousand since Labour took over; the figures were stark and I saw this situation as an affront to the conscience of us all. I repeatedly pointed out that, if business picked up, large firms were more likely to invest in labour saving devices. This meant that new and developing small firms were the best prospect for job creation. We tapped into research in the US which demonstrated that businesses with twenty or fewer employees were collectively their biggest source of job creation. The Labour Government wanted employment but had an antipathy to employers; they wanted investment, but hated investors (at any rate, British ones); they sought a dynamic economy without incentives – this was like running a racing car on one-star petrol. The road to ever rising unemployment was paved with good intentions and a total lack of understanding how the business world really works. What was needed was a partnership of motivated management and skilled workers, backed by investment. The tax increases had demotivated each of them.

In 1977 the Government produced a 'Green Paper' (that is initial proposals for legislation) on a Wealth Tax. Although later dropped, it cast a heavy shadow at the time over the future of many smaller businesses. Their owners realised they would be forced to take capital out of their firm to pay the tax instead of expanding. As a result many suspended development plans. As I said at the time 'In effect, the Government is castrating the Small Business sector and then complaining about its lack of virility! Their plans are a charter for unemployment by a government of unemployables.'

In order to give themselves a working majority, the first Labour government of 1974 had formed an alliance with the Liberals. Detaching the latter provided a potential chink in the Government's armour and they suffered a number of minor defeats. We managed to go one better.

---

[3] 1974 CMMD 75710.

The previous Conservative government had provided that companies with profits below £15,000 paid a lower rate of corporation tax. I moved an amendment to Labour's first budget to raise this limit to £25,000. We explained again that this profit was not, as many people assumed, the cash left over in the company at the end of the year. In fact, for most firms, much of this would be (as with the corner shop) money tied up in stock, work in progress and partly manufactured goods etc., as well as money owed by customers. We won by twenty five votes, and so brought a really useful benefit to many smaller businesses. Our victory was the Labour Government's biggest defeat thus far.

Small Business Bureau: our National Organisation for Small Firms

Up until about 1975, the voices of our Parliamentary Committee had been 'crying in the wilderness' but, by continually drawing attention to the potential of small firms and the effect of Government-inflicted damage on them, we had by 1976 begun the process of changing the political culture. We were making a useful impact in the House, but not much elsewhere. Various bodies ranging from the CBI to representatives of the self employed, regularly briefed us from their differing standpoints, but were not in the business of telling the public nor, in many instances, their own members, about the rôle we played in raising their concerns in the corridors of power.

We needed to set up our own organisation with working proprietors feeding us with real life examples of their problems and unfulfilled potential. My initial visit to Lord Thorneycroft, Chairman of the Party, at Central Office, seeking a 'start-up' grant, was without success. I fared better after some lobbying by members of our Committee. Office facilities would be provided by the Community Affairs Department of Central Office under Andrew Rowe – later himself an MP, but as for financial support, we must grow from our own resources as small businesses have to do. Years later Andrew told me Thorneycroft had called him in and told him to 'get this man off my back'!

We could not have been in better hands. It was Andrew's infectious enthusiasm, his contacts and his organising skills which turned our ideas into THE SMALL BUSINESS BUREAU (SBB). I became Chairman. Andrew, as Director and organising supremo, brought in Christopher Kirkham-Sandy in 1976, pulsating with ideas, to edit our newspaper. Through that and constituency meetings we were soon recruiting hundreds of direct members (four thousand five hundred members, plus many constituency associations) and, for a while, became the largest SB pressure group in the UK and our newspaper, which peaked at a twenty thousand print run, was I am told the then biggest small firm publication. Happily national newspapers often lifted chunks of our research, opinions and case studies. Geoff Lace joined us to manage the office and set up branches of the Bureau. (These branches made a lively and valuable early input to the SBB but, having done so, lost impetus with time and fizzled out.)

Margaret Thatcher in a statement launching the Bureau in February 1976 said 'In Parliament it is the Conservatives who are the champions of the small firm, the self employed, the individual and all those who want to use their own initiative. Now we shall be organised so that the special problems of smaller firms can be brought swiftly to our attention through the new Bureau. It will operate at Central Office under the direction of Andrew Rowe (Director of Community Affairs) and will work in close co-operation with David Mitchell, MP, and his colleagues of the Parliamentary Smaller Business Committee. This Bureau will serve two main purposes; first it will collate and analyse the views and special problems of small businesses, ensuring that I, the Shadow Cabinet and the Parliamentary Small Business Committee are fully aware of them as they unfold. Second, the Bureau will provide a direct link between individual small firms and our policy study team. Through its own newsletter it will report back to small firms who subscribe to it, letting them know what we are doing on their behalf . . . The prosperity of Britain will not be firmly based unless and until we encourage all those who can create wealth to do so.'

The first issue of this newsletter, 'Small Business', carried exclusive messages from Margaret and from Andrew inviting recipients to enrol at £3 a head (far too low but Conservative Central Office feared a switch to us from Party subscribers). The second issue offered to provide speakers for groups of small firm proprietors, for Chambers of Commerce and Chambers of Trade. Their remit (and mine) was always to listen as well as speak. Soon there was a rising demand for speakers. Before long we had seventy branches up and running, and several of our Parliamentary Committee stumped the country on the speaking circuit. It is fair to say I did not lead from behind and personally carried out over sixty SBB speaking engagements in the following twelve months. These ranged from a branch start up in Wales's Merthyr Tydfil to Inverness and Aberdeen, from Grimsby and Thanet to Truro.

Leaving for the 1976 summer recess, every Tory MP and all Parliamentary candidates (twenty three in Scotland) had a Dear Colleague letter personally signed by me, with a PS for those with whom I was familiar, covering briefing notes for constituency speeches on the Bureau and the work of our Committee in the House.

Gillian Greenwood, the indefatigable Constituency Agent for Montgomery, was one of those who organised a meeting to launch another SBB Branch in Wales, and had me along to speak. I got into some trouble for referring to Mid Wales as only full of sheep but Delwyn Williams, the local MP, was particularly supportive. On another occasion after speaking at a Round Table Dinner he asked what had happened to a school rumoured to have been closed in Gower. Delwyn commented that he remembered it as a school for nymphomaniacs, at which the hefty Branch President said 'I'll have you know, my wife went there'. Delwyn chanced his arm with the remark 'and who's a lucky boy'!

In one foray John Cope, Peter Morrison and I spent a fact finding day in Manchester, each of us on different factory visits, followed by a City Chamber of Commerce meeting, ending with a discussion with representatives of small business in Bolton – a fairly typical day.

The SBB proved a boon to our activities attacking the Labour Government in Parliament, inspiring numerous PQs, deputations to Ministers, a mass of illustrations for articles, speeches, letters to newspapers and several adjournment debates. (These take place for half an hour at the end of normal business, enabling a Member to raise a particular matter. Importantly, a Government Minister has to listen and reply.)

One frequent SBB complaint concerned the number of question-naires which bombarded small firms, and the time taken up reading them to discover whether your type of business was covered or not, and whether a reply was compulsory. From one probing PQ we discovered the Department of Industry had sent out no less than six hundred and forty thousand questionnaires, all requiring an answer; the Department of Trade, three hundred and thirty five thousand, whilst over at Employment they had lost count of how many![4] An engineering works employing forty people logged all post from Government in one month: it came to four hundred pages of booklets, forms and regulations. One wonders how they had time to make anything.

We received endless examples of burdens loaded on to small firms including Government licences to trade, double charging of launderettes for effluent disposal, price controls, census returns, the need to comply with the minutiae of the Shops, Offices and Railway Premises Act, and new Health and Safety at Work regulations which forbid you to do at work things which it is safe to do at home. There was vehement objection to the extra workload and the complex calculations arising from different rates of VAT (we made such a fuss about this that Denis Healey backed down on his plans to increase the number further). There were niggles about paying staff whilst away from work on trade union business or as Councillors or Magistrates — replacing common sense give-and-take with legal rights, however small the number of staff. Then there was the discrimination which granted tax reliefs for employees working overseas but denied them to the self employed. The list was endless. It would be dishonest not to admit that all parties and Governments, including Conservative ones, have contributed to these burdens. As the years roll by, the cumulative effect has become worse, most of all in the Blair/Brown era.

The essence of the problem for small firms both then and now is that, while many new regulations could be justified if you had a mind to do so, the cumulative effect is an unacceptable burden. Large businesses have specialist departments covering employment and company law, accounting and other areas where governments intervene. For the self employed and the small company, compliance is all time taken out from running the business. There was a revealing moment in a debate on an amendment John Loveridge and I were proposing which would allow firms with fewer than eighteen

---

[4] I am told that an earlier questionnaire asked for statistics on numbers of staff broken down by age and sex. One reply simply stated 'we have no knowledge of any of our staff broken down by sex.

employees to escape from the need to file accounts. The Labour Minister, Clinton Davis said he would send out 'guidance notes in a simplified form, illustrating clearly what new **burdens** – I mean **requirements** will be imposed'. A Freudian slip if ever there was one!

In 1978 we published our own SBB tax proposals in the form of a substantial pre-budget open letter to the Chancellor. Another year we tabled a seven point pre-budget motion in the House. Chris Kirkham-Sandy had me photographed with my hand steadying a six-foot pile of Acts of Parliament and Regulations with which the small firm had to comply. Shortly afterwards we initiated another small business debate in the House. Before it started, I discreetly laid them all out, stretching from the Despatch Box to the table of the Clerk of the House in front of the Speaker, dramatically identifying them at the end of my contribution. Afterwards, Labour's Minister for small firms revealingly muttered 'I never realised there were so many'.

I remember vividly a boat builder at the Kingsbridge meeting in South Devon explaining that he had a second order and the

David Mitchell beside a pile of government regulations

opportunity to expand on to an extra berth, but he turned it down. Why? Because it meant hiring more workers whom he might need to pay off when the second boat was completed, but the risks and costs of compensation for dismissal under the employment protection legislation made it uneconomic. 'If I cannot fire, I dare not hire' — yet more unnecessary unemployment.

The SBB did a survey of its members on the effect on job creation of six recent employment acts of Parliament. The first eight hundred responses told us that: for 17 per cent these had been of little or no importance, for 37 per cent a significant factor and in 41.8 per cent a major deterrent to more jobs. The most significant were the Employment Protection Acts, Redundancy Payments and Trade Union and Labour Relations Acts. We quoted these figures to good effect during one of the debates on job creation.

Mischievous good fun came with a competition in our newspaper on reasons for the Prime Minister to sack another of his ministers.

The Taxpayers' Charter

A further example of the value of the SBB to our Parliamentary Committee came in the form of case histories on the way officialdom behaved. It was rare for the pattern of one case not to be repeated in similar form. How would you like to be cross-examined on which pub you frequented, whether your wife drank and if so, what, how much money you spent in the pub, how much housekeeping money you gave your wife, whether she played golf, where you holidayed, and even how much you and your wife spent on clothes in each of the past five years. In 1976 on 6 March at 8 a.m. Mr George Button opened the front door of his bungalow in Dartford, Kent, to find two cars blocking the drive. Nine Customs Officers and two detectives entered his house by front and back doors and spent eight hours searching. The taxman had some suspicion that Mr Button had not been paying all the tax he should. They did not have a warrant, no evidence of fraud was produced and no charges were made. An Englishman's home his castle?

No wonder we fought against the extra search powers demanded by the Inland Revenue Staff Trade Union and obediently proposed by the Chancellor (this section of his speech appeared two days earlier in the *Sunday Times* above the union official's name). Geoffrey Howe

(Shadow Chancellor) icily enquired whether the Chancellor had written it for him! One extraordinary feature of the unprecedented powers to enter premises (John Cope 'the licensing of housebreaking by the Inland Revenue') was that the property owner need not be present, nor the police. Indeed, police powers for random searches in cases of suspected arson, burglary and murder were at that time more restrictive.

It was an apt sequel that the SBB initiated a demand for a charter of taxpayers' rights worked out by Chris Kirkham-Sandy. One format in which we put this out was as a parchment mock Magna Carta; this was presented to Margaret Thatcher by Bureau member Richard Vanbergen, colourfully dressed as a Town Crier on our stall at the annual Party Conference. The publicity ensured widespread reporting of complaints by SBB members over harassment by the Revenue. The charter set out nine proposals for protecting taxpayers, amongst them that the Revenue would no longer be allowed, unannounced, to change their interpretation of tax law, their manuals used for this purpose should be made public as a guide to taxpayers and accountants, an Ombudsman be established to consider appeals etc. with findings published, and Tax and Customs officials should not enter taxpayers' homes without a warrant.

I have no room to say enough about the introduction by the Inland Revenue of '714 certificates' required by every sub contractor working in the building industry from the self-employed plumber upwards. In effect this small plastic card became a licence to work. It is right the Revenue stamp on fraud and tax evasion and we certainly did not condone them. However, the SBB brought us shed-loads of cases where the 714 had been refused; absolutely right if there was tax evasion, but think for the moment of the self-employed plasterer with his bucket and bag of plaster, or a plumber required to comply with regulations over premises, stock records, $£¼$million insurance cover, the condition of three years' continuous employment in the UK – a strange world which penalised a man for being unemployed, even if resulting from industrial injury. One wonders if even Gilbert and Sullivan would have dreamt up the case the SBB brought us of the young sub-contractor refused his 714 because he had grown a moustache subsequent to his plastic photo. You can grow a beard or go bald and keep your British passport, but not your 714. It was Cyril Plant of the Inland Revenue who actually said in 1976 'with all the means at our disposal we must destroy the capacity to pursue self employment'.

In February 1976 the Socialist-run West Midlands County Council brought in a distasteful Bill. This sought widespread powers to trade, enabling the Authority to produce and supply goods and services in competition with commercial firms — the majority of which would be small businesses. Councils have considerable experience of spending money, but virtually none of making it. Losses could be expected and the proposals were silent on this way to subsidise competition against the private sector. Another unfair aspect allowed councils to fund their activities with sixty-year loans at rates below private sector borrowing costs. In effect, this amounted to using ratepayers' money to put rate-paying small firms out of business. Butchers, bakers, estate agents, garage owners, even flower sellers were vulnerable. The National Federation of the Self Employed campaigned forcefully.[5] When the Bill had its second Reading, Reg Eyre and Jill Knight, Birmingham MPs, savaged it — as did Paul Dean, now with a special rôle on behalf of the self employed. The Bill was soundly defeated, but it illustrated the need for constant vigilance on behalf of the small business sector. My own influence was, I believe, somewhat strengthened by my election in 1976 to the Executive of the back-bench 1922 Committee. It was fascinating and worthwhile to be involved in their key political discussions.

The SB campaign which a growing number of us had been running since 1973 had built up a sufficient head of steam by 1977 that, stung by it, Jim Callaghan's socialist Government began to react. Initially it was merely an additional Small Business Minister in the Lords (a new economic law that two can do as little as one?). Then in September he announced that Harold Lever MP (Chancellor of the Duchy of Lancaster) was to lead a special enquiry into the problems of small businesses. It was a shrewd appointment, for Lever was one of the very few Labour ministers who really understood the business and financial world. The first result that October went some way to meet our call for small business concessions in the Capital Transfer Tax. Further reliefs were under consideration for the 1978 budget.

---

[5] The National Federation of the Self Employed has developed into the Federation of Small Businesses (FSB) and is now the largest and most effective of the small business lobbying organisations outside Parliament.

When that came, instead of the usual brief aside, our sector took up a full column in Hansard. We had arrived! Later someone opened a bottle of champagne. Some wag asked if I had written Harold Lever's explanatory statement; I said no, but he had used my notes . . .

By far the most welcome aspect of all this was that we now had a growing cross-party consensus, including the Liberals, on the importance of small firms and what constrained their potential. In our view, this was immeasurably valuable because the business community really does need stability in order to plan ahead. It had been a team effort and I think it fair for us to claim a chunk of credit for the changing business culture of our time.

European Medium and Small Business Union – EMSU – a European dimension

During 1975 as part of the Parliamentary Committee's policy research I had enquired about concessions for small firms in each European country. The result showed that very small, generally family, businesses had a legally separate identity as artisans. Apart from that, there was a huge diversity in arrangements. Norway 'all our firms are small businesses', no concessions. Switzerland, each canton varied. France, cheap loans – more generous if the applicant had completed a course of business training. Germany, to help to increase efficiency and become more competitive. The Netherlands, to us the most interesting, had various loan guarantee arrangements administered since 1915 by their 'Middenstands bank'.

So we had some background knowledge and non-political contacts. Then in 1977 we at the Small Business Bureau were approached by Herr Christian Schwarz-Schilling,[6] a German Christian Democrat (CDU) MP and Vice Chairman of their Small Business Union, proposing to create a Pan-European organisation of political pressure groups operating within parties of the centre and moderate right on behalf of entrepreneurs, small businesses and professional people. After discussion we agreed the SBB would become a Foundation Member.

Chris Kirkham-Sandy and I attended a meeting in Bonn, along with representatives of parallel organisations in Austria, Belgium,

---

[6] As I write (2006) he has succeeded Paddy Ashdown as the EU High Representative in Bosnia.

France and Italy (later a Dutch group joined us). A further meeting in Frankfurt drew out the broad similarity of problems facing the businesses we represented 'suffocated by regulation, oppressed by taxes levied to pay for mismanagement by central government and other bureaucracies'. Later in Vienna we agreed the name and logo, European Medium and Small Business Union – EMSU – and a manifesto. The Continentals are much given to flowery phrases so this manifesto talked of the benefits arising from a pluralist society in contrast to state power and collective ownership, all as a bulwark against Marxism. Candidates in the approaching election for the European Parliament were asked to pledge support. Later a group was established there.

In July 1978 the SBB hosted the EMSU committee and agreed the statutes (rule book) of the organisation. Everyone understood English so there were few translation problems. The exception was in Paris. There, after chatting amiably in English over coffee, our French hosts insisted the formal meetings be in their language. In November that year we held an EMSU birthday party in London attended by, amongst others, Christian Schwarz-Schilling and Margaret Thatcher. Margaret's subsequent thank you letter commented that we had 'done splendid work in producing a six nation manifesto that looks as if it had been written entirely by ourselves'!

Finally we held a successful official launch of EMSU in Rome in April '79 with a surprisingly large turnout. Our SBB group was fortunate then and subsequently to have as one of our delegates the determined and quietly effective (now late) Phyllis Pearsall.[7]

Even when she became Prime Minister, Margaret continued to be supportive, attending amongst other events, an EMSU reception in June 1981, however I thought she looked less than best pleased when Schwarz-Schilling referred to her as 'the strongest man in Europe'.

---

[7] This remarkable woman, working from a bedsit, had single-mindedly walked, catalogued and drawn the streets of London to create the hugely successful A–Z Directory.

CHAPTER 9

Burgundy, king of wines

I take on French wine buying for El Vino, tasting / A buying
trip through the Burgundy vineyards / Corks or screw caps

AFTER FRANK BOWER RETIRED, I took over the buying of French
wines for El Vino – or to be more accurate – it was my job to
go to the traditional producing areas of Burgundy, Bordeaux and
Loire, armed with a list of future stock requirements and bring back
samples for final selection in London.

Pam would come with me to share the driving and to bring a fresh
palate to a finely balanced decision, or when mine became jaded.
When I taste, there are three things I consider, first the colour, then
smell and last, flavour. For me a white Burgundy should have a
relatively pale, greenish yellow colour; an orange yellow is bad news.
For a time there was a fashion for red Burgundy to be a pale red. I
would find a couple for our list, but my own preference is for a full rich
colour, at one time regarded as old-fashioned but now back in favour.

Next I have a good sniff, much easier with a tasting glass which
narrows at the top, concentrating the esters. The nose gives an
introduction to the flavour which follows. Some people believe
corkiness is bits of cork floating in the glass and some apply the term
to any wine they do not like! In fact, it is an invisible fungus in the
cork; this imparts a musty, dusty smell in varying degrees. Screw caps
eliminate this and are acceptable to me, provided they are used for
wines which will be drunk within one, two or maybe three years after
bottling. For that period there will be sufficient oxygen in the space
between wine and cap. For wines laid down to mature, it is important
to have the slow, gentle access of minute amounts of air through the
cork.

Coming to the actual taste, I use a little wine trade trick. This is
to suck air through wine held in the mouth. This doubles the impact
of the flavours showing up both good and, importantly, bad aspects
which may later become more pronounced. The two major constituents in my glass will be tannin and fruit acid. They are easily

recognisable for tannins dry the inside of the cheeks, whilst acid tangs on the tongue. For a good wine, I look for a balance of the two, tannin for firmness, backbone and keeping ability and fruit acids to develop fruitiness. All the time, on finding new wines in the vineyards or enjoying a bottle in a restaurant, I am automatically assessing a wine for the distinctive characteristics which others will like or dislike, but not what my coded notes describe as SON (something of nothing) as frequently offered.

Approaching from the north, the Burgundy area starts with Chablis, some two and a half hours south east of Paris, then after a break, restarts from Dijon down to the Beaujolais hills just north of Lyon. For me, the best times to go were at Easter or in January on the way back from ski-ing in Méribel. Suppliers were not busy and these times fitted into Parliamentary recesses. Visits were originally to négociants[1] from whom we bought through their London agents and later a small network of growers, vignerons I had discovered.

Imagine a hillside in winter with neat rows of pale brown vines, dotted about with small spumes of white smoke, each one issuing from a wheelbarrow-like contraption, burning the prunings of last year's vine skeletons. For me, this is an emotive picture as I move from one potential supplier to another.

At Easter I would start at the Hotel Maxime by the river in Auxerre. It is a little known, but lovely old town of cobbled streets, quaint tiled roofs and exposed oak beams. The town has three calls to fame: firstly, because Somerset born St Patrick had, as a young man, been enslaved by an Irish raiding party, worked as a pig herdsman, escaped to France, studied for the priesthood and eventually set out from Auxerre to convert the country of his erstwhile captors to Christianity. Secondly, its bridge was the scene of that moment in French history when Napoleon, having escaped from Elba and gathering a ragged army of his ex-soldiers, arrived on the north side of the bridge. Faced on the south by Maréchal Ney, sent by King Louis XVIII to bring the ogre in chains to Paris, Napoleon left his men and moved alone on to the bridge. Ney likewise. Napoleon called out in a loud voice, 'It is I, your Emperor;

---

[1] Négociants et éleveurs are firms offering a range of wines, often vineyard owners who supplement their own wines by buying in locally or making wine from bought-in grapes. Négociants are quicker than vignerons to reflect changes in market price either up or down.

come and serve me!' Ney hesitates, then, 'Oui'. Jointly they advance on Paris, the King flees and the hundred days before Waterloo have begun. Thirdly, Auxerre is of course the nearest significant town to Chablis and its smaller neighbour, St Bris.

The wines of Chablis are delineated into Petit Chablis, Chablis, Chablis Premier Cru and Grand Cru. Good Chablis should be crisp and dry, with an appetising hardness. Early on, I decided that Grand Cru did not justify its price hike and, worse, instead of stainless steel it was sometimes matured in new oak casks. In my own view this lost the typicity of Chablis and replaced it with the style of a poor man's Meursault.

For technical reasons we stocked only Petit Chablis and the Premier Cru, so it was my job to find a Petit as good as many a full Chablis, an interesting challenge and, surprisingly, not without danger. I tried to keep three suppliers in play; if one became a laggard, I would look for a new one. Hearing of a good supplier in the hamlet of Villy, I went searching. There was only one substantial house, 'obviously' that of the vigneron; ignoring the sign 'Chien Méchant' I went up the steps and knocked. A scuttering sound behind me came from the claws of a large Alsatian dog which, terrifyingly, pinned me to the front door. Fortunately a lady opened it and I fell into the house. She explained that the vigneron was her son-in-law next door. Back in London I put his sample with others on the tasting bench; it stood out in quality and value. El Vino continued buying from Olivier Savary at least until I retired.

St Bris, a village nearby to Chablis, produces Sauvignon, and since most conditions are similar, apart from the grape variety, it is valuable to taste the two wines together and compare the smooth butteriness of Chardonnay with the more aggressive Sauvignon – the latter with its hint of gooseberries, flowering currants or, dare I say – the cat box of a Siamese – but never let that put you off this wonderfully fruity dry aperitif. St Bris was a staging post for the Knights Templar on their way to the crusades. Large underground caverns and tunnels were used for storing grain and other supplies. Its underground chapel is now the cellar of one supplier with rows of bottles instead of worshippers . . .

I journey on to skirt Dijon and drop down into Marsannay, the most northerly wine village in the Burgundy area, traditionally admired for its Rosé. One should not pass by Dijon without recalling certain wartime events. The acting Mayor, a priest, was much criticised for being too correct, indeed co-operative, in his relations with the occupying German power. This led to a good deal of dark muttering against him. Then, in 1944, the Germans discovered he was, in fact, the leader of the Resistance for that entire region of France. Soon afterwards, he was walking down a one-vehicle wide street in Dijon when a car drew alongside; he was shot through the window and left lying on the pavement. By sheer chance, Doctor de Girardier, a surgeon at the Dijon hospital, father-in-law to one of the Beaune wine négociants arrived shortly after, got him into hospital and his life was saved. The Mayor's favourite tipple was Vin Blanc Cassis or, to be exact, Bourgogne Aligoté with Crème de Cassis (the blackcurrant liqueur). His name: Canon Felix Kir. Still today, throughout Europe, Kir, so named in his honour, is a popular aperitif; few realise that when calling for it, they are paying tribute to a brave French patriot.

The Côte de Nuits and Côte de Beaune make up the Côte d'Or, so named from the golden colour of its vine clad hills in the Autumn. Ruefully, the wine buyer may instinctively feel there is a different connotation! Driving south along the 'route du Grand Vin' is like driving down a wine list – passing through the villages of Couchey and Brochon, sold as Côte de Nuits Villages, in between lies Fixin, one of my minor favourites – fairly light, elegant with a flavour entirely its own. Then on to the heavyweight villages of Gevrey-Chambertin, Morey St Denis, Chambolle Musigny, Vosne Romanée, Clos Vougeot and the town of Nuits St Georges. The famous names of the Grands Crus flash by as I make my way to quiet, unassuming Louis Vallet at the House of Bourée et Cie, the methods of yesteryear producing good old fashioned but elegant results. Then to tall, courteous François Faiveley, so committed to quality he was the first man to install a hand sorting table before grapes enter the press house. He even put in 'hair dryers' to take off any moisture on the bunches. Also in Nuits I called on the two sisters who ran Lupé Cholet from their house beside the Route Nationale. The family had turned their orchard near the centre of town into a vineyard; being surrounded by a wall enabled its name to be prefixed with 'Clos', but there was no vineyard there when the Appellation classification was made in 1935. Thus it cannot be sold as Nuits St Georges, only as Bourgogne rouge, Clos de Lupé. I used to buy it, getting the style of a lesser Nuits St Georges for half the price.

Continuing south, the Côte de Nuits ends near a set of marble quarries, then starts the bigger Côte de Beaune, stretching down from the vineyards of Ladoix and Corton to Santenay and the gates of Chagny (with its famous Lameloise restaurant). Throughout the Côte d'Or, the red vines are and, for centuries have been only, Pinot Noir. Indeed in AD 1395 the then Duke of Burgundy issued an edict, legend has it, prescribing the death penalty, in fact a swingeing fine, for anyone planting the Gamay (Beaujolais) grape in his territory. I have often wondered whether this was a genuine desire to maintain quality, or the less noble protectionist tendency to keep out the more prolific Gamay.

Having mentioned four suppliers in the Côte de Nuits (over time others came and went) and more to come as I went south, you will recognise that the car boot gradually built up quite a lot of samples. Some suppliers would insist on carrying theirs to my car to be 'helpful', but in fact to see which of their competitors were involved, so I always stayed in a small hotel where the proprietor allowed me to accumulate my selections in his cellar before my return to London. At El Vino we listed over thirty Burgundies, inclusive of red and white, fortunately not all needing to be bought each year, but with three or four samples for many of them, I would end up with quite an embarrassing load.

Over the years a number of suppliers became good friends, such as Louis Vallet, Yves Doudet, Philippe Marion, Bénigne Bichot, Bernard Repolt, the Marcilly and Moingeon families, as well as Pierre Maufoux in Santenay.

There is a certain romance about descending, tasting glass in hand, into a labyrinth of old cellars with their rows of quietly maturing casks. More than that – for me, a sense of anticipation, for I knew the distinctive house style of a good many of the suppliers I dealt with, and needed that diversity of characteristics for the Company's list. Often I found it easier to recognise the house style than the difference between the wines of neighbouring villages! Also it is not my imagination, for I have found a curious similarity between some growers and the wines they produce. In Monthélie, next to Meursault, I had two suppliers of this lovely red wine – one slim, elegant and charming, the other a strong, powerfully built man. Each produced wines with just those characteristics.

Just into the northern end of Côte de Beaune are the villages of Aloxe Corton and Pernand Vergelesses. On the hillside between them are the vines of Corton-Charlemagne, my favourite white wine. You may search the world and find similar soil or aspect, but nowhere will the result replicate the special flavour of this wine, even from a similar hillside in the next village.

Moving south in the Côte de Beaune, past Pommard and Volnay, I would come to the other white wine greats, starting with Meursault, then the Montrachets. Originally all the latter were one estate. The tale is told that when the former owner died he left the world-renowned Le Montrachet to his son. Not without human failings, he left the next best and larger vineyard to his bastard son, now producing the well reputed Bâtard Montrachet. He felt the need to appease his mother-in-law, Madame Puligny; this wine is lighter, more elegant and well perfumed. It is easy to understand why the late and varyingly lamented owner had a debt of honour to the priest in the village of Chassagne – whose inheritance produces Chassagne Montrachet; both red and white are fuller bodied than Puligny but with less finesse. These characteristics can easily be upset – for winemaking, like music, is not a mechanical science – but requires experience and the instinct of the Maître de Chai – the maestro is all important.

For many years, the Marcilly family business was a regular port of call on a Saturday, since they would welcome me when the bigger firms were closed. It became a tradition that, after the tasting, I stayed on for lunch which rotated round the homes of the two married brothers and the unmarried sister. Once I had brought James Heath, our young bilingual office manager, with me. My French is perfectly adequate for business, but my social French is poor. We were sitting round the fire after lunch while I made heavy weather in my conversation with one of the wives. Suddenly the sister said something quick and sharp to her which I did not catch. James told me afterwards: 'You may be bored, but you do not have to look it' – an epitaph on my command of the French tongue!

An hour's drive south of the Côte d'Or lies Mâcon. This town has a host of nearby wine-producing villages. The northern ones are on limestone, planted with Chardonnay and the southern on granite, planted with the Gamay grape for Beaujolais. On my last visit the tale was circulating of the Mother Superior in a nearby convent who had it reported to her that a case of syphilis had been found. She responded 'Oh good, I feared we were back to the Beaujolais!' Be that, as it may, there is a huge difference between the cheap wine from the flat land and the cru Beaujolais on the hills. Each January, coming back from ski-ing, I would start with the southern-most hill where, before he expanded, Robert Farjat made five large vats of Brouilly. Hand picking means the vintage is spread over much longer than a week. During this time, the weather, and consequently the quality and ripeness, will vary. I would taste with him and choose which vat our bottling came from; some he held back for farm gate sales and the rest went to one of the big local négociant's firms who, for the quantity they need, have to blend together from many vineyards within the appellation. In this vineyard there is only ten inches of soil and then the vine roots are into the fissures in the granite. Older vines will go down for twenty five to thirty feet, or more, searching for moisture. In doing so, they build a network of fibrous roots collecting a range of minerals and trace elements. This gives the cru Beaujolais concentrated flavours without being rich or heavy. Wherever they are grown, vines are like men. The older we get, the less we produce but the better the quality!

Good friends included the Barbet family, Jean and his son Xavier, sequentially Managing Directors of Loron et Fils; they looked after the English market. Their old records told of Cru Beaujolais being sent to Paris by horse drawn barge, while the then boss took samples in pannier bags and rode ahead, calling on his round of customers, including members of the French royal family. Most of the wine would have been sold before the barge arrived. As I drove back to London I used to imagine a similarity between my car boot and old Loron's pannier bags ... On return to London, samples were grouped according to their slot in the price list and tasted over several mornings. Half bottles of the chosen wines were held in the cellar for checking against the shipment when it arrived. Yes – suppliers do occasionally make mistakes and I have sent wines back, or they have been discounted and sold off as cooking wine.

Sometimes my arm is twisted to take a small group to see and taste their way round Burgundy. On a precursor, my good friends Russell and Liz Sanderson came with me. Russell drove, at the back Liz watched the passing scenery intently. We stopped to pay homage to Le Montrachet, got back in the car, heard Liz shut the back door and drove on. It was not until we had covered about fifteen kilometres that I turned round to speak to Liz and found the back seat empty.

The closing door was the sequel to her collecting her camera! I must summon the courage to invite her again.

Burgundies are more complex to buy than clarets. In Bordeaux all the wine of a named château will be much the same. Per contra, in Burgundy wines are sold under the name of the village, which will contain many growers, each of them different in attention to their vines and methods employed in making the wine. Fortunately for UK purchasers, there is the filter of a professional buyer before wines cross the channel.

The Côte d'Or has many villages which are both wealthy and attractive. By contrast, the Mâconnais and Beaujolais hills offer much more rugged countryside, good hill walking and less expensive wine. I have to admit that sometime each year, even in retirement, I am drawn back to these attractive places with the recurring interest of each new vintage, also following up the changes in older vintages as they mature.

CHAPTER 10

Industrial relations

Raw Trade Union power exercised without responsibility;
widespread restrictive practices, closed shops, strikes / My
unsuccessful Industrial Relations (Improvement) Bill with
remedial proposals / Lessons learned from United States

I CONTINUED TO TAKE A LIVELY interest in Trade Union matters. It is
not easy to fit oneself back into the mindset of forty years ago. That
was an era of raw union power with immense influence on
governments, but little or none over their, often irresponsible, Shop
Stewards. Much of the electorate felt fearful and bewildered as well
as impotent, faced by this unbridled power. An opportunity to set
out my then views came in a debate on Industrial Relations directly
after the 1966 General Election. (This had returned Labour with an
enhanced majority.) I called for a drastic reduction in the major Trade
Union Restrictive Practices, which I proceeded to list, and secondly
a reduction in strikes, over 90 per cent being unofficial. The latter, I
claimed, would be achieved by making procedural agreements
between unions and management legally enforceable in the same way
as are Executives' contracts.

That year I researched and wrote a substantial booklet published
by Aims of Industry entitled 'FULLER EMPLOYMENT'. This
concentrated firstly on restrictive practices in the work place. The
four main ones I had identified were restriction on entry into a craft
or skill, demarcation where certain workers have a monopoly right
to carry out those skills, restrictions on the level of a man's output
and Union requirements for over-manning, including refusal to work
new equipment or insistence that the number of men displaced must
be kept on. However I concluded they held down British productivity and went a long way to explain why it took three men in UK
industry to produce the same output as one American worker.

I recommended that there be a Registrar with widespread
experience of industry who would select from among such practices,
examine them in detail, consider representations and if appropriate

invite the parties to discontinue them. If they refused, the matter would go to an industrial court with power to examine witnesses under oath and with legal authority to order discontinuance. Part of this approach was not out of line with the then current thinking in the Party.

Secondly, the booklet dealt with strikes. These had, in the first seven months of 1966, lost industry nearly two million working days. (Examples included half a million days lost over a swear word and a dispute over how long a female worker could spend in the lavatory.)

Here I recommended Standard Clauses negotiated between the CBI, TUC and Ministry of Labour to go in all contracts of employment. These would provide for the right to strike but only after a cooling off period, and the prior use of agreed procedures for settling disputes. Also, I was attracted by the idea of enhancing the personal nature of contracts of Employment with additional fringe benefits for those who adhered to them. Of the reviews of my 'Fuller Employment' publication, those in the *Financial Times*, *Daily Telegraph* and the *Yorkshire Post* were particularly helpful. It was not long after this that I became President of the Conservative National Trade Union Advisory Committee and, a bit later, Secretary of our Parliamentary Party Committee on Industrial Relations, presided over by Robert Carr, then Shadow Minister for Employment.

In my constituency I admired Sir Francis Portal, robust Chairman of the Overton paper mill, who successfully fought off a strike by SOGAT. This trade union demanded that the company sack ten women employees unless they joined their union. Sir Francis rightly commented 'This dispute was about individual freedom'.

I followed up this interest in Industrial Relations with a trip to the US which covered a Washington briefing from officials, and visits to New York and Detroit. I met the President of the union who had just brought the entire New York waterfront out on strike, then halted by an eighty day cooling off period. I was able to hold discussions with officials and shop stewards, sit in on the meeting of a factory committee to settle a grievance, attend an independent Arbitration Hearing and, on a non-disclosure basis, sat in on a confidential discussion between an industrial relations director and a trade union leader. That was an eye-opener as they stitched up a deal for union recognition, blocking out a competing union.

On my return, I reported to our Party back bench Committee on how impressed I was by the US success with legally binding contracts between employers and unions, independent arbitrators, cooling off periods and factory wide voting.

About this time I started a round of consultations with trade unionists within my constituency, not to express my views but to learn theirs. I was particularly pleased to be invited by the Andover Trades' Council to discuss industrial relations with their delegates. (Trades' Councils are the collective body representing local trade union branches.) The Basingstoke Trades' Council at first refused to meet with me but, after the Lansing Bagnall shop stewards invited me, they changed their minds.

Three years on from 1966 the number of working days lost through strikes in the UK had gone up first to over 2.2 million in 1967, then to 4.6 million in 1968, plus of course, time lost through non-availability of materials from strike bound factories. All this led up to me producing my Private Member's INDUSTRIAL RELATIONS (IMPROVEMENT) BILL in December 1969, using the Ten Minute Rule Procedure. This gives the proposer precious minutes of prime time on the floor of the House at 3.30 p.m. to explain their Bill. It may be killed off in an immediate vote or, more likely, be lost at a later stage, as was mine. Preparing the Bill involved briefing (and paying) one of the Parliamentary Agents who specialise in drafting non-Government legislation, finding colleagues to sponsor it and arranging for it to be printed if it has not been voted out on day one. Happily Tatton Brinton, David (now Lord) Howell, Kenneth Lewis, Patrick McNair Wilson and Teddy Taylor were among sponsors.

The Bill incorporated policies being considered in Party meetings along with ideas in 'FULLER EMPLOYMENT', supplemented by things I had learned in America, along with the results of my constituency consultations. Initially an unexpected hurdle appeared when I submitted it to a Clerk in the Public Bill Office. He raised objections on the grounds that the word 'improvement' in the title was tendentious, which is not allowed. Happily, higher authority in the Clerks' Department allowed it to proceed.

I had discovered that dismissal on disciplinary grounds was a very frequent cause of short, disruptive strikes, but what redress had a man who felt he had been unfairly dismissed? The short answer was – none, so his workmates would come out on strike to secure justice for him. Accordingly, Clause I of my Bill provided for the worker concerned to appeal to a local industrial tribunal, making a strike unnecessary. Another clause provided that all information given to shareholders of larger firms should also be circulated in a simplified form to their employees. The Bill provided that all new written agreements would be binding, unless agreed otherwise. Damages could be claimed if either employer or union failed to use their best endeavours to secure compliance with the terms of a binding agreement to which they had signed up. The last substantive clause provided for the setting up of a code of good industrial practice. This would not itself be enforceable, but compliance with it would be a criterion used by any enquiry into a dispute. My speech pointed out that some 30 per cent of disputes involved the question of which union, if any, should represent employees. 'The time has come when the decision should be taken by the men on the factory floor. That will be industrial democracy at work. Take the ballot-box into the factory. Let the men decide for themselves; a new way to peaceful solutions for a major cause of industrial disputes.' In short, my Bill provided for a modern and civilised alternative to strike action to resolve many situations which then resulted in lost time.

Following the 1970 General Election, the new government led by Ted Heath published a consultative document outlining indicative proposals for modernising Industrial Relations. These were subject to hysterical and distorted attacks including two national one-day strikes and demonstrations, both against the advice of the General Secretary of the TUC. The Conservative offices in Bristol and Glasgow were subject to attempted arson. The Chamber of the House was considerably fuller than usual for debates on these reforms and genuine passions were aroused on both sides. That did not prevent the odd light-hearted heckle from time to time. Two of these I still recall; one Labour member, as a preliminary to disagreeing with Employers' views, started 'I've had lunch with the CBI' – 'Anyone can see that!' from a Tory. Another time, Sally Oppenheim was holding forth on the evils of shop stewards and what happened on the shop floor. 'The only shop floor the Honourable Lady knows is Fortnum and Masons' quipped a voice from the back of the Labour benches, this to considerable cross-party amusement.

My trade union experience, limited though it was, had given me some insight into union attitudes. As in so many other situations, for example Ulster, fear was the key. Many trade unionists were still fearful that tomorrow might bring a return to the black years of mass unemployment between the wars. These had seared deeply into the minds and hearts of both their fathers' and their own generation, and still influenced them. They saw work spreading techniques as a way of keeping more of their members in a job, and still did not understand that adding to production costs priced them out of a job.

In Tory Party circles I still feel I had, at the margin, contributed something useful towards understanding those motivated in this way. I carried out a number of speaking engagements explaining the Government's policy, but, by this time, I had other responsibilities.

CHAPTER 11

Work of a PPS and more . . .!

Ted Heath's government 1970 / I become PPS to Keith
Joseph / The work of a PPS / The Centre for Policy Studies
is born / Keith speaks out against Ted Heath's policies / He
commits himself to challenge for the Leadership but
withdraws / Margaret Thatcher, Joint Trustee of Centre for
Policy Studies, takes up the baton

THE RESULT OF THE 1970 GENERAL ELECTION was unexpected.
Against polls and predictions, Ted Heath became Prime Minis-
ter, having overturned a Labour majority of a hundred and fourteen.
Soon names of Cabinet and senior ministers were pouring out of
Number 10. As expected, Robert Carr took over at Employment. I
had some hope, but no real expectation, of joining the lowest tier of
junior appointments (that of Parliamentary Under Secretary of State,
known in Civil Service jargon as PUSS or, irreverently, as 'Parly
Charly'). If this was to happen, clearly my best chance would be the
Department of Employment, in view of the part I had played in
Opposition.

However, it was not to be. No doubt the Whips' Office still had
my cards marked 'unreliable'.

Senior Ministers take on a PPS (Parliamentary Private Secretary).
This is purely a personal appointment. The position has been
variously described as 'unpaid fag' or 'bag carrier'. The principal
work is to act as a link between your Minister and back benchers, in
effect being his eyes and ears to compensate for him or her being
absent from the House, while working in their Ministerial Department. For the PPS, one great benefit is the opportunity and the
fascination of seeing the inside workings of a Government Department.

I was thrilled to be asked by Maurice Macmillan, newly appointed
Chief Secretary to the Treasury, to become his PPS, also by Sir Keith
Joseph at the Department of Health and Social Services. I sought
advice from the Whips' Office who recommended Keith, on the
grounds that he was in the Cabinet. Katie Macmillan answered the

phone when I rang to explain. Her response was instant; that Maurice soon would be in the Cabinet! Two years later her prediction was fulfilled, but in 1970 there could be no certainty about that and my choice was logical.[1]

I barely knew Keith before taking up the position. A barrister, Fellow of All Souls, Oxford, he had served as a Minister in Housing and Local Government and at the Board of Trade. He was slim, alert, tense and intense with a brain like a computer, but also a shy and very private man who rarely 'let his hair down'. At first he did not have a great deal for me to do, although always politely appreciative. I found the relationship so distant that after six weeks I sought out Robin Wendt who headed up his Departmental private office and explained my uncertainty as to whether I was the right man for the job. His response was that Keith was like that, but he was pleased with what I was doing. I felt there was an anxiety lest someone would presume on his friendship for their own advantage. As time went on, I compared my working relationship with Keith increasingly as a carthorse with a highly strung racehorse!

The work of a PPS is not widely understood, indeed one local newspaper headlined my position as a 'Secretarial Appointment'. All PPSs suffer one particular restraint, namely they must not speak in the House on matters covered by their master's Department. In practice, the rôle of PPS varies entirely according to the perceived needs of his master; I was now allowed to attend the morning 'Prayers', the name given to the informal weekly private meeting of the Secretary of State with his other Departmental Ministers. This is virtually the only opportunity Ministers have of meeting together regularly without officials being present.

Gradually I was allowed to become more involved, for example, attending selected meetings with officials, never to speak up but, sitting next to Keith, I could occasionally make a point with a scribbled note. Keith would glance down for about twenty five seconds and either slide the scribble back to me, or interject 'The PPS

---

[1] The Treasury is effectively the most influential department in Government, its staff often fast-streamed and move up to more senior positions in other departments. Maurice was a much more relaxed personality than Keith, hence more likely to open up in private, sharing his thoughts and inside knowledge of the 'goings-on' in other departments. In retrospect working with Maurice would have been more fun, but I doubt I could ever have become as useful to him as I was serving Keith, which became a real privilege.

is concerned about X'. Naturally such proceedings remained confidential, but they were very helpful in my job of keeping in touch with MPs back at the House.

I initiated regular meetings between Keith and the officers of our Party Committee in the House on Health and Social Security, often with our Whip in attendance. This proved particularly valuable to Keith, for it ensured that key MPs on the back benches were well informed on the purpose and the inevitable limitations etc. in the Department's legislative proposals. At meetings of the full Committee normally addressed by an outside expert, some of the points raised would identify for me those MPs with doubts on particular issues of policy, indicating there was a special need for me to keep in touch with them.

Those who watch televised sittings of the House will notice at the end of the Government benches, i.e. at the Speaker's right hand, a row of people separated from MPs by a four foot high screen. This is known as 'the box'; in it sit a Secretary from the Minister's private office and the appropriate Departmental specialists.

One duty of all PPSs is to accompany their master when in the Chamber, sitting half behind the Minister when he is on the Front Bench, whether participating in a debate, answering Questions, or making a Statement. The 'half' being to enable the Minister to say something half over his shoulder. For example, a Member may bring out some figure to prove his point. The Minister mutters 'check that' and the PPS goes over to the box to find out, then returns with a scribbled note, or simply to say quietly that he is correct, or he is wrong, here is the correct figure.

I shall never forget one hairy occasion when Keith was at the Despatch Box making an important statement on health matters. There was some agitation in the box and Keith's Private Secretary seemed to want me in a hurry. In some desperation she explained that the next two pages of the speech Keith was then reading had been transposed. Could I get him down and give him a correct copy. By good fortune, Marcus Worsley, an expert on Health and a former PPS, was sitting close by. I slipped in beside him and said something like 'for heaven's sake, get up and ask Keith a question, doesn't matter what – anything, I have to get him down'. As soon as I was back, Marcus rose 'Will my Rt. Hon. Friend give way'. Then, as Keith sat down, he asked for assurances on some relevant point. I swapped the briefs, Keith made some appropriate response and carried on as if nothing had occurred. Phew!

Other little jobs I had were planting questions – i.e. if the Department wanted some fact or figure to be put on the record, I would find an appropriate Member who would be pleased to table the question. Also, from time to time, I fixed up Keith's pairing arrangements, and I recall receiving petitions in the Central Lobby on his behalf.

Once Keith had a meeting to address in Gravesend. Unfortunately, some emergency detained him and he would not be there until later. I was despatched by car to read the speech on his behalf, or anyway to start it until he arrived. Keith had a slightly unusual way of speaking, often short, slightly clipped sentences, almost impossible for someone else to deliver. I sweated at it in the car, inserting my own pauses and music symbols to help make it run. Vast relief when ten minutes into my hesitant delivery, Keith arrived.

At this time I had a superb constituency Agent, Jim Coote, and arranged with him to hold a meeting in Basingstoke addressed by Keith. The pattern was to be a short speech, followed by roving microphone questions. Invitations were sent out to everyone we could think of who had any possible interest or connection with the work of the Department. It is amazing how many people are involved, often vicariously, in these associated fields – hospital staff, doctors, surgery staff, nurses, midwives, social security staff, St John's Ambulance etc. etc. We filled 'The Shrubbery' hall to capacity, approaching some six hundred people. The meeting was a huge success and Keith was delighted. In my view, two-way meetings of this sort take a lot of time and energy in preparation, but are immensely worthwhile. I urge more of our Shadow Ministers in Opposition and particularly our Ministers when we are in Government to do this. It will be a great benefit to them and to their audience.

One 'interesting' trip was to go with other relevant attendees at meetings of the Party Committee to Uppsala in Sweden for the day, to learn about their advanced hospital computer techniques. Alas, as we neared Heathrow, I realised that in my haste that morning I did not have my passport with me. I was allowed to leave, but the Swedish authorities were less forgiving. I was interviewed by a tall, powerfully built lady immigration official who barely listened to my explanation and launched into a diatribe over two passportless Swedish students who had been refused entry to the UK. Released, I caught up with the others to make notes for Keith. The Swedish computer system plotted and timetabled every part of a patient's progress, day and time of hospital admission, allocation of numbered bed, consultant time and place, etc. even down to treatment after discharge and automatic letter recalling the patient for post-operative examination. Similarly there were programmes to call women in for cervical smear tests. On our group's return to Heathrow, it was agreed to put me in the middle of our members at the passport desk, which worked well, in spite of one 'kindly' colleague saying in a loud whisper 'so that's how he got the money from the Pakistani gentleman'.

In 1973 I had a number of constituency letters (it may have been a co-ordinated campaign) saying that pensioners were all but starving. I asked the Department how much a pensioner drawing social security benefit should be expected to spend on food each week. Then I gave Pam £10 to spend for the two of us, shopping at local shops. I took sandwiches to the Commons. My conclusion was that, provided one used initiative and shopped around, an adequate healthy diet was possible, but for a partially disabled old age pensioner, only able to reach one nearby shop, it was pretty deadly boring.

I reported all this to Keith the next week and he commented that when he started work as a trainee with Bovis, his first job was digging a ditch. He had energetically put his best effort into it, until told by the foreman 'It's all right for you doing this for a fortnight, but don't show us up; we have to do it for months on end.' Dead right!

Initially, Keith's limited demands left me with plenty of time to pursue other interests, both with El Vino[2] and in politics, in and outside the House.

The 'racehorse' was a man who (fuelled on boiled sweets) drove himself relentlessly. Policy discussions were intensely invigorating, Keith frequently scribbling reminder/notes. Gradually the Department's programmes gave effect to his priorities. In many cases, these were relatively small groups he had identified as deserving cases which had missed out, for example, pensions for the over-eighties

---

[2] Mainly mornings, but with a briefcase of work accompanying me to the privacy of my room for later in the day.

who were not covered by the state pension system, the severely disabled who required twenty four hour care for whom he introduced the Attendance Allowance, the introduction of Family Income Supplement, benefits for widows in the forty to fifty years age group, free hearing aids for the deaf, and help for what he called the 'Cinderella' services – the run down long-stay hospitals for the mentally ill and handicapped. His justified reputation as a caring and compassionate man survived even the Treasury's required raising of prescription charges: these were skilfully crafted to exempt those unable to afford them, so fifty percent of all prescriptions were exempt.

Already the dichotomy of his position (later to become even more stressful) showed itself; on the one hand the imperative to reduce overall government spending, and yet being deeply moved by human suffering. The latter regularly gained the upper hand, with Keith beating a path to the door of Tony Barber, the Chancellor of the Exchequer. By 1974 he had extracted more money from the Treasury for Health & Social Services than any previous Minister.

In 1972 Keith gave a great deal of thought to why some children suffered an upbringing which left them deprived, bereft of the normal emotional warmth of a homely upbringing, their problems occurring in all levels of society – broken homes, stress, emotional difficulties and tension following marital breakdown – worst when the parents were also poor and badly housed. He argued that for them, adverse circumstances tended to be transmitted to the next generation, which he called 'the cycle of deprivation' – a theme to which he later returned with disastrous consequences.

By 1973, well after Ted Heath's famous U-turn on economic policy, Keith became increasingly uneasy about aspects of it. Alfred Sherman, an abrasive right-winger, but also a superb wordsmith and speech writer, suggested that a policy 'think tank' was needed where ideas and potential programmes could be put through the wringer of thorough examination and appraisal. Keith took up the idea enthusiastically, recruited Margaret Thatcher as a co-trustee and brought in Nigel Vinson, a successful entrepreneur who had recently sold his business, as a joint founder and third trustee of what was to become the Centre for Policy Studies. Keith had willed it, but it was the practical Nigel who made it all happen – finding premises, staff and funding for the office to open in Wilfred Street ready for the first Board meeting on 23 July 1974. In February 1974 the miners' strike had led Ted Heath to call an Election on the theme of 'Who Governs Britain?' But, once called, elections never remain one-issue contests and the Conservative Government was out. It was then that the office in Wilfred Street became almost as much Keith's political office as it was the CPS; Keith's fertile brain pouring out ideas deserving of further investigation, constantly seeking after 'the truth' in a world of competing ideas. About this time I described him to Nigel as being like a 'bluebottle trapped in a jam jar'.

I recall the stream of working lunches, bringing together leading figures from commerce and industry, along with ex and shadow ministers. Several Study Groups were set up, one on privatisation, another led by Geoffrey Howe developing ideas which became the next Conservative Government's Enterprise Zones policy, another led by Vinson working on the development of personal equity holdings which eventually led to Peps and ISAs.

A watershed came about in September 1974 when Keith delivered a thoughtful and well researched speech in Preston. This challenged the orthodox and widely accepted view of successive governments that the best way to prevent unemployment was to increase demand artificially – a policy later referred to colloquially as 'printing money'. Keith claimed this policy increased the already serious level of inflation and so, over a period, destroyed the competitiveness of UK industry and sucked in imports. This resulted in more of the unemployment it set out to cure. Of course, governments were terrified of a return to the mass unemployment of the interwar years, but Keith went on to analyse the current unemployment figures, pointing out that there were about three times as many vacancies as those notified to the Labour Exchanges. If you took into account the number of those registered as unemployed who were not fit, willing and available for work, together with the considerable number of the temporarily unemployed in transit between jobs, the relevant unemployment rate was only a fraction of the crude figures.

The speech (printed in full by *The Times*) set the cat among the pigeons, for it attacked both Labour's policy and that of Ted Heath in whose Cabinet Keith had so recently served. In fact, Keith's 'conversion on the road to Damascus', as he put it, happened between the two General Elections of that year. 'It was only in April 1974 that I was converted to Conservatism; I had thought I was a Conservative, but I now see that I was not really one at all.'

Many in the Party saw that a further General Election would not be long delayed and if Ted failed to win then, a leadership election would follow. Speculation developed that Keith would stand, as would Willie Whitelaw. It is a tradition that, if his master runs for high office, his PPS (or ex-PPS) is centrally involved. Soon small groups of MPs were coming to see Keith. I set up a card index (which now makes fascinating reading). It became apparent that Keith's reputation in government as the humane face of conservatism had created a welling up of support for him on the left of the Party, while his recent conversion to monetarism had brought support on the right. Whilst still not committing himself publicly, Keith did do so to Nick Ridley and a group of his friends. One morning Keith asked whether I thought that, if he stood against Ted, he would gain only derisory support. I responded that, on the contrary, he would definitely be 'in with a chance'. I have the clear impression that this was when his real worries set in.

At this time I was on the circulation list for later drafts of the series of speeches Keith was making up and down the country. He was due to make one in Birmingham and I remember saying to him that I had not seen the draft, and his response 'Don't worry David, there's nothing in it'. Alas for Keith, he had not recognised that, in returning to his earlier theme of the cycle of deprivation, he had added hugely sensitive passages referring to social classes four and five breeding faster than the rest of society, producing the 'problem' children of the future and a reference to the balance in the human stock of our population being threatened. There was an enormous and immediate furore. To me, the most worrying aspect was not so much what he had said, but that he had failed to recognise its political sensitivity.

It was a Thursday shortly after this when I mentioned that his supporters had become restive in that he had not formally declared himself a candidate for leadership. His response was 'give me another week'. The following Thursday he said he would make a definite decision within a week. He came in on the Monday looking as if he had not slept, indeed I am sure he had not. He then said 'I've made up my mind, I shall not be a candidate' and, after a pause, 'I would not get the answers right often enough'. A genuinely modest man, so unlike his public image. Personally I had become increasingly concerned as to whether Keith would be able to cope with the pressures and stress inevitable in leading our Party, and even more as

Prime Minister. For this reason, I did not argue and quietly let his decision be known amongst his supporters.

With Keith out of the race, it was natural that Margaret Thatcher, as the joint trustee of the Centre for Policy Studies, should step into his shoes, which she did with Keith's enthusiastic sponsorship. The rest is history, although the full extent of Keith's influence and huge moral support to Margaret throughout the testing time which followed has not been fully appreciated – both for the period before and early years in government.

Despite the many other pressures during this period, at some time during 1970–74 I became involved in interviewing for the Central Office candidates' list. I thought this to be worthwhile because I had become worried by the number of, in my view, inappropriate Parliamentary candidates – e.g. a merchant banker in a rural West Country seat, a charming stockbroker belt solicitor in the industrial heart of a northern town. As an election support speaker in another city centre, I listened open-mouthed as the candidate gave a lucid explanation of the balance of payments to an audience, most of whom had never heard of it, but were concerned about housing waiting lists, run down schools and yob violence. It seemed to me that we had too many round pegs in square holes and not nearly enough candidates with whom local people could identify: MPs like my friend, the late Donald Thompson, a local butcher, or Marcus Fox with his pronounced Yorkshire accent.

I was surprised by the number of starry-eyed young men who had never sat in the Gallery and watched even one debate, much less seen the detailed and sometimes boring work of a Bill's committee stage. In retrospect I was probably aiming at the wrong target and should have sought some way to influence constituency selection committees, too many of which I felt acted as if they were judging a speaking contest, rather than choosing a representative for their constituency. Unkindly I wondered if some were either choosing the man (alas, not woman) they would ideally choose for a son-in-law, or one they judged so clever he'd be yet another future Prime Minister. In my view suitability for their constituency, ideally a respected local with some useful expertise to bring to the Commons, is what was, and is, needed. Someone with whom many constituents could identify.

CHAPTER 12

A centenary or two

El Vino celebrates and remembers

Due to its situation, the El Vino branch at 47 Fleet Street in the heart of the newspaper world received considerable publicity. By contrast The Old Wine Shades in Martin Lane off Cannon Street is little known. Grandfather ALB bought the lease in 1900 from Henry Hallows, a wine merchant. At that time it was still known as Spragues Wine Shades. The *London Argus* of 9 November that year reported even then that the front part opposite the bar counter had its five foot high wooden partitions with the cushioned seats and tables 'black with age'. They are still the same. The smoking room, then partitioned off at the back, contained a curious old rack in which were held the long, fragile 'Church Warden' pipes of white china clay, kept there by the regulars, under each pipe the initials of its owner, also there the oil lamp which was passed round to relight the weed. There was at that time on the top floor one of the old decorated lead water cisterns which, according to the *London Argus*, bore the date 1663. This allowed Grandfather ALB to claim it was the only city tavern to survive the Great Fire of 1666. In view of this, it was reasonable to celebrate its Tercentenary in 1963.

We did this in some style, for the first time opening up our arched Martin Lane cellar for a tasting. Wines on offer were classified crus from Bordeaux and Burgundies including Clos Vougeot '55 at 24/6 (£1.23). I had old price lists on display, one undated, listed Chablis at 42/-, say £2. Château Haut Brion vintage 1921 at £5, Yquem '21 at £5 and 1865 Very Fine Liqueur Cognac at £18, ALL PER DOZEN, delivery free by cart! Candlelight showed up the massive oak beams and masonry arches of enormous strength, also the bricked up entrances to two alleged tunnels. I doubted the tale that one led down to the river and had been used for smuggling. However, when the outside of that wall was opened up circa 1970 due to adjacent building work, a section of the tunnel was exposed, and I have a photo of myself standing in it.

I have recently seen archival evidence which suggests that the original building, at least above cellar level, did not survive the Great Fire. This account suggests it was built in 1667 as a merchant's house, probably for a John Bateman who died in 1704, leaving it to his son Sir James, a Liveryman of the Fishmongers' Company, who almost certainly refurbished it and installed a new lead cistern with the initials JB and date of 1713, still there today. It is understood it later became the home of a coal merchant, living above the shop. Be that as it may, the building still survives as 'one of London's rarest domestic buildings of that era and of outstanding architectural and historic interest' according to a contemporary record of 1971.

By 1833 it had become a Wine Bar operated by John Henderson and known as 'The Shades'. This name may well link with the wine merchants' early practice of hanging out a freshly cut bush when a new cask of wine was being broached, hence 'a good wine needs no bush'. The wilting of the bush indicated how long the cask had been open. In those days the bottle was more expensive than the wine, so customers would bring bottles back to be refilled. By 1963 little in the cellars had changed, but in 1972 we converted them into a lunchtime restaurant. The ground floor remains unchanged, I love to draw attention to the plaster fireplace surround, brought down from the first floor above. This depicts the restoration of peace between Britain and America after the latter's war for independence. It shows hands linked and surrounded by a laurel wreath.

Beside the fireplace hangs a piece of doggerel, written impromptu by an anonymous customer on 19 December 1840:

Should e'er I desire to make myself merry
I'd call for a pint of Henderson's Sherry.
Of what else in this world can a man be ambitious
Than a glass of a beverage so rich and delicious.

A glass of such sherry would make a bear civil
With a pint in my pate I would face e'en the devil.
'Tis the soul of enjoyment, the spirit of love
The nectar that's quaffed by the blessed above.

There is more certainty in fixing 1879 as the year when Grandfather ALB started the Company, initially trading as Bower and Co. We held a centenary lunch in the Court Room of the Vintners' Company to celebrate and thank fifty of our suppliers, including

In an El Vino (Tasting House) Wine Bar, 47 Fleet Street

some who had more than once submitted samples unsuccessfully. We thanked them: bottlers, builders, cork merchants, accountants, solicitors etc. etc. for being eccentric enough to continue supplying us. We commented that our customers were sometimes demanding, exacting, irrational and impatient, wanting the best value in town, feelings which no doubt we in turn relayed to our suppliers. David Rutherford, at the time doyen of the London wine trade, proposed a toast to the Company. *Punch* magazine of July 1979 devoted a double spread to cartoons about the firm.

This celebration might never have taken place for I was at home one evening when the phone rang. Miss Fairbairn, the first floor tenant of 47 Fleet Street, told me that fire had broken out in our wine bar below her office and she had called the fire brigade, adding in a matter of fact voice that she thought I would wish to know.

As well as the casks of port and sherry behind the bar, we also kept a former sherry butt (capacity six hundred bottles) of our own blend of whisky standing on the ground floor. I realised immediately that this represented an immensely inflammable but unrecognised risk to the firemen. Pam and I jumped into the car and, disregarding speed limits, tore off. Fortunately there was no traffic in St James's Park, and I did at least 90 mph, only to find at the Trafalgar Square traffic lights a police van blocking our route. An angry policeman demanded to know what the hell I thought I was doing. Agitated and rather incoherently I explained, whereupon the back door of the van opened and I was signalled to come close. We shot down the wrong side of the Strand and arrived in Fleet Street with a screech of brakes opposite the fire engine. I ran inside and explained. By that time, our excellent City Fire Brigade had put out the fire, identified the probable cause as a cigarette end in a rubbish bin and were preparing to secure the door where they had broken in. The fire damage, although severe, was confined to a small area behind the bar. As soon as I had gone in, our policeman appeared at the car door and said to Pam 'Good thing for him there is a fire or I'd have had his guts for garters'.

CHAPTER 13

Into government

*The nitty gritty work of a junior Minister / My shopping list of
fifty two items on behalf of small business, some
successes / The Loan Guarantee Scheme / I badger Jim Prior
for more concessions on employment law / Bureaucracy and
regulation do not create wealth but by lightening these burdens
and taxes the climate can be created for new businesses to start
up. Not only 'can be created' – the Thatcher governments did
it, and I am proud to have played a small part*

THE GENERAL ELECTION OF MAY 1979 followed swiftly after
Labour's Callaghan government lost that vote of 'no confidence'
in the House (see pages 81–2).

The result was inevitable for a government which, in the life of
one Parliament, had halved the value of the pound in voters' pockets,
doubled tax on the average family, broken all records for bankruptcy,
doubled unemployment and borrowed more money than all the
British governments since the war. I romped home with the biggest
majority ever recorded in the constituency at 21,746. They were
heady days! – especially for me on being appointed a Junior Minister
as Parliamentary Under Secretary of State (PUSS) in the Department
of Industry now led by Sir Keith Joseph. Incidentally there was no
induction course on how to be a Minister.

MPs are not permitted to carry on in business when they take
office and I had less time to clear my desk at El Vino than I had
anticipated. My brother was not best pleased to find himself as sole
Managing Director, but in a very short time had mastered his new
role. As a precaution, in case I joined the Government, I had
prepared detailed notes on the work I had previously done and
delegated part of my work to the Company Accountant and to James
Heath, the Office Manager. It was a great relief to me that Pam, who
had been running a small mail order business we had taken over, now
became a Director to represent my side of the business. She also took
on responsibility for the wine shipping and sundry other parts of my
work. Indeed, she threw herself into it more than I had suggested,

passing the Wine Education Trust exams. For several months, I would find wee notes waiting for my return home such as 'Where have you hidden so and so?' 'What's the name of Y . . .?' etc.

Ministers are constitutionally responsible to Parliament for the work of their Department. This means, among other things, Questions (PQs) every four weeks, general debates on the work of the Department, statements and debates on proposed Department legislation and adjournment debates (the last business of the day, then often at a late hour). Not least, there is the massive correspondence with MPs on matters raised by their constituents.

All of this, and much more, is organised by a Minister's Private Office – a Chief Private Secretary plus supporting staff, each covering a different part of your responsibilities, plus a diary secretary and typist. Hardly anyone can communicate with you directly in your Department unless the Private Office has set up the meeting. For most engagements you will be accompanied by a member of your Private Office and generally an official responsible for the appropriate part of the Department's work. Most telephone calls are logged. This may sound almost prison-like, as if a Minister cannot be trusted, but it is necessary to protect the Department since a Minister can commit the Government. These procedures ensure he is protected from those who may allege he has made promises to them when he has not.

The normal pattern is for Junior Ministers to work to a Minister of State who, when necessary, reports to the Secretary of State. For my responsibilities such as Regional Policy and aids to industry, I worked to Lord Trenchard, Minister of State in the Lords, but for Small Business policy direct to Keith Joseph. The relationship between a Secretary of State and a Junior Minister is of considerable significance. Officials would be less than human if they did not quietly probe the extent to which the latter's judgment was supported by his Secretary of State. The results soon determine how often a Junior Minister's decision is questioned.

Also the relationship with the head of one's private office is crucial. I inherited someone who had happily served my socialist predecessor, but the relationship did not gel with me. After some six week I saw the Permanent Secretary, Sir Peter Carey, and asked to interview three potential replacements. For them the job itself is often an indication of career 'fast streaming', also having been chosen rather than inherited does create a subtly different relationship. I chose Tony

Willis (AW) and few problems ever arose, although I remember once feeling that he had crossed the line between advising and telling me and I snapped 'Yes, Minister'. The point was taken and a happy working relationship restored. His number two, Jane Gutteridge, concealed a quiet determination behind a seemingly timid exterior. They made an effective team – more so than I realised when they got married a few years later. AW is now studying for the priesthood – one more surprise!

The Department of Industry's offices were then in Ashdown House, Victoria Street, within easy walking distance from our house in Eaton Terrace. Apart from the first day, I needed to be collected by car because of the red boxes coming back to the Department.[1]

Soon after my arrival, I was asked by Sir Peter Carey to arrange to see him with a list of all my investments. I was conducted across by my Private Secretary. Ministers are not supposed to wander around on their own. (Subsequently I caused consternation by daring to go AWOL to speak to an official on the floor above.) Sir Peter looked down my meagre list and said I could keep a Dutch investment trust and Grace Bros, Australia, but the rest must either be sold or put into a blind arms-length trust for as long as I remained a Minister. Next we talked about my chairmanship of the SBB and membership of EMSU. Not unreasonably he said I could not both make representations on behalf of small businesses and receive them! (Micky Grylls MP took over the SBB from me.) However I could continue with EMSU. John Loveridge was elected to take on my other role as Chairman of the Parliamentary Small Business Committee; this was in good hands for he had run three successful businesses.

A few weeks on, a reporter interviewing me described my office, one wall covered with maps showing the tax-concessioned Development Areas, another, unemployment and job vacancies etc. 'It looked like the Operations Room preparing for an assault'. Apparently I

---

[1] That first day I was more fortunate than Paddy (now Lord) Mayhew (later to become Attorney General and subsequently Secretary of State for Northern Ireland). On his appointment as PUSS to the Department of Employment, then in St James's Square, he was mildly put out when no-one was there to welcome him. Approaching the desk he said he was the new Minister and was taken aback by being looked up and down by the Commissionaire who said 'I fear you have the wrong building Sir -the Methodist offices are down the road!' Mistakenly he had come into RTZ's offices next to his new Department.

In my office at the Department of Industry

claimed (rightly) that it was hard work and frustrating with the long hours only worthwhile if something concrete was achieved. I was then cross-examined on those frustrations; was it the Civil Service? 'Good Lord, no they are very helpful, it is the system'. In fact, most of my frustrations arose because I came to the Department with a shopping list of fifty two changes I wanted to achieve, then quickly realised that most of my list were matters belonging to other Departments, principally Treasury, Employment, Environment, DHSS etc. Understandably, these other Departments had to discuss all the implications with Industry Department officials. I was greatly impressed by their determination to do a thorough job, but that took time – lots of it!

I had been in the Department about three weeks when Keith Joseph asked me whether I was enjoying it. I said yes, but I had not finished my second red box until 2 a.m. Keith responded 'As a Minister you must expect to work till then'. Thinking about this that evening, I concluded that if I did so regularly, I would soon be useless to man or beast. I vowed then to put down my pen at midnight:

something I generally stuck to for the next nine years.[2] However, I invented the 'Speak Box', a wonderful device for saving me time. The red box was put on my desk and each Private Secretary told me what they proposed to put in it. I absorb information quicker through talk and making myself a one-line note, rather than reading endless sheets of paper. So 'This is to inform you the Minister of Agriculture is meeting your constituency NFU' (National Farmers' Union); me 'I don't need to read that'. 'This responds to your request for information on XYZ'; me 'I need that' – and in it goes. Interestingly, if it was late in the day, often it was they who said 'You won't need to see this'. A red box would be finished in perhaps half the time. I should have done it more often.

One of the first things I did was to ask for information on the number of UK small businesses and whether it was rising or falling. The initial answer was 'we do not know, but we could devise a questionnaire' – no way! However, the next week I was introduced to one of our statisticians, the excellent Mr Pom Ganguly, who explained it would be possible to bleed a sub programme off the VAT computer at Southend. Properly refined, this would tell us the number of new firms coming on to the VAT register and the number coming off. Of course, it would not cover the smallest businesses which were exempt from VAT, but the overall movement in numbers was unlikely to be much different. This was set in hand, and grim reading it became as, month after month, numbers fell.

As the year progressed, there were four things I recall taking up much of my time. First, continuing a running dialogue with the organisations representing small firms (I was inevitably more familiar with them than were the Department officials). Secondly, seeking to persuade officials of the benefit from implementing my wish list of small firm changes. Third, on Regional Policy. Here we inherited a system which provided (financially) Assisted Area Status to 40 per cent of the country (it had been easy for past Ministers to gain local popularity by increasing the coverage). This had meant that aid was spread too thinly. We changed that to concentrate it on the 25 per cent with greatest need. The result amply demonstrated the political

---

[2] A red leather covered Ministerial box, or boxes, follow you each night; they look romantic until you open them! Generally they contain responses to matters you have raised, submissions on problems with advice on options, endless photocopies of what is going on elsewhere, letters for approval and signing, also briefing on the programme for next day.

axiom that you can get away with not giving something which is thoroughly justified, but face an enormous rumpus if you take away some existing benefit, however small. For me, this resulted in a stream of deputations, often introduced by the local MP. Fourth, a considerable amount of time was spent on Regional visits.

I have the programme for one such visit by me:

> 7.30 a.m. Picked up for train, visit Midlands factory – look and listen. Meet Local Small Firms Advisory Service. Recommend its service to Press and local radio, plus photocall.
> Lunch Chamber of Commerce, listen and speak, then second factory visit.
> Evening train to some bank for a dinner meeting re finance for small firms, return home 11.50 p.m.

I was generally made welcome, but came up against really hostile questioning in areas of high or rising unemployment. I relished my visits round the country as a valuable two-way exchange of information. Listening enabled me (and equally important, the accompanying Department Official) to discover local concerns and priorities, for example an extensive fact-finding tour of the West Country highlighted the shortage of small industrial premises of 750–1500 square feet.

The world recession led to a serious run down in the steel industry with consequent job losses. Keith Joseph's very reluctant approval of BSC's plan to close their giant Consett steel works created an abysmal situation for this somewhat isolated North East town. In the Department I met representatives of the local authority, introduced by their MP, and agreed a visit. I was the first Minister to (so to speak) put my head over the parapet into what might be an ugly situation. The night before I went up unaccompanied and unrecognised and over cups of tea, a pub visit and a fish and chip supper, listened to local gossip. It gave me an understanding of the mood in the town (a flashback to my father, four times unemployed in the depression). I heard most talk about what people planned to do with their redundancy money. The next day I opened officially a large site for small and new businesses, including a start on two quite significant factories: a small message of hope in a sea of gloom.

Listening was useful on my various visits, but in my view it was also vital to explain what our Government was doing, why, and the eighteen months to two years timescale for results to come through.

This was the time when Britain was recognised as the 'sick man of Europe'. We suffered from comparative long-term industrial decline. This was now exacerbated by over 20 per cent inflation, much of this caused by well-meaning policies pursued by Governments of both parties. They had stimulated consumer demand by massive government spending, financed it by huge borrowing – in effect printing money. Instead of creating jobs in the UK, this consumer spend went on a flood of imports, most of them in fair competition from within the Common Market (not the Far East). In addition, huge sums had been spent on wholesale subsidies to prop up declining industries.

One explanation I used for explaining our credit squeeze and higher interest rates – to restrict the money supply – involved the Roman emperor Diocletian. He had wanted a huge increase in military spending without anger from increased taxes. His solution had been gradually to double the coins in circulation, only to discover then that this had halved their value or, put in today's context, prices had doubled. The earliest example of rip-roaring inflation. I explained that soon we would hear the phrase 'money is tight' and not long after inflation would drop significantly. Indeed, before the end of 1980 we already had three months with inflation down to single figures.

My first rôle as Small Business Minister dealt with reform in matters covered by the Department of Industry. In my first six months some three quarters of a million questionnaires (I calculated a column as high as Big Ben) had been stopped from landing on the desks of small businessmen. Changes ensured that smaller firms no longer had to file detailed accounts at Company House. A freephone management counselling service was in operation organised by the Department but operated by experienced businessmen; this proved to be particularly valuable to those starting up a small firm. In a new development we established a link between this service and a pension fund. They would often provide finance for sound small projects which were unattractive to most investment institutions due to the disproportionate cost of assessing them (small, but that is the nature of seedcorn!).

One pet project of mine was trying to persuade first our Department officials and then the Treasury that we should introduce a Loan Guarantee Scheme so that small firms could borrow from the banks when they had a sound business proposition, but insufficient assets to pledge against the loan. Officials were understandably worried the banks would put their potential bad debts into the scheme and lend recklessly if the Government covered their losses. We were at an advanced stage when I left the Department. The announcement was made by Geoffrey Howe in his 1981 Budget and implemented in the capable hands of my successor John MacGregor. Eventually the Treasury approved the scheme with 20 per cent of any bad debts falling on the lending bank.

Geoffrey Howe's first two Budgets did a power of good for small firms, particularly start-ups. His cut in top rate income tax from 83 per cent to 60 per cent actually more than doubled the take-home pay for those who really succeeded and motivated thousands more to start up their own business. Reductions in company tax on small firms enabled many to finance their own expansion without borrowing. Simplification of VAT was widely welcomed, along with exemptions from Capital Transfer Tax on passing small businesses including farms on to their next generation. The Department of the Environment played its part by speeding planning decisions, Office Development permits had been swept away, restrictions on industrial developments eased. All nationalised industries and local authorities had to prepare a 'domesday book' of under utilised land so it could be made available. In a controversial and widely publicised speech I made a special plea to those who served on Planning Authorities to judge small firm applications not on the basis of planning zones, but whether by reason of noise, smell, traffic generation or unsightliness an application would damage the purpose of the land zoning, whether it be residential or agricultural land.

Jim Prior, Secretary of State, Department of Employment, recognised that the then current Unfair Dismissal procedure under Employment Protection legislation inhibited small firms from taking on new employees. I made a number of representations to him. Happily he concurred with an exemption for firms with fewer than twenty employees. At first he kept a requirement that the employee so taken on must be informed in writing of this loss of protection. Many small firms would not have picked up this requirement so I sought to have it dropped. Eventually Jim agreed to accept an amendment moved by John Townend, even telling the House (Hansard 23 April 1980) that he had been 'badgered' by me over recent weeks 'Never met anyone who is more persistent over a point'. It must be rare, if not unique, for a Secretary of State to admit in public that he has been persuaded to change his mind by a Junior Minister in another Department. The comment from AW was amazement that perseverance had won the day, adding that for some civil servants a more accurate description might be 'horrified'.

I have four other recollections which have stuck with me, all concerned with the competitiveness, or lack of it, of British industry. There was a visit to a knife manufacturer in Sheffield where I watched as the molten hot metal was put in to a cast, a string pulled to release a heavy weight to crash down and the raw knife removed, all this done one at a time! Another day spent in the Lancashire textile industry where I was proudly shown an excellent new weaving machine, hurrah, but the machine it replaced was so out of date it was going straight to a textile museum! I visited a thriving modern factory somewhere in central Cornwall. My eye was caught by a recently purchased robot carrying out amazing tasks. Then out tumbled the fact that three firms had been invited to tender. The quote from the British company arrived a week after the Japanese purchase had been installed and a Japanese gentleman had arrived to check all was well and to repaint any parts bruised in transit. The last of these horror stories was a visit to a UK car manufacturer. As I walked round the plant there were a good many men standing around without appearing to do anything. I was hugely embarrassed when I innocently asked whether it was the tea break.

What a contrast when I visited a Japanese tyre manufacturer. Everyone in sight was beavering away, all dressed in a company uniform. There were big notices of production targets. I was completely taken aback to discover that two of the identically clad staff who met me on arrival were the Plant Manager and the Accountant. This visit was not to the Far East but in Britain in the North East, in Sunderland. Even more dramatic was a visit to a Liverpool, or maybe Birkenhead, manufacturer of jeans. I have never seen women work at such an exhausting pace as those working the trouser presses, straightening the trousers, down came the press with a puff of steam and moments later ready for the next – but each of these women was working two presses! I felt uncomfortable to see the speed at which they chose to operate the machines. The secret? They were on piecework, paid according to their output, but paid tax free with the firm paying the whole income tax on these earnings.

I mention these so varied experiences not to point fingers, but simply to illustrate the days when and why Britain was indeed the sick man of Europe. But now change was on its way. True, tax-free earnings did not become a part of the commercial scene, but Geoffrey Howe's budgets slashing income tax gave every earner a significant incentive. March 1980 saw me off to Luxembourg to sign a contract with the European Investment Bank for a £20 million loan for certain small and medium sized industrial projects in Assisted Areas of the UK. After the signing ceremony, our Ambassador very kindly provided lunch. It was either on this or a subsequent occasion (borrowing for Housing in Northern Ireland) that an amusing situation arose. I found myself sitting next to the number two in the Embassy. Later the Ambassador's suitable words of welcome started by saying how pleasing it was to have two Government ministers round the table, Mr Fowler and Mr Mitchell. However, Derek Fowler was not Norman, the Secretary of State for Transport, but the similarly named Treasurer of British Rail! I was not put out, unlike the embarrassed Ambassador.[3]

Ministers continue to have their constituency work. Happily, sometimes this covers common ground; Prize-giving at Basingstoke's thriving technical college was one such opportunity. I applauded the work of the college in preparing young people for careers in industry and commerce, emphasising the benefit to the whole community from our commercial life. 'Too many young people believe that if you wish to serve the community in a worthwhile way, then you do it best through social or welfare work. It is natural for young people to draw on the well of human compassion and have this in mind when choosing their career. I make a plea for recognition that those who work in business, industry and commerce also serve their community, first by producing what their customers want, second by creating wealth (or providing services for those who do). There is a direct link between commercial success and an enlarged tax base. It is this which

---

[3] Not nearly as embarrassed as our Ambassador to the UN who was contacted for a media survey late one December as to which gift he would most like for the New Year. Properly mindful of the limitations on acceptance of gifts by those in the public service, he responded 'a box of crystallized fruit'. He was taken aback to hear the results of the survey broadcast on New Year's Day with the US Ambassador opting for progress on the roadmap towards peace in the Middle East, Russia, a rapprochement with the US, and the UK Ambassador a box . . .

funds our hospitals, schools, pensions etc. I deplore the fact that so few people recognise the direct link between business success and the ability of this country to help the weakest in our midst.'

It was after I had left the Department that by sheer chance I bumped into Pom Ganguly in the lift and learned that his figures from the VAT computer were regularly showing significant numbers of new business. Later I was to discover these had averaged a net gain between 1980 and 1985 of over five hundred new firms a week, plus the self employed not large enough to register for VAT, and I learned from other sources that eventually well over nine hundred thousand more jobs had been created in firms employing twenty or fewer. This turnaround was helped by our new £40 a week Enterprise Allowance for start-ups and by £640 million of borrowings under the Loan Guarantee Scheme.

No wonder people no longer spoke of the German miracle so much as the Thatcher revolution, something her detractors find it convenient to forget.

CHAPTER 14

Bordeaux, queen of wines

A buying trip encircling Bordeaux / The strategic difference
between French and New World wines, benefits and
downside / Whither the future?

Wine cheers the sad, revives the old, inspires the young,
makes weariness forget his toil.

Lord Byron 1788–1824

T HE HISTORIAN F.S. OLIVER DESCRIBED politics as 'the endless
adventure'. I judge this equally true for each new wine I taste.
Perhaps particularly Bordeaux, for every district and château is
different and each vintage is like the human thumb print, distinctive
and unique.

The contemptuous twelfth century Gascon word for the pale red
wines of Bordeaux was 'Clairet'. It is from this that the English word
for red Bordeaux takes its name. In years gone by, it was not unusual
to give more body and colour to the wines by the addition of wine
from the Rhône valley. There still survive labels from Château Latour
which in the 1860s proudly proclaim it as 'Hermitager' or 'Hermit-
agé'. Be reassured, the strict Appellation d'Origine laws of today
ensure such things cannot happen now. I can be sufficient of an
iconoclast that occasionally I think this is a pity, but it is better to
keep such thoughts to myself!

There are four things which determine the style and character of
a wine. These are the grape varieties, the soil, the weather and the
wine maker. Unlike most vineyard areas, virtually all the wines of
Bordeaux are a blend of two principal grapes: Merlot which
contributes colour, fruit and richness, and Cabernet Sauvignon with
its backbone, staying power and greater complexity; with, to a lesser
extent, Cabernet Franc giving a gentle mellowness with a pinch of
spice. The reason for this blending is because the Merlot flowers early
and so is at risk from a severe late frost. Per contra, the Cabernets
flower later but the hundred days twixt flowering and vintage leaves
them at the mercy of autumn weather, with the risk that the grapes

155

never fully ripen. Even worse, hail or windless warm weather after rain swiftly brings rot and total ruin to the crop. It is too great a risk to have only one grape variety.

On the right bank of the Gironde (facing downstream from Bordeaux) the farthest vineyards start near Blaye. Normally this is where I would start my tasting and sample selection. The small town of Blaye is dominated by a huge moated Vauban citadel which commands the estuary. There is now a hotel at its centre. For me, sitting at dinner watching the sunset across the sea is a good place to reflect on my first day of discoveries. The vineyards here are on a soil of sand or grit with occasional gravel crests, the resulting wines tend to be light with a reasonable concentration of flavour. Next I move upstream to the fortified port of Bourg; here the soil has more clay which helps to make rounder bodied wine; these are slightly more expensive but good value. It is near here that the big Dordogne and Garonne rivers join to become the Gironde Estuary. The Romans made wine here circa 50 BC. Now Roland Charbonnier, a hands-on vigneron, at Château Clos du Notaire suits my taste with 75 per cent of the vineyard planted with Merlot. Further up the right bank lies Pomerol with its iron oxide sub-soil; I have found these wines to be generally firm, with good body, backbone and full flavour.

Continuing upstream near the Dordogne, I come to the hill of St Emilion with its flatter surrounding countryside. Ironically the town is named after Saint Emilio, a teetotal monk from Brittany who settled here. The dominant grape is Merlot with its dark colour and smooth, fruity roundness. The wines are classified upwards from simple St Emilion through St Emilion Grand Cru to Grand Cru Classé and, at the top, the great wines of Premier Grand Cru Classé. There is a huge variation in the quality of simple Grand Cru. This is because there are many small, differing proprietors, some making excellent wine but, alas, others not.

The Château of Pavie, St Emilion Premier Grand Cru Classé, is at the foot of a short precipitous cliff with a cave alongside and a vineyard on top. I have a photo of myself in it, holding the roots of a vine from the vineyard above; I judge that to be well over thirty feet down. Nearby is Château Gaffelière, also Premier Grand Cru Classé. As with many châteaux it makes a second wine, Clos de la Gaffelière, from the younger vines plus any vat not quite up to the demanding standard of the Premier Cru. I bought it for, as with most second wines, it has the same style and characteristics as the great wine although without its concentration, or its price. Age is important, the older the vine, the bigger its root system and the more minerals, trace elements and complexity it will have.

On one visit to the neighbouring village of Montagne St Emilion I discovered Château Coucy and introduced it to the English market. Apart from good wine, I was interested to learn that a former English owner had chronicled the most authentic account of the nearby battle of Castillon in 1453. Apparently the English were trapped within the junction of the Dordogne and a tributary. The French on the hillside above were, for the first time ever, armed with cannon. In the ensuing rout General Talbot and his two sons were killed along with three thousand others. Thus abruptly ended English control of Aquitaine and, with it, Bordeaux.

On my first visit with Frank Bower, I was fascinated to see the different ways in which white and red wines are made. I had assumed white wine came only from grapes of that colour. Not so; if you cut open a red grape its flesh is the same greenish yellow as a white one. Only the skin is different. Indeed, there are more red grapes than white in most champagnes. All the colour and much of the character of a red wine comes from the skin. White wine is made by pressing the grapes, drawing off the juice, generally adding cultivated yeasts and fermentation soon follows. This process turns sugar into alcohol, giving off carbon dioxide. How different with red wine. Here the grapes are squeezed enough to burst them and put in a vat, yeast added, and during the ensuing fermentation the colour gradually leaches out of the skins into the juice. Next the skins rise to the top and form a cap. That is not much help when you want the skins in the fermenting mass to bring out the colour and the tannins, although not too much. This is where the skill (or is it art?) of the winemaker is crucial. He may pump juice from the bottom of the vat and spray it on to the cap. Others will push the cap down into the juice, sometimes mechanically. I know one Maître de Chai who lowers a solid oak beam until the cap is immersed. Many small growers push the cap down using a wooden disc on the end of a long broomstick. This can be dangerous; every year somewhere a small proprietor will inhale too much CO_2 and faint – sometimes falling into the vat! Next, the harsh young red wine is put into wooden casks where it starts to soften before bottling.

Reds on the left bank commence with the gravelly background flavour and elegance of the Graves district here, the most famous is the First Growth Château Haut Brion, right in the suburbs of Bordeaux. The Bordelais are not amused when they are reminded that Talleyrand[1] purchased this Château solely because his chef advised him that it made the best sauces in France!

Moving down the left bank of the estuary from Bordeaux, one comes first to the Médoc and then Haut Médoc, within which are in sequence the four greatest wine villages of Margaux, St Julian, Pauillac and St Estèphe. In Margaux will be found the great Château Palmer, part owned by the Sichel Family who also own Château d'Angludet nearby. For many years, the hugely respected Peter Sichel, a good friend, would be an early contact and a mine of information. He was the only man to advise me from time to time not to buy. His four sons continue their successful business and Angludet always features in my own cellar.

Between the Margaux and St Julien villages lies a stretch of Haut Médoc. Here I found the Cru Bourgeois Château Lamothe Bergeron with its 'eye to the estuary', said to be an advantageous endowment. It has some of the characteristics of its two greater neighbours and, anyway, in a good vintage I like its concentrated flavours.

My next stop was, and is, with Anthony Barton and his charming and capable daughter Lilian at their superb Châteaux Léoville and Langoa Barton. When yet another 'vintage of the century' fever had pushed prices through the roof, Anthony is remembered as having set an example of moderation. Château Langoa, with the family house, is classified a third growth and Léoville a second. Charles Cocks (1812–1854), an Englishman, wrote an authoritative classification of Bordeaux wines based on the then market prices. It was published in 1846 by Longmans. Its French translation came four years later by Feret in Bordeaux, who update and still publish this claret bible. It was adopted by the Bordeaux Chamber of Commerce for the famous classification of 1855, a classification which still stands today.

Its formal adoption was not without controversy, as shown in Biarnez' poem:

---

[1] The enigmatic Talleyrand, an aristocrat who was President of the Assembly during the Reign of Terror. Earlier a Bishop, defrocked, he had four preoccupations in life; a love of women, good food, politics and an affection for London.

... What a perfect blend, full of warmth, full of flavour,
So I can't understand what fool taster from Vaudeville
Can have ranked as a Second, the wine made at Léoville.

Going on to Pauillac with its three great First Growths: Latour,
Lafite, and Mouton Rothschild, I am reminded of a hot dry summer
which had thickened the grape skins so that the subsequent wine
would be over-tannic. Some light rain was improving both the
quality and the quantity. It appears the Baron Rothschild was walking
through the vineyard with his Maître de Chai and commented that
it was raining money. 'Not so,' responded his cellarmaster 'if it were,
your umbrella would be the other way up!'

Adjacent to Château Latour is Château Pichon Longueville
Comtesse-de-Lalande owned by the irrepressible Madame de Lencquesaing. Beside making one of the greatest of the second growths
of the 1855 classification, the Château has an interesting tale to tell
concerning its ownership. For this I am indebted to my friend John
Avery (a fellow Past Master of the Vintners' Company). Under the
rules of the Code Napoleon regarding inheritance, an estate has to be
divided amongst the children. Here the family could not agree
amongst themselves as to which of three should inherit the Château.
Eventually after seventeen years, they agreed to draw lots and put
three tickets in a biscuit tin. Madame May de Lencquesaing won.
Alas, she has now retired and the château has been sold.

Not very far behind Mouton the appellation returns to Haut
Médoc and here lies Château Cissac, currently owned by Louis
Vialard. Because the vineyard is larger than average, the price tends
to offer good value. I recall an evening tasting, followed by a meal
where we were joined by his export director, a charming Dutch-
man. Over coffee he instructed me about a quicker route back to
my hotel and offered to lead me through the lanes to the main road
– an offer I gratefully accepted. Having collected my samples and
said my farewells I was pleased to see the backlights of my lead car
waiting for me. We set off at a reasonable pace which, to my surprise,
became faster and faster, making it difficult to keep up, finally a
sharp turn on to a gravel road. There was something wrong and I
turned back to find my usual route. Next morning the cook arrived
at the Château complaining loudly that she had been pursued by
that mad Englishman and asking if I should be reported to the
police?

In 1975, Pam and I arrived in a torrential thunderstorm for our first visit to Château Haut Marbuzet, St Estèphe. Mud was spewing out from between the rows of vines on to the road and I recall watching a woman picker crossing the road, one hand holding up her skirt and the other carrying her shoes. As proprietor Henri Duboscq opened the door to us, there was a violent clap of thunder and the lights went out. He stammered a 'please wait' and rushed away to the press house which had been struck by lightning. Later we met his enchanting wife Liliane and his two young sons (now partners in running the business). This was an inauspicious start to what has become a lasting friendship with one of the most charismatic proprietors in the Médoc. Henri once described to me those four most famous areas of the Haut Médoc in an amusing way which really does illustrate the difference between them: Margaux, the wine of gentle femininity, soft, round and seductive; St Julien, an austere femininity, the iron hand in a velvet glove, adding mischievously 'a real Thatcher of a wine'; next St Estèphe, the macho of the Haut Médoc, powerful, masculine, with backbone and staying power, sometimes combined with a rich opulence (e.g. Château Haut Marbuzet). Pauillac combines all these qualities, a district which holds Château Lafite, Latour and Mouton Rothschild cannot fail to be the repository of all talents.

As I write, French vineyards, even including Bordeaux, face an uncertain future, in part of their own making, but to a significant extent due to rigid restrictions and burdens imposed by the French authorities. In the UK and a number of other markets there is rising demand for wine, but far exceeded by the huge increase in new world production (e.g. from 1999 to 2003 Australia increased its area under vines by 76 per cent).

Some thirty classified crus in Bordeaux with world famous names will always survive. There are another fifty or so which have a loyal following; they too should be survivors, and their number may well be increased by young growers with up to date technical know-how, taking over from an older generation. These will survive by producing wines with individuality reflecting the distinctive terroir from which they have come. This all ties up with the big difference between French vineyards and the New World. The latter are defined by the grape variety and the name of the producer, whilst the better French wines are defined according to the exact plot of land on which the vines stand. Hence the uniqueness of each of their wines and the immensely enjoyable, indeed 'endless adventure', which comes from this diversity. A friend for dinner and an interesting bottle which provides a conversation piece is a joy, or a dinner party with that special bottle with the cheese (and before dessert, please!). The big question is, where do the six thousand five hundred plus other small growers fit in? Some will have a local or niche market, others will be grape growers supplying fruit for brands, some, part-timers with another job but, for many, the next ten years will, I fear, see their vineyards disappear.

No account of my visits to Bordeaux would be complete without reference to white wine. Here the demand for dryish whites has been shrinking over a number of years, along with the number of surviving growers, in part thrust aside by the increasing success particularly of New Zealand whites. Too many of these French whites have been nice, easy drinking with little to make them stand out. Of course, there are exceptions, witness the superb white from Château Malartic Lagravière as just one fine example.

The story of the best sweet wines has been different, with a strong following for the better known Sauternes and Barsac (the latter are normally a little lighter and more elegant; they form a defined part of the Sauternes district). Grape production here is very different. Generally the grapes are left on the vine until last, hoping for warm, windless sunny days with damp misty mornings. This is a combination which would bring disastrous rot in red grapes but with the white, mainly Semillon variety, it produces 'noble rot' – botrytis. Much of the bunch becomes stuck together, the fungus lives on the juice of the grapes reducing the quantity, hence concentrating it to produce the wonderful luscious perfection of great Sauternes.

Whether it is Sauternes or any other wine, a problem arises; if only two or three glasses are required, too much is left in an open bottle which will not keep. I resolve this by emptying a small twenty five centilitre fruit juice bottle with a screw cap and filling it with red or white wine out of a bottle I have opened for dinner. Once full, this will generally keep for some while. Not a widely known trick, but it enables me to enjoy a third of a bottle of wine when, alas dining on my own. Surely a meal without a glass of wine is like a day without sunshine.

CHAPTER 15

Northern Ireland

Parliamentary Under Secretary of State Northern Ireland Office,
known in Northern Ireland as Minister for the Environment, my
responsibilities 10,000 staff, budget £430 million / Baptism of
fire – Minister thrown out of Council meeting / Jim Prior
follows Humphrey Atkins – comparison of their ways of
working / Ulster MP murdered – subsequent reaction / Building
bridges with District Councils / Housing in a divided
community, more owner occupation / I relax planning controls
for business, become only Minister to meet Gerry Adams / The
Honours system / A real game of 'Yes, Minister'

I WAS SKI-ING IN MÉRIBEL when a message came through to phone
Tony Willis. He was his usual breezy self, but with a note of
excitement in his voice 'You are to phone No.10. This is the number.
There must be a reshuffle, so please phone me back.' I got through
and found the Prime Minister saying she was 'making a few changes
and I'd like you to go to Northern Ireland'. At that moment the
phone went dead! I redialled, wondering how much the PM's time
was valued per minute. On reconnection she said my experience of
small business would be particularly valuable in Northern Ireland. She
wanted to announce the change at 6.30 p.m. (it was then 4.30). I
gulped and said something like 'if that is how I can be most helpful,
of course I'll do it'. She added 'finish your holiday and report to
Humphrey (Atkins, Secretary of State) in Belfast.' I came out of the
call box and repeated the conversation to Pam who was not wildly
enthusiastic. It must be remembered that we are talking of January
1981 when the PIRA and INLA[1] were regularly committing
outrages. I recall that, driving home, Pam and I discussed how we
would respond to various imagined threats. The only one firmly in
my memory is my determination that if ever I were to be taken
hostage, no ransom was to be paid.

---

[1] PIRA, the Provisional IRA, the younger, active part of this paramilitary organisation.
INLA, Irish National Liberation Army, a brother terrorist organisation.

With Valerie Steele, Private Secretary, Northern Ireland

The phone rang almost as soon as we were back and Valerie Steele introduced herself as my new Private Secretary from the Department of the Environment at Stormont, Belfast. An initial briefing would be delivered next morning and she would collect me on Monday morning. I replied that there was no need to come all this way, I would let her know what time my flight arrived. In a very firm, no–nonsense tone of voice she said 'I shall be in the car when you are collected'.

An uneventful flight, but some prescience in the announcement 'as we may experience some turbulence as we descend into Belfast, will you please fasten your seatbelts'. When I arrived unknown at Aldergrove airport, we walked down the passageway and two men with large feet formed up on either side and escorted us to the rear of two cars waiting outside. Of course, my new Private Secretary was right – what a scoop if the wrong man had been welcomed.

We drove across Belfast to Stormont, the seat of Government. I was happily surprised both at how normal everything looked in the city and what a wonderful setting it has, with green hills rising up on almost three sides and the sea nearby. I was led up to my Departmental office in the Parliament Building and advised that the

Permanent Secretary, Ken Bloomfield, would join me shortly. He proved capable, easy to work with, had a wonderful sense of humour but was promoted after a few months. His place was then taken by John Irvine, a tough and effective Scot who ran the Department as if it were a business, heads of Department as though they were Directors, himself as MD/Chief Executive, treating me as Chairman. I soon felt at home with him.

My responsibilities covered planning, housing policy, trains, buses, airports, the fire service, water, sewerage, roads, road safety, traffic management and ports, enterprise zones and conservation etc: all the local government functions of English District, Borough and County Councils along with many of those of the Westminster Department of the Environment, but not those of an English Parish Council; these, together with dustbin emptying, were covered by elected District Councils. The *Basingstoke Gazette* sent a reporter over to cover a day's work and headlined the report 'The Minister for Everything'! However, I discovered that District Councils had one other, to me, very important rôle: that of consultation. I decided this was something I wanted to develop as much as practicable. Accordingly I asked officials to set up a programme for me to visit all the twenty six District Councils. My message was to be quite simple: I am not local, I'm not pretending to know what should be the priorities for your area so you tell me. If what you want is within my budget and is not discriminatory in its purpose as between majority and minority communities, then it will be high on my list of projects for your District.

Officials set in hand the programme of visits for twenty five of the twenty six districts. They explained I would not be able to go to Magherafelt. I asked why not. There seemed to be some reluctance to explain. Eventually the story came out. In those days, when a Minister went on a foray away from Stormont he received two briefs, one from his Department, in my case outlining what the Council would be seeking from me, perhaps a bypass, and advising me on priorities, practicalities, costs etc. The second came from the office of the Secretary of State, briefing me on some of the people I would meet, possibly in the hope that someone might be appropriate for the Secretary of State to invite to serve on a public body, sometimes detailing past scandals or allegations. Of course, all such briefing was heavily marked 'Confidential'. A Minister in a previous Parliament had carelessly left his briefing behind. It was found and copied to all the Councillors, who were not best pleased, indeed furious. At its next meeting the Council passed a resolution never again to receive any Minister. It took me over a year, but I did get there in the end, and very useful it was.

I was soon on a swift learning curve for I had no previous knowledge of the Province and many things surprised me. For example, standing on the cliffs of the Antrim coast on a clear day and seeing buses in Scotland, I had no idea that it and the ties were so close. Next, finding that the conflict was largely rooted in tribal tradition and culture, though religion was an important element. The majority, just under two thirds of the population, were Unionist, leaving nearly forty percent to the minority community. This latter had increased from ten percent to thirty percent between 1860–1875 through migration from a depressed agricultural economy in the South to the labour starved and hugely successful linen, cotton and shipbuilding industries in the North.

After the Republic secured its independence from the UK, its government under William Cosgrave determined to stamp out the IRA. It announced that, for every assassination, it would execute a number of IRA prisoners currently in jail whose death sentences had been suspended, on condition there were to be no further murders. I state the facts without moralising. After seventy seven such executions the IRA largely called off their campaign of violence and, in effect, disbanded. Even when De Valera, the fiercely Republican leader, took office as Prime Minister in 1932 he took a strong line against continuing illegal activity by a violent rump. Why was it then that violence was renewed? To answer that, one need go no further back than the Northern Ireland constitution of 1920.

At this point, a short recall of history is unavoidable. When the North secured its own constitution, this said that 'Northern Ireland will remain part of the UK so long as the majority so wish'. No other part of the UK had this question mark over its future. The message was clear to those who wanted a united Ireland; there would be the possibility of change. The message was equally clear to the supporters of the Union, 'Lose an election and you will lose your nationality'. The whole of the island of Ireland has long had very high levels of migration (there are more Irish in the US than in Ireland). Understandably the Unionists were terrified of losing their majority and were determined this should not happen. So, partly by unthinking tribal loyalty and partly by deliberate gerrymandering, they are said to have rigged local election boundaries, rigged housing and jobs so that most emigration would come from the minority community. As a result of this, a survey in 1972 showed the Protestant proportion of the population virtually unchanged since 1921 in spite of the higher birthrate in the Roman Catholic community.

Inevitably, the result of this discrimination was the gradual build up of a simmering resentment in the minority community. By the 1960s pressure was growing. First there was the influence of the US Civil Rights Movement, then in 1968 the Paris student riots lit the spark and violence flared up. In August 1969 Harold Wilson sent units of the army to support the police who were being overwhelmed. From 1970 Ted Heath continued this support. In 1972 he demanded that Brian Faulkner, Prime Minister of Northern Ireland, accept the transfer of law and order powers to Westminster. When this was refused, Ted suspended the Northern Ireland constitution and initiated Direct Rule with Westminster Ministers heading up the Northern Ireland Civil Service departments. So that is why I found myself with a staff of just over ten thousand and a budget of circa £430 million pounds, responsible for almost all the functions of local government throughout Northern Ireland. At Westminster I was the Parliamentary Under Secretary of State, but in NI known as Minister for the Environment. The arrival of Westminster Ministers ended much of the discrimination against the minority and went a long way to explain the drop in violence between 1972 and when I arrived in 1981. For example, shooting incidents fell from over ten thousand a year to under four hundred, and deaths from four hundred and sixty to approximately one hundred. As with most people on the mainland, I had no idea the figures had been so horrifically high.

My normal pattern was to catch an early flight from Heathrow to Belfast on Mondays, fly back for any unavoidable three line Whip and return next morning; otherwise home on Friday. There had to be a Minister in Northern Ireland at all times, so we rostered every fifth weekend. During the week Ministers stayed in the former Speaker's House (unkindly referred to as Trust House Twenty) although perfectly adequate. The weekend duty Minister had the use of a converted coach house maisonette at Hillsborough in the grounds of the hundred-acre Hillsborough Castle, formerly home to the Governor of Northern Ireland and now the Secretary of State's residence.

I was fortunate that Alan and my other escorts-cum-bodyguards were congenial people to have alongside since two of them accompanied me every time I left the office. I was also fortunate to have inherited Valerie Steele, my Northern Irish Private Secretary who also accompanied me on most visits away from the office. There was virtually nowhere we went where Valerie did not have a friend, a relative or an old schoolmate whom she knew and their useful bits of inside information were invaluable. Several Ministers brought English Private Secretaries with them. I can understand the comfort this gave them but I can only put on record that, time and again, having an insider at my elbow saved me from 'putting my foot in it'.

One early trip was set up for Newry, on the border, to plant a tree inaugurating pedestrianisation, followed by a meeting with Councillors and rounded off with a meal in the 'Copper Kettle' restaurant. PIRA blew up the restaurant the night before, however my visit went ahead and a meal was hastily organised in the Council offices. The Catholic Chairman, John McEvoy, generally known as 'Big John' was an impressively capable and fair minded man whom I was delighted to see brought forward to become, later, the Chairman of the Housing Executive for the Province.

My baptism of fire

I had only been in post about six weeks when a planning application came in from the Gaelic Athletic Association for a playing field on the outskirts of Ballymena, Ian Paisley's[2] home town. I then discovered that this strongly republican organisation had headquarters across the border in the Republic, its rules required that during matches they flew the flag of the Republic and no members of HM forces nor the Royal Ulster Constabulary (RUC) were allowed to be present. Obviously this made it a sensitive decision. I went and looked at the site, which was well outside the town; it was mainly rough ground but in planning terms I could see no reason why it should not go ahead. Officials then pointed out that the following Tuesday I was due to pay the first of my goodwill consultation visits

---

[2] The Reverend Ian Paisley, Leader of the DUP (Democratic Unionist Party), bitter opponents of a united Ireland.

Department of Environment Press Officer, Mike Worsley, Pam and Minister

to the Ballymena Council; understandably they suggested I say nothing about my decision until ten days or so after my visit.

I took the view that if I did that, no-one would ever trust me again. My decision about the application would be announced the night before. Officials pointed out that I would get a somewhat dusty reception since Ballymena was a DUP stronghold; accordingly I arranged to arrive half an hour ahead of schedule. Outside the Town Hall were some twenty people who shouted and booed as I went in. The Mayor, Sandy Spence (later we became on friendly terms) started his welcome to the new Minister. Up jumped the DUP leader of the Council to move that TV cameras be admitted. The Mayor again started his speech, to be interrupted by a motion that I be asked to leave as a person not welcome to the majority in the town. The Councillors sat at a horseshoe shaped table in front of us and, with one exception, denounced my actions in forthright terms. The exception was an Irish Nationalist whose brogue was so pronounced that I couldn't follow what he was saying. Several speakers referred to me as bringing disgrace on the town and comfort to Her Majesty's enemies.

The last Councillor to speak unfurled a union jack as a waistcoat, spoke (as had others) of his war record, and denounced the Republic for having denied the Allies their agreed use of the Southern ports during the war, with more about comfort to Her Majesty's enemies. The Mayor summed up by suggesting the debate had been conclusive. I jumped up and said that before a vote was taken, it was usual for the other side to be heard. The Mayor concurred.

I explained that, as a Minister, I was not there to play sectarian politics. I had looked at the site, there were no planning grounds for refusal, that was why I had approved it, indeed if the application had been from the (fictitious) Protestant Protest Association it would have been passed without difficulty. I re-emphasised my impartiality as a Minister and added 'you would at least expect me to have the courage to come here today, after the decision was announced, and be prepared to defend it'. The motion was passed and I, along with Valerie, was escorted out of the Chamber. Outside the number of jeering protesters had grown to around two hundred. We were caught on the flank wall as the crowd surged forward, and swiftly escaped to the cars, having collected a few bruises on the way.

Looking back, I realise that this was the best thing that could have happened. 'Minister thrown out of Council' was the main story in most Northern Irish papers and both TV channels led with my straight to camera explanation to the Council. On ensuing visits around the Province it was frequently said 'You'll get a better welcome here than you did in Ballymena' – not difficult! It was only later I discovered that the Council had set me up with special invitations to TV, radio and journalists to watch and report my anticipated humiliation.

Many legends arose from the 17th Century siege of the town called Londonderry by Unionists and Derry by the minority community. When, later, I went there the invaluable Valerie advised I use the term 'this fair city'. In 1688 a Catholic army led by the Earl of Tyrconnell had arrived on the other side of the River Foyle and demanded surrender. The elderly Mayor and Councillors were minded to agree, but the Protestant Reverend Walker, incensed by this suggestion, roused the town's Apprentice Boys and had the emissaries thrown out and the drawbridge raised. A hundred-and-five day siege ensued before the near starving inhabitants were relieved. Later the towering Walker Monument had been built on the top of

the raised west wall of the city; here it looked down on the largely
Catholic Bogside, a position which epitomised the Protestant
ascendancy. In 1973 PIRA had blown it up. At the same time I was
wrestling with the Ballymena planning application, the Apprentice
Boys of Derry put in an application to rebuild the monument. The
Secretary of State hoped it would be turned down because the
Government picked up the bill for restoring bomb damage. I argued
that there could be no planning grounds for refusing because it had
long been there. I gave consent on the same day as the Ballymena
decision, expecting a huge outcry. At least there would be a sectarian
balance of disgust at my actions! In the event, to everyone's surprise,
this decision was accepted without protest by the town's Council. I
think much of the credit for this belongs to David White, an
outstanding local official of our Department and a member of the
Plymouth Brethren, who was trusted by both sides. Later a survey
found that the west wall could no longer safely take the weight of the
proposed superstructure; hence Building Consent had to be refused
but a less ostentatious monument was subsequently able to go ahead.

Humphrey Atkins was succeeded as Secretary of State Northern
Ireland by Jim Prior in September 1981. It was interesting to discover
their differing ways of working. There is a reporting chain between
the Junior Minister's Private Offices and that of the Secretary of State.
Humphrey was a very hands-on Secretary of State, for example if I
reported at his weekly private gathering of Ministers that I planned a
new initiative, Humphrey might say it sounded interesting, that I
should bring my officials over the next week and we would look at
the details. When Jim Prior arrived I had assumed that was the
normal pattern and reported a proposed new initiative on Housing.
Jim asked how it was to be financed and the anticipated cost. 'Shall
I bring my officials over next week?' I asked – 'No – so long as you
are satisfied with the figures'. That made it fully my responsibility. As
you can guess, I went back and re-checked every figure with
renewed thoroughness.

Harsh realities

I wish I could produce pen portraits which record a scene as if
photographed. One would certainly be the day Harold McCusker,
Ulster Unionist MP for the border constituency of Armagh, had

come to see the Secretary of State and beforehand joined Ministers for lunch in our Trust House Twenty. He came in, was given a drink, and then took off his jacket, took off a bullet proof waistcoat and resumed his jacket. 'Thank God I can spend an hour or two not wearing that thing'. He went on to explain that he had come from the funeral of the last of the selectors who had chosen him as Unionist Parliamentary candidate, most of them murdered.

Back at the Commons one Friday in November 1981 I found myself with the Reverend Robert Bradford, the MP for South Belfast, almost alone in the Members' Tearoom. It was a good opportunity to get to know rather better one of the most sensible, level-headed Northern Ireland Unionist Members. We chatted for half an hour or so ... Imagine my shock and horror a couple of weeks later when Robert was murdered by PIRA on his way to his regular constituency 'surgery'. His funeral the following week took place in the large Dundonald Presbyterian Church and, timed to coincide with it, there were a large number of spontaneous Services, some in churches, others at local war memorials. Most included two minutes silence. For example, in the rural Clogher Valley alone two and a half thousand attended and at the Cenotaph in Omagh almost four thousand gathered for an hour long service. It was the same up and down the Province, a tribute to Robert coupled with vehement protest against the Government's allegedly inadequate security policy.

Neither the Secretary of State's, nor my attendance at the funeral had been announced, but as soon as his car appeared, part of the large overflow crowd surged forward jeering and shouting 'Traitor' and 'Murderer'. My car was behind his and, for a while, it looked as if we might not get through. We entered the church by a side door near the front. As soon as Jim was seen, part of the congregation started hissing. As the service ended, the Reverend Ian Paisley went outside to appeal for calm, asking the crowd to remember it was a funeral service and to allow Jim to leave. However, about a hundred gathered near his car and, when he reappeared, they pushed forward, kicking and hitting his car and bruising him. Some fifty RUC struggled with the demonstrators and got him safely away. In my case there were scuffles and bruises but a great deal less than for Jim.

Back at Stormont Castle, the Secretary of State's headquarters, I joined him for a cup of tea as we discussed the events of the afternoon. His (English) Private Secretary came in to announce that a 'rabble' were being held at the barbed wire outer barrier, demanding to speak to the Secretary of State. I volunteered to investigate. To my horror I discovered some thirty Unionist Mayors, Deputy Mayors and Council Chairmen, many of whom I recognised from my District Council visits, outside the gate ('rabble' indeed!). Dismayed at their treatment, I had the gate opened immediately and led them into the hallway of the Castle. I explained the Secretary of State was tied up and had asked me to welcome them and take a note of their representations and queries. Understandably their complaints were about security and protection from acts of terrorism. Three or four acted as spokesmen, while I listened and took notes. Some forty minutes later they left, mollified to some extent that they had been listened to and my assurance that I would give the Secretary of State a full account of their concerns.

Housing in a divided community

I decided that after building a good working relationship with the District Councils my next priority would be housing, particularly in Belfast. Public sector housing in Northern Ireland is run by the Housing Executive so, paradoxically, Council houses are known as Executive houses. I was particularly keen both to make possible and to encourage more home ownership. I did this because I felt that, in a divided community with many disaffected people, one healing influence would be owner occupation. With it should come the feeling and the reality of a stake in the community in which they lived. The Housing Executive already had in hand a number of initiatives to encourage sales. I was pleased that one of my first engagements was the handover ceremony of the deeds to the thousandth Housing Executive home bought by its tenants. I was even more delighted when I had been Minister for fifteen months to hand over the keys to the ten thousandth happy owner-occupying couple. Spreading wealth, Thatcherism in practice!

Apart from the effect on morale and sense of pride in ownership, I saw three other benefits coming from the mounting sales we achieved. Firstly, wherever possible, tenants were now encouraged to borrow from the Building Societies and only use loans from the Executive when unavoidable, a reversal of the situation hitherto. This meant nearly a hundred million pounds of new money from sales coming into the Executive's coffers by the time I left. By May 1982, eighty per cent of sales were financed in this way and allowed the Executive to start work on an extra two thousand dwellings. I recognised publicly the huge credit due to John Gorman, the public sector housing's Chief Executive, and his team when we sold more 'Council houses' in Northern Ireland pro rata than were sold in the rest of the UK!

A second reason why I see owner occupation as desirable is better use of the existing housing stock. The average public sector tenant continues to occupy their subsidised house until carried out in a coffin, whereas owner occupiers down-size when older and move further afield, allowing the same house to be occupied by a series of owners more appropriate to its size. (Of course I encountered the usual spurious argument that selling public sector houses increases the number of homeless – as if changing ownership decreases the nation's housing stock.) With part of the money from Executive house sales we soon had under way the biggest slum clearance programme in the history of Belfast, indeed probably of the whole United Kingdom, accompanied by the largest new build programme in Belfast since the days of Queen Victoria. The third benefit was quite simply that pride of ownership ensures this housing stock is likely to be more lovingly cared for. Sensibly, the Executive cleared a huge backlog of tenants' minor repairs by allowing them to undertake the repairs themselves up to a cost of £50; a stitch in time . . .

I was also anxious to see more co-ownership (part owned, part rented); we even gave grants to help people on the priority waiting list with their deposit. Another initiative encouraged and helped new Housing Associations. The Catholic St Matthew's Housing Association of Short Strand, a strongly Nationalist area of Belfast, invited me to hand over the keys of the fiftieth house they had refurbished. It was one in a long terrace of houses which lined both sides of the street. A small crowd gathered across the road while I made appropriate remarks. I was about to go in for a conducted tour when the chief of my security team growled 'five minutes only'; apparently two known terrorists had appeared and, disturbingly, disappeared from the end of the street. As I came out, the Chairman of the Housing Association said how sorry he was not to be able to show me their next planned rehab because I would be interested in the words carved into the lintel above its window 'No Home Rule 1913'. Plus ça change!

One of the sensitive issues which arose each new year was fixing the percentage increase in Executive property rents. This could be decided by the Board of the Housing Executive or imposed by myself as the Minister. Any increase which exceeded tenants' expectations meant noisy condemnation of whichever of us had been 'guilty' of imposing it. On the other hand, rental income was important in funding good maintenance and new build. Officials in my Department had already negotiated with the Treasury in Whitehall on the minimum amount acceptable to them. The meeting to fix the increase was held in the Executive's office, presided over by their Chairman, Charlie Brett, a very fair and hugely respected solicitor. He indicated that, in his view, I should make the decision. I suggested that there should be a discussion as to what sort of figure the Board thought to be appropriate. I do not recollect the details of the discussion, but clearly they feared a very large increase and did not want to be blamed. Somehow I ended up by suggesting that they 'make me an offer'. Charlie Brett strongly advised them not to, but the majority overruled him and offered a figure below what they expected me to impose. Such had been the speculation of a big rise that, to their Chairman's fury, they offered a figure I was able to accept. Charlie Brett became a good friend, but you would be right to assume that I did not 'get away with it' the next year and had to impose the increase.

One major Housing problem concerned the Divis estate. This consisted of seven hundred and ninety five medium to high rise flats and maisonettes, together with a tower block. Started in 1966 and completed in 1972, this complex was a genuine, if belated, response from the Unionist government of the time to the substandard and slum conditions which had gradually overtaken much of Belfast's older housing. When constructed, the twelve interlinked blocks of Divis had been a popular and fashionable design, built around gardens with the added cachet that their covered walkways linked to St Peter's Cathedral so that 'parishioners could walk to church without even getting their hair wet'. Now, in 1981, it had deteriorated into a disaster. With the 'troubles' the gardens were said to be a dumping ground, the 'covered streets in the sky' concept had helped turn the estate into an inward-looking, terrorist-dominated no-go area. A campaign had started for demolition[3] and officials were studying the options. To me, it sounded utterly unreasonable that an estate built so recently should even be contemplated for demolition. Indeed, how on earth would I defend that in the Commons? Clearly I had to see it to understand the situation. An early morning visit was arranged. We had just started to walk one of the internal roads when I looked up across the burnt-out cars which littered the garden to the next level up, to see that my every movement was being covered by the rifles of an Army patrol. This was no way for the Housing Minister to be seen going about his duties and, in my view, created a hugely unsatisfactory image at a time when Ministers were emphasising the return of normality to the Province. Accordingly, I had the visit aborted immediately and returned to the office somewhat dispirited and anxiously casting round for ideas.

Here again the value of an Ulsterwoman heading my Private Office proved its worth. Valerie knew the Roman Catholic Deputy Chief Constable and suggested she ask him to approach the parish priest to see if he would be kind enough to take me round. It was all discreetly arranged with only a handful of us. We started with the priest's housekeeper whose immaculate flat was beautifully kept and I would happily have occupied it, had it been in London. We walked along the passage and, where a door was ajar or had the key in it, I was led inside and introduced as the Housing Minister who wanted to see what their accommodation was like. It was early enough in the day that when we went upstairs (uninvited) in one maisonette there was an elderly couple getting dressed, a younger couple still in bed and small children playing on the stairs. I was embarrassed by the extent of the intrusion but, apart from that, no visit could have been better arranged for my purpose of seeing and understanding the real problems of the Divis. Before I left Northern Ireland, plans were being developed to isolate blocks, break up the connecting roads, install modern security controls etc.

During the worst of the Troubles the 'peace line', a physical barrier of brick walls and chain-link fences, separated the Catholic and Protestant tribes (parts of it still do) each determined to guard

---

[3] I had already turned down the proposed demolition of Parklands, a vandalized block of flats on the outskirts of Belfast. Although assured it was valueless, I insisted (to some hilarity amongst officials) it be put up for sale. It sold for £240,000 and is still in good use, but its siting and potential were totally different from Divis.

zealously its territory, providing security for, and only for, its own tribe. Some sixty thousand people (yes, sixty thousand!) across the Province had been forced to flee their homes between 1969 and 1973; now with the high Catholic birth rate but no extra territory to accommodate them, it became essential to build new, out of town estates. One major development on greenfield sites at Poleglass raised considerable objection from its Unionist controlled District Council of East Lisburn. To show their displeasure, the Council refused to empty the dustbins. The rubbish piled up and the first rats began to make their appearance. I called in the Mayor and the Town Clerk and explained that it was part of my duties as Minister for the Environment to ensure this situation did not continue. Accordingly, they had two choices: either they would carry out their statutory duties starting that week, or I would have it done for them, inevitably at very much greater cost! They did it.

Self build was a minor but useful part of new housing. I was invited to dig the first sod on one such estate near Londonderry and another outside Ballymena. The self builders were mainly craftsmen who contributed their differing skills, often with family help. The sod cutting ceremony drew a curious crowd. There is in Ulster and the rest of Ireland a legend that Catholics dig with their left foot and Protestants with their right. The first incision had been prepared for me. Which foot should I use? I wriggled the spade down into the soil below the turf and then took a deep breath and pressed the handle down with my chest. Laughter all round . . .

Planning for enterprise

I soon became involved in making the decisions needed to set up Enterprise Zones both in Belfast and Londonderry, in many ways these were similar to elsewhere in the UK. We had two sites in Belfast jointly of over five hundred acres and two in Londonderry. In these designated areas all industry and some commerce paid no rates, secured a 100 per cent tax allowance on development and the highest level of capital grants anywhere in the UK. All of this was greatly assisted by virtually no planning restrictions, exemption from Training Board levies, no Development Land Tax etc. Readers will hardly be surprised that I gave special emphasis to encouraging the start up of small businesses in the four Zones. Speaking to a local Chamber of Trade, I emphasised that almost all the large firms of the time had started as small ones. Moreover, there were too few new and small firms 'because for thirty years Governments had over taxed, over regulated, over controlled and demotivated the business community upon whom society depended for jobs'. Enterprise Zones proved islands of opportunity in which to escape so many of these disadvantages – and they proved highly successful.

Having in the past grumbled a great deal on behalf of small business about delays and over-restrictive planning controls, I had now the authority to do something about it. So in August 1981 we had new planning guidelines issued, these aimed at cutting red tape and speeding up decisions. In the case of new small firms, applications should generally be granted except where there were specific grounds for objection due to noise, smell, unsightliness or traffic generation. A year later decisions had speeded up to an average of eight weeks instead of twelve. John Hume, the leader of the SDLP,[4] was anxious to secure my support for a planning application in Londonderry, which had the next highest unemployment after Belfast. We fixed this on one of my Ministerial duty weekends. Pam was over, so we both went and met John and his wife Patricia, before hosting them for dinner. John came with me site viewing, leaving our respective wives at the hotel. As soon as we had gone, Patricia suggested Pam might like a short tour of the city. They were still gone when John and I returned, and after waiting a further half an hour I had become more than a little uneasy. All was well, but it emerged over dinner that her tour had included the Bogside and Creggan housing estate areas, at this time considered so dangerous I could only have a stopless tour of the Bogside in an adapted car with half a ton of metal shielding. It was just as well I did not know what Pam was up to in my absence! However, it was a real bonus to have her description of the housing conditions she had seen, not to mention vulgar graffiti whose subjects of attack included John Hume.

Only one Minister met Gerry Adams of Sinn Fein

As a result of a major initiative from Jim Prior, the autumn of 1982 saw the establishment of a Northern Ireland Assembly in the

---

[4] Social Democrat and Labour Party, the moderate nationalist party.

Stormont Parliament building. Amongst those elected were five from Sinn Fein (the political wing of the IRA) including Gerry Adams. This was a new situation in that neither the British nor the Dublin Government recognised Sinn Fein. At his Ministers' meeting next morning, Jim Prior indicated that Sinn Fein should be treated the same as any other Assemblymen, i.e. if they wanted to come and make representations which concerned their electors, we should deal with them in the same way as all other Assemblymen, albeit Sinn Fein and SDLP representatives were at that time boycotting the new Assembly. About a fortnight later Gerry Adams asked to bring a deputation from the Moyard Housing Action Committee, an estate which was claimed to be in so bad a condition that it should be demolished.[5] Clearly the Secretary of State's instruction applied and my Private Office set the necessary arrangements in hand. I did not relish the position in which I now found myself. No Minister had met a representative of Sinn Fein for ten years.[6] The Unionist community would be incensed and, in all probability, doors would be shut in my face. Undoubtedly the goodwill I had been building up with District Councils where there was a majority (Unionist) representation as I had with the minority (Nationalist) would be shattered.

Apart from that, we had not yet decided the future of the block of flats concerned so, if we did decide on demolition, Sinn Fein would (persuasively but wrongly) claim the credit – and so encourage the notion that aggressive campaigning, demonstrations etc. paid off. I decided that to receive just Adams and the Moyard Housing Action Committee was unfair on the SDLP and Alliance Party Assemblymen for that ward. Accordingly I invited them also to join the meeting.

This lasted over an hour and afterwards the three Assemblymen and Mrs Margaret Keenan, the Action Committee Leader, were

[5] The sewerage system was said to be inadequate, not surprising when, for example, someone had lifted a manhole cover and dropped a TV set into the drain. Another factor was that, before any demolition started, existing tenants would require to be rehoused and that would involve queue jumping over Falls Road tenants, who were already programmed for decanting. So later Moyard took its turn.

[6] In 1972 a young Adams was involved in political talks with the then Secretary of State for Northern Ireland, Willie Whitelaw. These had led to a Provisional IRA ceasefire. The whereabouts of that meeting having come into the public domain, it was switched at the last minute to the home of his Minister of State, Paul Channon, later Secretary of State for Transport.

photographed on the steps of the Parliament building below my office. Needless to say, the news that I had met Gerry Adams was the lead story on the 6 p.m. TV news. Amongst those watching it was Garret Fitzgerald, Taoiseach (Prime Minister) of the Republic. He promptly rang Margaret, apparently in a state of seething fury. In essence he said – You are always claiming we do not do enough to isolate Sinn Fein but now you have one of your own Ministers actually receiving Gerry Adams, when we never talk to him.' The next day a revised instruction from the Secretary of State said Ministers would not meet any Sinn Fein Assemblymen. Hence I became the only Minister to meet Adams. My impression was of a charismatic man holding himself in, letting the deputation speak for themselves, but each time I deliberately broadened the discussion, it was Adams who interrupted to say 'but Minister, we have come to see you about Moyard'.

A bit of everything

Part of my responsibilities covered the island of Rathlin, reputedly where Robert the Bruce, whilst sheltering in a cave, famously observed a spider ... At its Western tip, it has a lighthouse, a thoroughly Irish lighthouse, the only one I have ever heard of which has the light at the bottom of the tower. Although six miles out to sea, the island was part of my responsibilities. Their main link with the North Antrim coast was a boat which carried passengers, household provisions and cattle for fattening on the island. Unfortunately, Board of Trade inspectors had picked up an account in the local paper of an over-large wedding party on board, and had decided that the boats should have Plimsoll or weight lines, otherwise they could not even carry groceries. To implement the regulations would cost several hundred pounds or, failing compliance, a fine of up to £1,000 for the first offence. For five weeks the principal boat had ceased operations. My initial representations were rebuffed. Back at Westminster the Tea Room provided a useful point of contact with Scottish MPs in relation to their many islands and, after them, I had a quiet word in the Division Lobby with one of the Department of Trade Ministers. Happily this led to my being able to announce that, depending on the size and suitability, boats would be permitted to carry up to forty passengers, plus seven and a half tons of cargo, which equated to roughly fifteen head of cattle. For this the boats would be classed similarly to those operating to the offshore Isles of Scotland.

An amusing story from my visit to Rathlin concerned a complaint about the state of the only road on the island, asking for money to be spent on it. There were only a few cars, mostly untaxed, so I said that when taxes were paid, I would consider repairing the road. Needless to say, I heard no more.

I thought that fish were not my responsibility but one afternoon at a waterworks on the River Roe there was a minor accident when one of the staff cut themselves badly and an ambulance was called. Naturally his colleagues rushed to see if they could help. The time had been just before 5 p.m. Afterwards, one of the men looked at his watch, realised it was finishing time and went home. Waking in the night and going over the events of the day in his mind, he suddenly realised he had been in the middle of filling a small drum of concentrated poisonous chemical used in minute quantities as a water purifier. He rushed back to find, as he feared, that he had not turned off the supply tap; the small drum had overflowed down the drain and thence into the river, a tributary of the Foyle. All the fish in this stream were killed. The next day the MP, Willie Ross, came demanding to see me. Of course compensation would be paid but then I found myself on a crash course of discovery in which I learned that fish, or anyway salmon, only spawn in the river in which they had been born. Since most of this year's fish had been poisoned, there would be few to come back next year and, no, you could not bring in fish from elsewhere . . .

A frisson ran throughout the Unionist community and wider when, in October 1981, P&O decided to end its hundred and seventy two year long service between Belfast and Liverpool, with the loss of three hundred and fifty jobs. Although there were other services from Larne to Scotland, this was the only service connecting England to Northern Ireland, so it had a particularly emotive meaning to the Unionist community. The problem this created fell to my Department. Privately P&O told me the service was potentially viable but because of 'an attic full of old Chinese (Trade Union) restrictive practices', they were losing approximately £1 million a year. I had to make it clear that the government was not prepared to subsidise the service. There followed a period of hectic activity as officials sought to find another operator. This proved extremely difficult, but worth the attempt. Eventually in April 1982 a new company, Belfast Car Ferries, employing two hundred and twenty, started operating the route with the renamed 'St Colum'. Pam performed the naming ceremony and the new service started next morning. I commented that if as many people used its services as protested to me about the P&O closure, it could not fail!

The Honours system rarely impinged on my work. At the appropriate time senior officials submitted their list following their normal pattern. I sent it back (yes, I can be difficult) saying 'I want the man who walks the rail track between Newry and the Irish border and has to decide whether it's a discarded beer can or a bomb ... The (as it turned out) woman who manages one of the worst estates of the Housing Executive, and the foreman of the gang who clean up the broken glass and debris after an evening riot so the roads are clear for the morning rush hour traffic – and more of the like'. It was unconventional, but I felt these were the unsung heroes who so much deserved recognition.

Renaming St Colum Ferry. Belfast to Liverpool route

'Yes, Minister'

One form of the real game of 'Yes, Minister' is most frequently played out when it is known that a Minister will shortly be moving on; an approaching reshuffle is one opportunity, a General Election is even better. In my case it was the latter.

The New Town of Craigavon[7] had not lived up to the hopes and plans of its founders. In the heady days of great expectations, substantial amounts of farmland had been compulsorily purchased. During my time in the Department we did a reappraisal which identified a significant number of farms no longer required. The rules on disposal were governed by the result of the Crichel Down court case. There a dispossessed landowner had successfully sued the compulsory purchasing authority for selling off surplus land without first offering it back to him. For the Craigavon owners, the established procedure meant that they had been paid compensation of the then market value x years before, and could now recover their land on payment of the new current value. Although a blunt instrument, this was seen to be reasonably fair. How fair it was to the individual farmer depended on what he had done with his compensation money over the intervening years.

However, a small number of farmers had consistently refused to negotiate the terms of compensation and had simply carried on farming their own land, thus 'cocking a snook' at officialdom. For this heinous and infuriating offence, officialdom had an appropriate answer. Punishment would fit the crime in a way Gilbert and Sullivan would approve. They would now be paid the original value of their land which would immediately be returned to them on payment of the current value. I forget the difference, but say £1,000 per acre. For this my approval was sought and refused. I argued that I could not and would not defend saying to these farmers 'we don't now need your land; you (who have never left it) can have it back on payment of £1,000 an acre'. Officials were politely outraged. These people were to be rewarded for having refused to co-operate with

---

[7] Great care was taken to involve representatives of the local community. For many of them discussing expenditure in millions was entirely foreign; one businessman described to me a meeting where the agenda included £2 million of expenditure, and an item for the purchase of a white donkey for £50. The first went through in ten minutes, the latter took over an hour and was rejected.

officialdom. 'What a dangerous precedent'. 'Not following the Crichel Down rules' etc. 'Yes, Minister, we understand what you want but we are sure the Department of Environment in London will not allow the rules to be broken; we will discuss it with them and report back.' Silence, a long silence. I remember about it in my bath and write a note asking for progress; after some delay it appears. The Department of the Environment in Whitehall do not have any comment to make but, 'Yes Minister, we are sure the Treasury will have objections.' A General Election is approaching. I depart the scene but arrange lunch with Chris Patten, my successor, in order to brief him on the current issues he would inherit – the least of which is 'no doubt in a couple of weeks' time you'll find in the bottom of your box one night a proposition ...' He did, and thankfully supported my view.

Standing back for an overview

I had not been in post as a Northern Ireland Minister for very long when Enoch Powell, by then a Northern Ireland MP, asked me how I was getting on. I said 'fine; both communities have made me welcome, but there is no logic in this place from one end to the other' which drew the response 'that is because you have only been here six weeks; by six months you will recognise that it is all too tragically logical'; and so it was.

In the land of the blind, the one eyed is king, thus back home I was invited to speak at Rotary, Chambers of Commerce, Chambers of Trade, Conservative meetings etc. Their quest was for knowledge, an explanation for the baffling situation where, on one side, many gave tacit support to the bullet accompanying the ballot and, on the other, where prejudice and bigotry appeared to defy common sense; a land where, as Lloyd George put it, every time he thought he had solved the Irish question, the Irish changed the question.

The vast majority of people in Northern Ireland were not in a conflict situation and only want to live peaceably with their neighbours seeking, as in the rest of the UK, a secure job, a decent house and opportunity, unmolested, to lead a fulfilling family life. What is different is that those who live in that part of the UK which is NI, see themselves as belonging to one of two different nations; the majority as British, but also a sizeable minority who feel themselves to be profoundly Irish. For the latter read also the myths, legends and actual claim in the then constitution of the Republic that it was the government of the whole island of Ireland. At its most simplistic, the idea that because the island is a single land mass it must be peopled by one nation does not stand examination. Neither Norway nor Sweden wish to be one state, nor Spain and Portugal.

In fact, just as in England, there are place names which go back to the time of Anglo Saxon raiders and colonisers. They came, settled and merged as part of a single population. What made the later waves of settlers different was that they arrived after the Reformation in a Roman Catholic country. This created a religious separation which backed up their tribal origins, not unlike the position I had first come across in early post-war Holland where the majority in a country village would often be of one or the other religion and would discriminate in favour of their own.

What then is the key to this 'tragically logical' situation? It is fear; people in both communities feel threatened. Fear by the minority community of once again being discriminated against by a Unionist dominated Stormont government, and fears by the British Irish, the Unionists, that their mother nation would happily disown them. These attitudes led me in every speech I made to call for more understanding, sympathy and less censure.

I think it is well established in other majority/minority situations elsewhere in the world that the greatest stabilising factor is the presence of a confident majority able to accommodate minorities without fear of losing out. Indeed, this is well illustrated within Northern Ireland where those Districts whose Councils have a clear majority one way or the other had few problems. Often in these Districts the Mayor or Chairman of the Council rotates from one party to another – the tension comes where the control of the Council is in near balance. As an illustration, take Magherafelt where in my time a much respected member of the RUC had been shot. The next Council meeting had a resolution deeply regretting his death, to which a provocative amendment had been tabled to insert 'and Bobby Sands', a hunger striker who sometime earlier had starved himself to death in the glare of huge media coverage. The ensuing Council meeting broke up in disorder, blows were exchanged and two opposing councillors ended the night in hospital.

One might expect in a society divided roughly one million and just over half a million that a confident majority would exist, but while the minority have their confidence reinforced by support and encouragement from within the Republic, no Unionist has heard a parallel murmur 'culturally and emotionally you are part of our nation, it is our hope and aspiration that Northern Ireland will continue to remain British'. Indeed, in the Unionist community there has long been a malaise, a loss of morale, a feeling of being unloved, unwanted and beleaguered, so there has been no confident majority. For both communities their ideal has been control of the Province, their worst nightmare – control in the hands of the other community, with continued direct rule through Westminster ministers being the second choice for most people. There has been, since I left Northern Ireland, a gradual but perceptible change of attitude; both communities have elected the more extreme parties but these have themselves become more moderate, the Unionists' second choice losing some of its attraction as London has accommodated the Republic's desire for a greater say in the affairs of the North.

I left Northern Ireland after the election of June 1983. I suppose I am inordinately proud of the fact that both the official Unionist leader, Jim Molyneux, and the DUP leader, Ian Paisley, as well as an editorial in the *Irish News* – the newspaper of the minority community – all paid tributes to the work I had done. I am told that, until then, this was the first time such voices have come from both sides of the community divide.[8] Like many other NI Ministers, I was sorry to leave Northern Ireland and Jim Prior, for whom I had developed great respect. However my posting to the Department of Transport was to bring new, interesting and very different challenges.

When I served in NI, some perceptive friends over there used to say the troubles would only end with Ian Paisley and Gerry Adams shaking hands on the burnt out ruins of Belfast. As I write in the spring of 2007 this, without the ruins, may be coming true provided both parties can contain and retain their more extremist elements without a paramilitary breakaway. Please God it be so, and this land haunted by its past may know real and lasting peace.

---

[8] Footnote: However, this did not stop the IRA having me on their target list, as I was warned by the police on two separate occasions.

CHAPTER 16

Women at the bar

El Vino – Court cases over women standing at the bar – now taught
in Law School / El Vino wins twice, loses in Court of Appeal

S CARCELY A MAJOR NEWSPAPER IN THE WORLD did not carry the
story, from the front page and an editorial in the *The Times*, to a
newspaper in Bulawayo. They carried tales as untrue as, 'El Vino, the
bar that does not admit women', to those grateful for our rule that
ladies were waited upon at table, rather than having to push and
shove at the bar. My brother and I are the only people who know
the true story as to how all this came about.

Before 1939 there was only a handful of women journalists in Fleet
Street. During the war, women filled many of the vacant posts and were
warmly welcomed in our establishment. Stools were provided so they
could sit at the bar. Naturally, handbags were stood on the bar. Alas these
had a habit of falling over and sometimes breaking and spilling a glass or
two. Frank Bower, Director and Manager of the branch, instructed that
handbags must be put on the floor. Tables were served by a girl bringing
a tray of drinks. Unfortunately from time to time, the waitress on her
way through the bar area tripped over the bags or their straps, sending
the tray of drinks flying to the floor. Frank instructed that women were
to be waited on at tables with the old world courtesy at that time
customarily shown to a lady. So it continued happily and unchallenged
until the 70s with the appearance of a more aggressive feminism.

June 1970 saw a determined group of 'The Monstrous Regiment
of Women', as one newspaper reported it, march on 47 Fleet Street
demanding to be served standing at the bar. There was then pushing
and shoving with a regrettable loss of cool. Geoffrey Van Hay, the
urbane and impeccable Manager, was half throttled with his tie pulled
round his neck; I am told that loaded soda siphons were brought into
play by staff with some customer reinforcement. The appearance of
two large members of the City constabulary restored order. The front
door was locked, regular customers used the side door and all
returned to normality.

Next a more serious skirmish occurred on the day the 1975 Sex Discrimination Act came into force. That day nine young women trooped in to challenge the house rule by ordering drinks at the bar. They were politely told they would be served only if they sat down. They departed eventually, proclaiming they were 'extremely insulted, grossly hurt and very distressed'. No doubt they would have been more distressed if their desire to make a scene had failed! One woman complained it was the rudest encounter she could remember; was this shortness of memory or reflecting a very sheltered life? The Manager, Paul Bracken, was informed that a summons would be taken out, supported by the National Council for Civil Liberties (NCCL). Eventually in 1978 a Miss Sheila Gray brought a case with the support of the NCCL. I am told that no judge could be found at the City of London Court who had not been a customer, so the case came up at the Westminster County Court. An editorial in *The Times* suggested we had been chosen for this test case because Fleet Street stood in the very heartland of the media, furnishing it with an amplifying system. Judge Ruttle (I am told, teetotal) accepted the evidence of my brother, whom he described as manifestly honest and responsible, and found that our rule was in the interests of sensible administration as well as courtesy and chivalry, and did not amount to a breach of the statute.

The next day my brother announced that as a gesture of goodwill El Vino intended during our centenary celebrations to institute an annual award for the woman journalist of the year.

Another day, yet another case. In July 1981 Mrs Tess Gill, a solicitor, and Mrs Anna Coote, a journalist, co-authors of a book for campaigners for women's rights and backed by the Equal Opportunities Commission, brought their case on similar terms at the City of London Court. Judge Rankin, the County Court Judge, found both their alleged dismay and their evidence somewhat artificial and found for us on grounds that women did not receive less favourable treatment and that any difference was of minimal importance.

However, November 1992 saw the Equal Opportunities Commission, whose Deputy Chairman was Geoffrey Howe's wife, Elspeth, financing the case in the Court of Appeal. The three judges hearing the case all felt it necessary to declare an interest, being, or having been, our customers. They held the firm to be in breach of the Sex Discrimination Act. At this time I was at the Department of

Environment in Northern Ireland, but I understand the evidence of a *Times* journalist made a considerable impact, pointing out that reporting rumour and gossip was part of her livelihood and that this centred on the bar area, from which she was excluded. Overnight a rule of the house became a mere tradition which has, however, continued happily for the majority of our lady customers. One amusing sideshow to all this was the scope for cartoons, varying from a lady at a gents' urinal to a signwriter changing our shop fascia from 'El Vino' to 'Elle Vino'.

Tailpiece – That evening Geoffrey Howe came up to me in the Commons Division Lobby and said 'David, send me a couple of cases of your Fleurie, it will help with the costs of my litigious wife'!

CHAPTER 17

Department of Transport

British Rail: new Chairman's re-organisation, investment, badgers
saved, moving freight road to rail, 'minded to close' Settle-Carlisle
line / Bus services de-regulated / Promoted Minister of
State / Shipping: unfair competition, Trinity House, Spanish boats
fishing on the UK quota / Port of London Authority , Pilotage,
Sinking of the Marques, Cut price airlines, Channel Tunnel

L EAVING NORTHERN IRELAND AND THE MANY friends made there was
somewhat of a wrench, not least because I had served there long
enough and decisions were implemented sufficiently fast, that I could
see a lot of the results on the ground whilst I was still there. With a
Westminster Department it was more likely my successor would
shudder at or enjoy the consequences.

My appointment as Parliamentary Under Secretary of State for
Transport in June 1983 coincided with the advent of Tom King as
Secretary of State and the addition to the Department of all the civil
aviation, shipping and marine responsibilities formerly with the
Department of Trade. I was given railways, ports, road freight,
aviation, shipping and marine matters including coastguards, pilotage
and, certainly not least, Trinity House. Two years later my coverage
was changed to rail, buses, taxis, London Regional Transport and
Channel fixed link (tunnel). In January 1986 I was promoted to
Minister of State, Nick Ridley's second in command as Minister for
Public Transport with the same list of responsibilities. From this it
will be seen that at one period or the next, I covered all the main
responsibilities of the Department except for roads.

As an Under-Secretary I had shared a PPS who did for me broadly
the duties I undertook for Sir Keith Joseph while his PPS. I recall
Marion Roe who was so good she was nabbed from me by John
Moore whilst he was Secretary of State. When I moved up to
Minister of State I ceased to share and invited Patrick Thompson MP
for Norwich North to fill the post. He proved to be outstanding,
unflappable, competently on top of the work and a good friend (as
he and his wife Kathleen remain).

British Rail

British Rail was a major part of my responsibilities. The Chairman, Sir Peter Parker, was about to retire. During the summer of 1983 I was involved in the search for a successor; a number of experienced businessmen were approached but none was enthused by the prospect. One with knowledge of the industry advised strongly that the post should go to a professional railwayman and recommended Bob (Robert) Reid, at this time Chief Executive. I was tasked to find him. It turned out he was on holiday, walking in the Dolomites whilst staying with the Italian family who had sheltered him as an escaped prisoner during the war. I judge this appointment must be the most valuable of the many decisions taken by Tom King before he was reshuffled to the Department of Employment in October that year. Nick Ridley became the second of four Secretaries of State I would serve on my way to becoming the then longest serving Tory transport minister ever.

Before the Second World War, the Great Western, LMS, LNER and even Southern Railways were respected private companies, proud of their achievements and viewed with some affection. Nationalisation in 1948 had brought amalgamation, creating an organisation too large[1] and unwieldy to be efficient, in spite of staff loyalty and dedication, but alas also with an attic full of Union inspired restrictive practices.

Bob Reid's appointment brought swift and decisive change. Out went a management structure based on the old regions and in came executive directors, each responsible for one of five sectors: the Inter City main lines, London & South East (responsible for commuter services), Provincial Railways (later named Regional), Freight and Parcels, each a profit centre with its own bottom line. Until this time the BR Board had always set its own policy objectives. Now, in October 1983 Nick Ridley, after consulting Bob Reid, wrote an official letter to the Chairman setting out for the next three years the objectives the Government wished BR to pursue. Principally, these called for reliable, attractive and punctual services at twenty five percent lower cost to the taxpayer. (BR exceeded this target and delivered twenty seven percent) Armed with clear objectives, the job

---

[1] As well as their core business, BR Board had their own two ferry companies, twenty seven hotels and a large property portfolio etc. inherited from the previous companies.

of the Board became implementation, helped by being largely freed from political and government interference, except for approval of major investment projects.

These objectives, which at first sight appeared difficult to reconcile with each other, would only be achieved through significantly improved efficiency. Two things were to bring this about. First Bob Reid's new commercially focused sector structure, second a different approach to investment. Hitherto BR had a limited sum agreed with the Treasury; this was replaced by a more open ended arrangement, dependent on an appropriate financial return.

The first investment project coming in for my approval concerned replacement of the worn-out diesel trains on the Tonbridge to Hastings line. The situation was very unusual because its tunnels had originally been constructed using only four instead of the six layers of bricks specified. Subsequently they had been lined with two additional layers and so special narrow trains had always been built for this line.

The obvious alternatives were to continue with trains the same size, or to single track the line through the tunnels, using standard size trains either diesel or electric. There was no appraisal of the diesel option, so I sent the submission back. When it was returned, the economics for diesel were virtually the same as for electrification, making it an option I should have been offered. I casually mentioned this when seeing Bob Reid on another matter. His immediate response begged me not to approve diesel because BR had to get rush hour trains out of London every twenty five seconds, but inserting diesel with its slower acceleration would affect all the services on that line. No-one had indicated this to me. You will readily understand why I built up an increasing respect for Bob Reid's blunt common-sense and sheer professionalism. Subsequently I wrote to him, conveying my formal approval for a spend of some £23 million for electrification with single tracked tunnels, adding it had taken overlong to reach my decision, in part because of deficiencies in the submission. Somehow all this reached the ears of No. 10 and the PM commented appraisals 'cannot command confidence unless they are properly argued and are economically sound'. Subsequently the Department seconded Philip Wood, a particularly thorough and competent senior official, to BR to help them in this area. After that the quality of submissions vastly improved, as did my turn–round

Viewing Badger Crossing following electrification of the Tonbridge to Hastings Line

time, for which I won undeserved praise. Indeed, on one application, I gave an immediate turn-round when BR applied for their Sealink Isle of Wight ferries to be replaced only months before their privatisation: 'No, a matter for the new owners'.

Following the electrification of the Tonbridge to Hastings line, I was saddened to hear that badgers were being electrocuted where their runs crossed the track. I prompted BR to see what might be done. After consulting the RSPCA, they came up with a plan to create a series of ten foot gaps at the main badger runs, with the third rail current carried across by insulated cable. Unexpectedly there was a large public response and I became better known for some time, not as a Minister so much as 'the man who saved the badgers'.

It makes my blood boil when I hear people condemn the Thatcher years as those 'when the railways were starved of investment'. It is said that if you repeat something often enough, people will believe you, so I suppose the propagandists work away on that basis. Actually I approved nineteen multi-million investment projects, six for electrification schemes including Kings Cross to Edinburgh[2] and more on new passenger trains, locomotives, signalling etc., not to overlook some eighty stations opened or re-opened. It all added up to the biggest railway modernisation programme since the change-over from steam to diesel. Indeed, in the four years 1983–87 I approved just on £1,000 million of railway investment plus £500 million for BR Chunnel related needs. By 1988 I was even chasing BR to bring forward more investment for my approval. The inhibiting factor was not financial limitation, but the fully stretched capacity of BR to manage these investment programmes efficiently. Many proposals involved replacing slower, heavy old rolling stock with fewer, because faster, vehicles with lower maintenance cost on both the train and track. Another saving came from the change from many loco-hauled trains to more with multiple small engines under the carriages, enabling trains to be both more reliable and split, so one train from London could serve two or even three destinations.

Alas, one unhappy side effect was a reduction in British Rail Engineering Limited's work and staff needed for repair and maintenance. Approval for closures came to me. I agonised over them. When I consented, I was always encouraging BREL to assist in new job creation projects. We had a good deal of success at Horwich near Bolton with an enterprise agency supported with a loan guarantee; here they created between three and four hundred jobs. Shildon became a similar success story. I felt a particular misery over closure of the giant and historic railway works at Swindon. Those who worked there had an exceptional record of job flexibility and high productivity. Unfortunately heavy overhead costs dictated closure with many redundancies. Fortunately many were re-employed in this expanding town's other successful businesses. I fought hard to retain some specialist workshops and secured a partial success. I went there for a second meeting with the shop stewards involved, only to be thanked but they preferred to have redundancy pay coupled with the good job prospects in the town! I was astonished and hardly knew whether to laugh or cry. I still treasure a cast iron GWR loco shield as a memento of thanks for my efforts from one of my visits.

---

[2] ECML had to go up to Cabinet for approval; it was after all the biggest single rail investment for twenty five years Happily it was delivered on time on budget.

The benefits from Bob Reid's sector management were soon beginning to prove their worth. The most astonishing result was Inter City, consisting of the main fast lines where it was hoped to minimise the amount of losses. Cyril Bleasdale, its sector director, worked up an entirely new business plan which came to be executed by his successor, John Prideaux. Inter City was soon running more trains at a hundred miles an hour than any railway in the world, except France which has the huge benefit, for rail, of long distances. Better still, it became the first and, at the time, the only profit making railway anywhere in postwar Europe. The Provincial sector and London & South East had the heaviest loss making routes, effectively railways to provide socially necessary services subsidised by Government.

I paid a number of visits to Scotrail to support Chris Green, an inspired team leader, with their big modernisation programme. I had made it my policy to get out and see for myself. I do not believe a Minister can properly understand the issues whilst sitting at a desk in Whitehall. Similarly when Chris Green moved south to run the London commuters' sector, he did not believe he could properly assess the service being experienced by commuters unless he travelled with them, therefore for his first three months he did so, staying in differing overnight hotels around the London suburbs.

This led in 1986 to London & South East being rebranded Network South East, accompanying a large programme of suburban improvements. Cynical commuters suddenly found their run-down stations being repainted and their trains gradually being refurbished. New marketing ideas produced the Travel Card, giving access on one ticket to train, tube and bus. I found myself willingly dragged in to open new stations. I offered a couple of personal initiatives, one provided a bottle of champagne to the Waterloo Enquiries Bureau if they could speed up their services from fifty to ninety percent of calls answered within thirty seconds – they did. I then presented Network South East with 'The Minister of State Cup' to be awarded every six months to the London commuter line which had achieved the best all round improvements. A number of impressive results followed.

Striking miners had effectively brought down Ted Heath's government and were hoping to repeat this with Margaret Thatcher. Some early preparation against this, strongly advocated by Nick Ridley, involved increasing coal stocks at the power stations. During this second miners' strike the Prime Minister chaired a Cabinet

Committee monitoring the overall situation. I attended, and it was fascinating to watch her ability to cut through any discussion to identify the absolute key priority issues and shred any waffle. My job was to report on coal movements by rail. BR management were quietly effective in identifying opportunities where driver, guard and signalmen were all prepared to work. One trainload could be well over a thousand tonnes so this was an important aspect. I always wrote down the exact figures relating to trains, tonnage etc. I had reported, passing them before leaving to the keeper of the Minutes – who was appreciative.

The sector system reinvigorated carriage of freight by rail and brought it into profit. It has always seemed to me to be wholly desirable to shift as much lorry traffic as is practicable from road to rail. I learned there was a scheme in existence for providing grants of up to sixty percent towards the cost of loading and unloading facilities and trucks, sidings etc. for freight terminals. I set out to encourage this, and have to confess to spending more taxpayers' money on this than any previous minister. For example, we took thousands of lorry movements off the roads of East Anglia by linking a grain terminal to the Norwich – Peterborough main line, switching forty five thousand tonnes of grain a year to rail. Five hundred lorries a day were taken off the M4 by contributing to a rail link for a quarry in Somerset. My approval of about a hundred of these grants gave me great satisfaction in terms of improvement to the quality of life and environment for those living on these routes.

Settle–Carlisle Railway

One of my more lasting memories is of the huge controversy over the future of the rail line between Settle and Carlisle in the North West.

The bizarre start to the saga of this route is intriguing. At the beginning of the 1870s there were two main lines from London to Scotland, LNER, plus London and North Western [NW]. They were shortly to be joined by the Midland Railway, mounting an impudent challenge from St Pancras through middle England, on to Leeds and soon considering its route from Settle to Carlisle. Since Midland already had a line joining the NW at Clapham Junction in North Yorkshire, Midland sought an agreement with them to run on their track to Carlisle. NW agreed, but imposed unacceptable conditions. Midland's Chairman, fed up after months of haggling, decided they would build their own line. Their solicitors secured the necessary Act of Parliament whilst their surveyors examined the route. The latter's report indicated rugged countryside requiring more civil engineering work than any line yet built in the UK. There was a collective sigh of relief when NW came back, offering an acceptable agreement.

The next drama came when Midland's solicitors explained the Company had secured an Act of Parliament which now required them to build the line, so they must do so! Their only escape would be to secure Parliamentary consent to abandon their Act. The House of Lords debated and refused, so the railway line no-one wanted had to be built. It was a monumental task, involving fourteen tunnels, twenty one viaducts, three hundred and twenty five bridges, various farm crossings and numerous culverts, all achieved using only pick and shovel – the last railway in the UK to do so.

In 1983 British Rail announced its intention to close the line on the grounds that much of its seventy two miles was a duplication of the West Coast main line, now electrified and so cheaper to run. The income was about £1 million, whilst its operating costs were £2.7 million, a figure which changed from time to time! Crucially the viaduct at Ribblehead needed repair at the huge cost of £4.3 million, all on a line they did not need or want. Notably 80 per cent of the passengers were tourists coming to enjoy the spectacular scenery, courtesy of a taxpayer subsidy. By the time the formal closure application arrived from BR it was accompanied by a storm of protest and the establishment of the Friends of Settle Carlisle Association and, later, a Joint Action Committee. As Minister, I decided to see for myself. BR laid on a special viewing coach from Carlisle and I was given a detailed introduction. Most of the places where we stopped had groups of protesters. The most memorable was at Appleby. There I was met by the Mayor in his official robes, accompanied by the Town Clerk and Mace Bearer, and conducted to the ancient Moot Hall. There followed one of the most effective presentations ever. First the head boy and head girl from the local grammar school set out how important the line was to young people attending college and university, also that closure would damage job opportunities. Next, a hotelier on the damage to tourism, on to Express Dairies, the

Settle Carlisle Railway. Minister being shown the condition of the Ribblehead viaduct

Chamber of Trade on damage to business prospects and, finally, an OAP on the needs of the elderly. The whole presentation of short, concise contributions, each a representative of their user group, was sincere, straightforward and highly impressive.

At another halt, I walked over to a woman hanging out her washing, to ask whether she used the line or her car. Before the train moved on, a reporter went and explained I was the Minister for Public Transport to which she responded 'If I'd known, I'd have taken my knickers down'. At next morning's Ministers' meeting, I was quizzed about this – apparently the context of her washing line had not been mentioned!

On to the Ribblehead Viaduct, where I was swung under this vast structure from the track above with two engineers in an inspection bucket to see the condition of the apex of an arch. I have no head for heights and was nearly sick . . . (Someone muttered about an impending by-election.)

I came away from Settle with several conclusions of my own. One was that there were conflicting views within BR, that the local population, whether they used the line or not, were united in protest, and particularly that the line's real value lay in exploiting its tourist potential, including the splendid feats

of Victorian railway engineering, its views of the Yorkshire Dales
with their tracery of dry stone walls, and the sheer grandeur of
scenery north of Ribblehead.

I began to formulate a plan in my own mind. Clearly BR were
geared to moving passengers from A to B, not to exploiting tourist
attractions which were the line's real potential. As someone put it to
me 'BR has demonstrated with its bungling, its ageing trains, poor
service, inadequate publicity and total disinterest that it is the last
organisation which should manage this line'. That was unfair, but had
more than a grain of truth in it, for BR – intent on closure – had lost
interest in it. What it needed, I judged, was a consortium including
the flair of a professional leisure company, an imaginative tourist
operator, co-ordinated support from various public bodies operating
in this field, along with financial support from both the local
authorities and the private sector. It would be particularly valuable to
harness the support of those opposed to closure.

No doubt such a body would be brimming with ideas, for example
special viewing coaches, sponsored dining cars, one of the Halts
equipped with wall to wall cinema screening to show the exciting
tale of the making of the line, another the history of steam,
instruction for school parties, nostalgic steam-hauled days out for
pensioners, T shirts and souvenirs. All of this I came to believe could
be a more secure future for the line and the local economy, rather
than being solely the unwanted child of BR. As a longstanding
member of the North Yorkshire Moors Preserved Railway, only
eighteen miles long, I knew that it and the Severn Valley line both
had as big a revenue as BR on Settle to Carlisle.

I discussed the possibility of the National Railway Museum at York
using the line to demonstrate working examples of its exhibits, an
idea its Director welcomed. I even speculated to myself on the
money to be made through licensed 'bookies' taking bets on steam
train races.

A discussion with British Steel brought forward an offer, gratis, of
the steel rods needed for the Ribblehead viaduct repair. BACMI, the
trade association for the road making industry, offered material at
cost. The English Tourist and Regional Boards would consider the
provision of visitor centres. The Historic Buildings and Monuments
Commission were willing, in principle, to make a substantial grant
towards Ribblehead viaduct repairs. Likewise the Rural Develop-

ment Commission was prepared to consider help, as were the Countryside Commission and the National Heritage Memorial Fund. A number of companies offered help including commercial sponsorship. The local authorities, which had been subsidising BR services on the line, offered some increase but, alas, accompanied with restrictive conditions.

I was not the only one suspicious about BR's figure for the costs to be incurred on repair of the Ribblehead viaduct. One evening, a retired BR engineer came to see me with an extraordinary tale concerning the line to Barmouth in North Wales. This crossed an estuary, the line being supported on wooden pillars which were regularly safety checked. He, or another who had this task, had checked one when a train crossed and, with a bang, a zig zag crack appeared right across the pillar. The line was immediately suspended, creating fear and uncertainty amongst the hoteliers and boarding house proprietors in the town. BR engineers prescribed steel pillars, encased in concrete at a huge cost which seemed certain to condemn the line. The problem had been caused by sea worms (*toredo navalis*) boring holes the size of my finger. My visitor had persuaded local BR management that this expense was unnecessary. Instead he advocated pumping liquid cement under pressure into the network of worm borings, then wrapping plastic sheet round the pillars to prevent a recurrence. This had been successfully achieved. He explained that the towering arches at Ribblehead were originally filled with rubble which, over the years, had shrunk down. All that was needed, he claimed, was to smother the rubble in liquid concrete and fill the columns in the same way at a cost of £900,000 to £1m.

Meanwhile the volume of protest at the prospect of closure steadily increased with well over twenty thousand objectors including a 'legitimate' dog.[3] Both County Transport Users' Consultative Committees held successive hearings, coming down heavily against closure.

BR reacted by undertaking to keep the line open for five years while Ron Cotton, their newly appointed Project Manager, a born marketeer, successfully exploited the raised profile the row was generating. Tourists poured in from across the world. On one visit I

---

[3] Under the 1962 Transport Act, the word 'user' is employed, so an objection from such a dog can be lodged via its owner!

had standing room only, surrounded by Canadians. BR doubted this would last. Local supporters claimed it would.

In a Statement to the House in May 1988 I announced that the Secretary of State 'is minded' on the evidence before him to consent to British Rail's proposal to cease operations. Also that he had been advised to delay the final decision until the end of November to enable any new evidence to the taken into account. The potential for this included a substantial brochure of background information being prepared by Lazard Brothers on behalf of the BR Board due out in August. This invited those interested in purchasing the line to come forward. Secondly, significant interest from tour operators supported by a joint study by PIEDA and L&R Leisure Consultants commissioned by the English and Cumbrian Tourist Boards with support from several local authorities.

Word that I would make a Statement and the rumour it would be favourable had been going the rounds, indeed, the West Yorkshire Transport Authority and others had already planned a celebration steam-hauled excursion from Leeds to Carlisle on Saturday, 25 June. Their invitation to me to participate still held. There was discussion about this in my private office, the conclusion of which was, 'Of course you can go, Minister, if you want to put your head in a noose, but none of us are joining you'.

I boarded the train at Leeds and, when at Garsdale station, cut the tape to open a refurbishment carried out by local volunteers; the only interruption came from the back 'and no bloody trains' in a loud, broad Yorkshire accent. I found myself in an extraordinary position, the Minister who had announced the 'minded to consent' to BR's closure proposal, but with warm local support for my known efforts over many months to find a solution; the local papers had carried what they called my 'impassioned appeal' to the private sector for help.

On 11 April 1989, Paul Channon, Secretary of State for Transport, announced he had refused BR consent to close the line. He evidenced more people using the line, a weaker financial case for closure, and an anticipation that the Ribblehead viaduct would be much cheaper to repair than was first thought. Finally he believed there was scope for better marketing of the line with private sector involvement. In addition, I have some reason to believe that No. 10 thought closure would cause enormous trouble and resentment, so doubted if it was worth it.

Subsequent years have brought privatisation with its many critics, but even they have to accept that better marketing has hugely increased passenger numbers. The Settle–Carlisle line is no exception with, I am told, some forty percent more passengers over the past ten years (1996–2007). Just as important is freight carried on the line, most notably coal imports from Hunterston port in Scotland to the Yorkshire power stations around Leeds.

Throughout this time there has been a great deal of support from user groups, local residents and enthusiasts. They can take considerable satisfaction in knowing the line's future is secure. I hope my own contribution was of some value – at least this memoir tells the inside story as participated in from the Minister's desk.

Bus deregulation

Nick Ridley allocated Bus Deregulation and Privatisation of the National Bus Company to me. He always maintained as a Grade I principle that choice and fair competition are the customer's best friends, a view I fully share, not without reason . . .

Flying to Northern Ireland on the BA monopoly air shuttle was like travel on a London bus. I enquired whether coffee could be made available and was told no, the excuse being that BA's catering facilities were too far away. The really annoying thing was the smell of the pilot's freshly brewed coffee drifting around the front passenger seats. When our government ended BA's monopoly on the routes to Northern Ireland, competition arrived in the form of that redoubtable entrepreneur, Michael Bishop, with his British Midland Airways service providing catering. Instantly, out went BA's Shuttle and in came 'Super' Shuttle with newspapers, breakfast and, behold, coffee. No witchdoctor in Africa waving a juju stick could create a greater magic than competition for domestic air travellers. Similarly long distance coaches used to be protected from competition by a system of licensed monopolies. In 1980 we had thrown all these routes open to competition; consequently fares went down and over six hundred additional services operated with hugely improved standards, more comfortable seats, coffee bars, video shows etc. and lavatories. As a result passenger numbers had then increased by no less than 45 percent.

What a contrast with the humble bus. Here the industry was in chronic decline, journeys had shrunk from 42 per cent of all travel to

8 per cent over the preceding thirty years mainly, but not only, due to more cars. Fares had risen a lot faster than inflation and between 1972 and 1983, subsidy had rocketed from £10 million, not to £30 million or £40 million, but to £522 million. When I read my brief I sent it back, since this figure must have been wrong, but no – it was correct. No responsible government could fail to take action.

The two main planks of our plans were to end the system of route licences then required for every route; these had provided the bus operator with a mini monopoly. The second big change forced local authorities subsidising loss making, but socially necessary, routes to put them out to competitive tender. This replaced the annual haggle between Council officials and local bus operators over the price for the ensuing year. Previously there had been a certain amount of splitting the difference, but no way of assessing a fair and reasonable charge.

Nick Ridley was a Secretary of State whose decisions were, wherever possible, rooted in Conservative philosophy and principles. Neither these nor Nick's resolve changed because of opposition. Hence his ministerial team would not find agreed programmes withdrawn, leaving them with 'egg on their faces' as happens to some hapless Junior Ministers. This was just as well when it came to bus deregulation, since almost everyone in sight opposed Nick's policy and was anxious to tell me why.

Opposition from the Labour Party and trade unions was, of course, to be expected, but it extended to employers, local authorities, the Passenger Transport Executives, municipal bus operators, the National Bus Company, branches of the WI, and some religious bodies. Even the then Bishop of Durham oddly condemned our proposals as an 'act of faith'.

The only national body supporting us appeared to be the small voice of the Consumers' Association. I admit I empathised with Landseer's picture The Stag at Bay. Our plans provoked an exceptional amount of distortion with assertions of a massive reduction in the bus network and cuts in essential rural and suburban services. For example, Lancashire claimed 60 per cent of its routes were uneconomic, needing subsidy, they then frightened pensioners by claiming that bus passes for the elderly, blind and disabled would be abandoned – all untrue, as were widespread claims that unsafe vehicles driven by cowboys would risk passenger safety (ignoring the continuing need to have an operator's licence after vehicle inspection by the traffic commissioners). Speaking in Blackpool I referred to this as 'a Lancashire hotch potch of distortion, served up with a helping of poisonous deception and garnished with untruths'.

In the Second Reading debate opened by Nick Ridley and wound up by me, I ended with Eliza Doolittle's famous line 'In Hertford, Hereford and Hampshire, hurricanes hardly happen'. In Hereford there had been a transport hurricane because the County Council had volunteered in 1980 to be a test bed for our proposals. The result had been a 2 per cent increase in rural mileage, lower fares, more people travelling by bus, fewer complaints and a huge 38 per cent reduction in ratepayer subsidies needed. Norfolk found that competitive tendering slashed the £500,000 subsidy previously needed to £150,000. Was the tale apocryphal of another Council, on being told that its drivers were speeding past queues with a smile and wave of the hand, replied 'It is sometimes impossible for drivers to keep to the timetable if they have to stop for passengers' (see p. 26).

The Bill had a long Committee stage which I, along with my fellow Transport Minister, Michael Spicer, carried through, ably assisted by the very capable Michael Ancram from the Scottish Office. Several supportive members of the Committee volunteered to undertake meetings round the country to reassure public opinion that people should not be worried by the rumours of approaching disaster. I recall outstanding support both in Committee and in speeches round the country from Matthew Parris, Martin Brandon Bravo, Colin Shepherd – Hereford's MP, and others.

I commiserated with one hapless official from the Scottish Office who had to travel down each week to advise on Scottish aspects of the Bill. He said it had been worthwhile for an incident on the overnight sleeper. His cabin was next to the steward's office. He overheard a man complain that his wife had been put in cabin number twenty three instead of next to him at number eight. The steward expressed his regrets, but advised all cabins had been allocated. Money must have changed hands for there was a distinct change of tone as the steward agreed to fix matters. At this point, a second male voice was heard which apparently belonged to the man due to be moved. The steward explained the situation, with the response of a burst of laughter and, 'George, are you passing Mary off as your wife?'

My responsibilities for privatisation of the National Bus Company were also interesting and stimulating. The Treasury wanted it sold as a single entity on advice that this would raise the most money. Nick rightly insisted it be broken up into about fifty bus companies, each of about three hundred buses so as to ensure plenty of competition. A load of second hand buses was not the easiest parcel to sell to a prospective buyer, especially with Labour saying any future government of theirs would re-nationalise it. Inevitably the first sales had to be at bargain prices, but once a number of sales had been completed, confidence grew and, to my delight, thirty eight were bought by their company's employees, mainly via existing management. I relished Devon General led by an ex-bus conductor who became its successful Managing Director – another example of the Tory concept of spreading wealth throughout our society instead of concentrating it in the hands of the State. Eighteen months later, it was a real pleasure to prepare a letter for all colleagues in the House reporting that, as a result of competition in the deregulated bus world, an initial 85 per cent of bus miles were found not to need subsidy and, in consequence, in that first year, £40 million of ratepayers' bus subsidy costs had been saved. In addition competition (not all sustained) fathered a lot of innovation with the new minibus services operating in over three hundred and fifty areas.

It is fair to claim that an industry in chronic decline was reinvigorated to the evident benefit of its users, nevertheless rising prosperity leading to yet more car ownership will bring new challenges, particularly for thinly used rural services. Maybe shared taxis will have a bigger rôle to play.

Shared taxis – my failure

Having seen shared taxis operating successfully in America, Northern Ireland and Barbados and discovered the benefits for myself, I thought it a good idea to introduce the same arrangements in the UK, starting in London and at Heathrow.

The law, as it had stood for over two hundred years, said that anyone could share the taxi they had hired with anyone they chose to invite. However, it was illegal for the taxi driver to take the initiative, for example on picking up a passenger at Waterloo for Victoria, he could not call down the queue 'Anyone else for

Victoria?' To facilitate sharing, we changed the law in the 1985 Transport Act. The system we introduced with fares split between passengers going to compatible destinations gave the cab driver more money, whilst passengers paid a fare reduced according to the numbers sharing the cab, so two would pay sixty five percent of the normal fare, and four only forty five percent each.

Of the two trade unions involved, the T&GWU (cab section) was bitterly opposed, the LTDA ambivalent. A T&G deputation came to see me and were rather bewildered when I said I had been a member of their union and initially welcomed them as 'brothers'! Their view was that, if four people shared a cab, then three of their members would have lost a job. They saw it like a static photo, totally failing to recognise that, for example, at £8 a head then from Heathrow to the City instead of £32, there would soon have been a big switch to taxis at the expense of tubes and coaches.

The MP for Basildon who had a concentration of taxi drivers in his constituency had me along to address their Essex Federation. Unfortunately, on the way we met a bad traffic jam and arrived about forty minutes late. There was a bar at the back of the hall; quite a few had availed themselves of it during the over-long wait and were in a jovial mood. I had just started my, by then, well rehearsed explanation of the new opportunities which would shortly be available, when someone, still at the bar, bellowed 'It's all right for Ministers like you in your £400 Savile Row suit what no cabbie can afford . . .' I retorted that Marks and Spencer would be flattered, unbuttoned and swung open my jacket, revealing the M&S St Michael label – to a roar of laughter.

Shortly after, we introduced a scheme giving drivers a chart of fares, varying according to the numbers of passengers. Also we had marked out special taxi queuing points for shared cabs at Heathrow for central London and between the main London railway stations. The T&G instructed their members to boycott the scheme and many LTA drivers followed suit. At Heathrow, which was high profile and provided the biggest potential market, such adventurous cabbies as dared to make for the shared taxi rank hastily retreated amid the jeers and taunts of their fellow drivers. Within ten days the scheme had virtually collapsed.

I understand there has been a limited scheme on somewhat similar lines tried out at Heathrow and in the mornings at Paddington. Good luck to them.

Elsewhere in England and Wales, three different forms of taxi sharing became available, first providing local services just like a bus, including the opportunity to bid in competition with bus operators for a contract to run a lightly used, socially necessary service subsidised by the local authority. Second, promoting cab sharing to compatible destinations from taxi ranks such as outside a railway station. The third new opportunity is a system of advance reservations where a taxi operator prepared to go out and seek extra business can match up two or more bookings to a similar destination. The latter could be a boon for those who live in a village where the remaining shop has closed and who want to go into a bigger village or town to shop. Organising the latter could be a useful earner for an enterprising taxi operator, rather than waiting for business to come to him. I do not know how widely taxi drivers have seized these opportunities, or even are aware of them, but at Heathrow and in London it was my big failure. A journalist friend commiserating with me said a good rule for Ministers was 'If you don't succeed, remove all traces you ever tried'! Which is broadly what happened without any assistance from me.

Shipping: our fleets facing unfair competition

The British shipping fleet is an important national asset, its sponsor the Department of Transport, and hence my responsibility. It was a time of world recession and the industry faced fierce competition.

In 1984 I had a deputation from their trade body, the GCBS (General Council of British Shipping) complaining about cut price quotations from clapped-out or ill maintained foreign vessels Added to that, it was feared some of them were a risk to the ports they entered and potentially an environmental hazard to our coastline, particularly in the case of oil and chemical tankers. Such vessels posed a threat to the commercial viability of our own fleets, which properly complied with the high standards required of them.

I made a commitment to effective action and arranged for our marine surveyors to re-examine our system of enforcement; not only the recent increase from a quarter to a third of vessels entering our ports, but also moving from random selection to priority for ships not recently inspected and those where past inspections had found something wrong. In short we moved to concentrating on potential offenders. In another small initiative to attack unfair competition, I went to Norway to seek a change in a requirement of theirs that UK vessels had to employ a pilot when servicing the needs of their North Sea oil platforms – a requirement waived for Norwegian ships. We made some progress.

Years later in the millennium year I applied to become a Freeman of the City Livery Company linked to Shipping, the Worshipful Company of Shipwrights. Fortunately I was accepted, perhaps because my father had been a naval architect and shipbuilder, or most likely because someone on the Court remembered my spell as Minister for Shipping in the Department of Transport. I was admitted to the Livery the following year and happily have found myself in agreeable and interesting company.

Trinity House

Trinity House, an ancient and prestigious body, with its responsibilities for marine safety round our coasts, came my way obliquely as a Transport Minister. Their Lighthouse Board is responsible for the buoys which mark the safe channels for vessels entering UK ports, for marking wrecks which may endanger shipping and for lighthouses, etc. They were, and are, financed by lighthouse dues, a levy on every commercial vessel entering a UK port, then bringing in an income of £42 million per annum. In short, the costs of Trinity House providing these services were an unavoidable burden on the shipping industry whose good health came within my responsibilities. Nor were the representatives of this industry slow in lobbying me to hold down the levy at a time of recession and fierce competition. Trinity House were rather unfairly described to me as 'A self perpetuating oligarchy of retired ships' captains handling a multi million budget'.

The working head of Trinity House was its Deputy Master, or Executive Chairman. Their Master, the Duke of Edinburgh, was not just a figurehead, he took a lively and knowledgeable interest in their affairs. A number of visits convinced me their staff were very skilled, experienced and truly dedicated to their task of ensuring marine safety. It was, however, apart from a few would-be modernisers, an inward looking organisation working with outdated equipment and, to me, showed little sign it recognised this. As but one example, they maintained some eight hundred buoys, lit by acetylene gas lamps fed from bottles stored on board, their lighthouses were lit by electricity generated by diesel engines. In neither case were they exploring how to apply the new and cost saving technology of solar panels.

It seemed to me, and Nick Ridley concurred, that the Lighthouse Board needed shaking up with new blood bringing expertise in finance, modern business methods and technology. A tentative suggestion that something of this sort was needed did not go down well, although my recommendation that they speed up their appointment of an experienced Finance Director was accepted. The office arranged a working dinner with the Chairman. I emphasised my locus and concern re costs also, I fear, exaggerated the murmurs within the Department that these functions be taken away from Trinity House, adding sympathetically that this was something I personally would like to avoid. One way to preserve the situation would be if he allowed me to recommend, effectively to appoint, half the members of a reconstituted Lighthouse Board. He undertook to sleep on it and discuss it with colleagues. Later he came back to me and reluctantly concurred, providing he would have a casting vote as Chairman. I readily agreed but pointed out that, if ever he used it, on his own head be it if things went wrong. I believe he never felt the need to do so.

The first of my recommendations was Sir Michael Colman, Finance Director of Reckitt and Colman and, after advice from officials, three others who brought respectively top level experience of ship and port operations, of business and high technology and the practicalities of navigational aids experienced overseas. My recommendation of Michael Colman of Malshanger near Basingstoke came from experience of working with him in other fields. There I learned to respect him as a successful team leader with a wonderful ability to disarm potential antagonists and secure their support. I can well imagine my four directors meeting privately to identify their next target, then coming to the Chairman seeking his advice on his plans to exploit this or that opportunity, along with promises of support when he brought the issue to the next Board meeting; probably it would be Michael's gloved hand quietly steering things. Be that as it may, what did come about was a ten year modernisation programme, pulling the Lighthouse Board into the twentieth century, greatly aided by David

Orr, I think Operations Director, who drove forward much of this programme. The first 'dividend' from the changes was a ten per cent reduction in lighthouse dues which I was able to announce in 1988.

I was delighted to learn that later Michael Colman's work for Trinity House led them to confer on him the signal honour, for an outsider, of making him one of their own 'Younger Brethren'.

Fishing fleet failure – pride goes before a fall

The Merchant Shipping Act of 1988 was mainly concerned with Marine Safety, much of it responding to lessons learned from the appalling tragedy when the *Herald of Free Enterprise* sank off Zeebrugge. A lesser but still important part of the Bill sought to put right an injustice facing our fishing fleets. This arose because Spanish fishing boats were re-registering themselves as British. This enabled them to count their catches against the UK quota allocated to us by the EEC. For those 'poaching' in this way, it involved little more than putting up a brass plate to provide a UK address. There were already some fifty vessels directly involved, and others where British boats had been bought by Spaniards to enable them also to count their catch against our quota.

The Bill dealt with this abuse by making it a legal requirement that all vessels must re-register but would only be accepted when at least seventy five per cent of the vessel was owned by British citizens, resident and domiciled in the UK. This restructuring was warmly welcomed by fisherfolk and by MPs generally. Sweet is the taste of a wrong put right.

Alas, it was not to be. Enter the owners of the *Factotame* on behalf of themselves and ninety four other Spanish owned fishing vessels which did not comply with our 1988 Act. In a test case they claimed our Registration requirements were incompatible with the Common Market Treaty of Rome and applied to the UK High Court for a Judicial Review. The High Court referred a number of questions to the European Court of Justice This ruled that each Member State had to comply with the Treaty prohibition against discrimination on the grounds of nationality and also in the treatment of trading companies where the Treaty covers the right to Freedom of Establishment.

This was effectively the *first time* a British Act of Parliament had been overruled by the supremacy of Common Market law, adjudicated by the European Court of Justice and confirmed by the law Lords at Westminster. For me, and for significant parts of our fishing fleet, it marked a sad albeit historic moment.

The Port of London Authority

The Port of London Authority brought together three differing activities: management of the tidal Thames, a property portfolio, mainly warehousing, and Tilbury docks. These diverse activities, operating as separate divisions, were merged in an accounting fudge, covering a up a substantial cross subsidy to Tilbury. Nick Ridley set the ultimate goal of division into three separate companies and my job was to cover the changes needed to prepare for this. I interviewed the short list for the new Chairman of the Board, singled out Sir Brian Kellett and recommended him to Nick. He had been consecutively Director, Managing Director and Chairman of Tube Investments Limited, a major and successful company. Brian Kellett's quietly spoken, somewhat diffident manner belied both his track record and his effectiveness. It was a happy choice; he was a great persuader who carried people with him and, as important, concurred with the changes we sought to achieve.

To help him on the property side I appointed to the Board Christopher Jonas of Drivers Jonas, the well regarded City surveyors of that name. Sir Brian formalised the divisional structure so each had its own Chief Executive working to their own non-executive Board member. The separation of the accounts for each division exposed very clearly the nature and extent of Tilbury's loss.

The docks at Tilbury had long been a sad story of bad industrial relations, restrictive practices and constant strikes as shop stewards tried to avoid the contraction and unemployment their own activities made inevitable. After I left Transport, large-scale government assisted severance pay and the end of the Dock Labour Scheme in 1989/90 enabled Tilbury to renew itself. It was pleasing to have been involved in kick starting the PLA on to its new route.

Pilotage

Pilotage was for a time another area I covered. There were on-going problems concerning the then vexed and complicated matter of ships' pilots around our harbours. Oddly, my most notable recollection concerned Mr XYZ, a particularly likeable senior official. He was conscientious almost to a fault, more anxious than most to ensure I was fully and completely informed. Sometimes this meant that I understood the situation until I read his briefing – indeed there seemed no simple question he could not make sound complicated. One morning his name appeared in my diary for the day, but without the usual indication of what we were to discuss. What followed astonished me. He came in, stood in front of my desk, made half a bow and said he had come to apologise. 'For what?' I asked. I had, he said, been found guilty at the ABC Court of acting against the course of Natural Justice in respect of a matter associated with shipping. The details escape me now, but apparently he had made an Order on my behalf which affected certain people working out of ABC port. I was astounded; I had no knowledge of this Order, nor that a Court Hearing was taking place. I am a strong supporter of the doctrine of Ministerial Responsibility which, in those days, meant that a Minister who got it wrong on a serious matter would resign, witness Lord Carrington pre Falklands war. This incident partly undermined my commitment to that doctrine, although it is really a matter of how serious a blunder it has been. This was not such a case.

Tragedy and disaster – the sinking of the *Marques*

In July 1983 I had received a letter from Andrew Rowe MP writing on behalf of a constituent, Mark Litchfield, owner of the *Marques*, a three-masted sailing barque some eighty five feet long, built in 1917 as a small cargo-carrying vessel. In more recent years it had been used for sail training and more lucrative film work. (To millions of television viewers she had been known as the heroine of *The Onedin Line*, had participated in *Kidnapped*, *Poldark* and *Dracula* TV programmes. She was the famous *Beagle* in the BBC film *The Voyage of Charles Darwin*.)

The letter said she was due to sail shortly to undertake a valuable filming contract and afterwards to participate in the Tall Ships Race from Puerto Rico to Bermuda and on to Halifax, Nova Scotia. However before sailing the *Marques* needed some essential certification, and for this the Department of Transport required the vessel to be dry docked for a full inspection to ensure she was sound below the water line. The delay this involved would lose them the filming contract. Andrew asked for my help in seeing if there was any way in which the Department's needs could be met by reducing the timescale and cost involved in taking the vessel out of the water. He pointed up the unusual circumstance that the *Marques* had only recently had her hull rebuilt in a Spanish shipyard, overseen by a well qualified English naval architect. In the light of this, it seemed unnecessarily bureaucratic to require the time and expense involved in a re-examination of the hull. Would I do what I could to help?

A meeting was arranged for our marine surveyors to come and explain the situation to me. I asked them to consider whether the English naval architect's qualifications were such that he would be acceptable for employment as an inspector by the Department, or one of the other specialist bodies licensed for this certification. Also to consider what, if anything, could be done, keeping within their professional judgment on safety. Later I had a note from Andrew Rowe's secretary that matters had been satisfactorily resolved. I learned subsequently that the naval architect, a qualified marine surveyor, had been interviewed in depth by our surveyors and his evidence accepted as to the condition of the hull. So I did not expect to hear further.

You may have difficulty in imagining the extent of my shock and horror on hearing the news that the *Marques* had sunk during the Tall Ships Race with serious loss of life among both crew and youngsters on a sail training course. Sleepless nights were not helped by the Department's Permanent Secretary saying to me that there was a heavy lead water tank on board and he would not be surprised if it had fallen through the hull. Bit by bit more information became available. Apparently she had completed her filming assignment without incident and had gone on to win (with the benefit of her handicap) the first leg of the Tall Ships Race. The boat was on the edge of the notorious area known as the 'Bermuda Triangle', the weather was very hot, stiflingly so for those below decks and, as a consequence, various vents and hatches including the main hatch, were open to provide ventilation. Suddenly an unforeseen and violent squall had struck the vessel and threw her heeling over almost on her side. The open vents and hatches admitted the sea and she virtually nosed herself under water. Apparently it was all over within minutes. Almost all those below deck were unable to escape. Nineteen out of twenty eight souls perished, including the captain, his wife and baby son.

I had earlier been to see Nick Ridley and told him I had drafted my resignation letter. He explained that, because of my rôle in the matter, there would be a formal Court of Investigation into the loss of the *Marques* and advised me to await its findings.

The Court met in a Plymouth hotel in October 1985. I was called to the witness box, not the dock, but it felt like it. I was taken through my witness statement, asked various questions and returned to the well of the court. The Inquiry sat for sixty four days and concluded there was no evidence of structural failure and that the *Marques* was in a proper state of repair and maintenance. The English naval architect was justified, so far as the structural condition was concerned, in providing a Declaration to the Department on compliance with the certification rules. Various other matters had emerged, including that the Captain may have had forged qualifications.

Had there not been survivors to testify as to what had actually happened, I would have found myself in an appalling situation; now I can only sympathise with the families of those who died in what was a genuine accident at sea.

Aviation

The issue which most interested me was Nick Ridley's policy of getting competition into the European market. This involved an ongoing attack on the cosy price-fixing cartels which protected each country's national airlines, however inefficient, from competition. The process had started with a sustained campaign which persuaded the EC Commission to liberalise Europe-wide flights between a number of regional airports. This did not go far enough, so much time was spent in trying to 'beef up' the Commission's proposals.

Nick identified Neelie Kroes,[4] the Dutch minister who had been brought up in a transport business, as a supporter. I found her a valuable, determined and very practical ally and, in May 1984, clinched a deal with her in The Hague which ended the airline cartel between our two countries. This opened the way for full competition. As a result, discounts of up to 50 per cent began to be offered between London and Amsterdam. Unlike the UK, surrounded by

---

[4] Now EU Commissioner for Competition

water, there was nothing to stop a German choosing to drive to Amsterdam instead of Frankfurt. Soon German and Belgian travellers flocked across the Dutch border. It was not long before Lufthansa's resistance started to crumble, to the discomfiture of Sabena Airlines.

It can now be seen that this became the key which opened the door for the cut price operators now epitomised by Easy-jet, Flybe and Ryanair, to the benefit of millions of our fellow citizens.

The Channel Tunnel

The biggest civil engineering project ever undertaken in this country

The romantic dream of a channel tunnel had already been around for a long time with its supporters and opponents when Palmerston damned it 'for it would further shorten a distance to France we already find too short'.

In 1802 the plans of a French engineer for a two-deck, lamp-lit tunnel with horse drawn carriages had keen support from Napoleon. The idea was received with less enthusiasm by the War Office. By the mid–1800s, the success of tunnelling by railway and canal builders[5] had brought encouragement to promoters, banks and the South East Railway Company. The latter's track along the coast between Folkestone and Dover provided an opportunity at the foot of Shakespeare Cliff for the starting point. Disraeli recognised the tunnel's potential and, in spite of Queen Victoria's personal disapproval, set up an Anglo-French commission to prepare for the necessary treaty. This led on to the first Channel Tunnel Act of Parliament in 1875. Five years later tunnelling started amid huge controversy. Within two years it was stopped on a legal technicality by Joseph Chamberlain (Board of Trade), supported by the War Office.

Throughout the next ninety one years there was a string of unsuccessful attempts to restart the project. Then, in March 1973 the Heath government published a 'Green Paper' (a government document for discussion). The same year preliminary boring was undertaken,[6] paid for by a mix of public and private finance, only to be

---

[5] For example the three-mile tunnel under the Pennines for the Huddersfield Canal and the Woodhead rail tunnel on the Manchester to Sheffield line.

[6] Three hundred metres or so are now incorporated in the Chunnel's service Tunnel.

Viewing the site of the proposed working entrance for tunnel drilling

aborted by the Wilson government of 1975 during one of the then, not infrequent, financial crises. Later Margaret Thatcher was to observe that, had the Tunnel we have now been financed by government, it would undoubtedly have been similarly cancelled.

I was incredibly lucky to be part of the team turning this 'romantic dream' into reality. As Minister of State and number two to Nick Ridley on matters of the 'The Fixed Link' I was involved in the choice as to which of the proposals would be backed by government. Later, I carried out part of the detailed negotiations with the French government, inaugurated the Inter Government Commission with Monsieur Douffiagues (my opposite number), wound up the major debates on the legislation and took the Bill through its detailed examination in Standing Committee. I had also the interesting hands-on task of chairing the Fixed Link Consultation Committee in Kent.

In November 1984 Nick Ridley had met French Ministers in Paris. They agreed that both governments were willing to facilitate a link, provided it was financed by the private sector. This was important, not least to stop public money being used to create unfair competition with existing air or sea operators. Privately Nick was sceptical, but less so as the banks became more bullish. In March 1985 we met two of the French Ministers involved in London and agreed a programme of work for officials of both countries. An open invitation was issued in April inviting promoters to submit their proposals by the end of October.

As the outline of bids emerged, there was intense discussion and assessments within the Department and across Whitehall. It was a useful benefit that Nick Ridley had nine years' experience as a civil engineer. The Prime Minister hankered after the ability to get in the car and drive from Folkestone to Calais. This fitted in with both the proposal for a bridge and Euroroute's short bridge to an artificial island, a less lengthy tunnel, then another island and a final bridge to the French coast. As the assessment developed, the bridge was discounted for obstructing channel navigation and some uncertainty over untried materials and cost. The tunnel between two islands had considerable attractions but posed problems re navigation which I thought exaggerated. More serious was the problem of exhaust fumes; ways could be found to remove diesel smuts but not a build up of carbon monoxide – a problem sure to be exacerbated when a road accident led to a severe undersea traffic jam. James Sherwood of Sea Containers, using his Sealink UK company, a privatised British Rail subsidiary, was a late entrant with larger twin tunnels for road and rail. However, lack of French support together with safety and ventilation concerns told against it. Frankly, it also suffered because Sherwood, with his shipping interests and forceful opposition to any fixed link, was viewed by some as suspect. The final decision to go for the Channel Tunnel Group's twin rail tunnels with through trains and vehicles carried on shuttle trains was accused of lacking imagination; it was without the appeal of driving one's own car but it combined the least technological advances with the lowest risk. Compellingly for Ministers it was assessed as the most likely to succeed. The choice was announced in Lille by Margaret Thatcher and French President François Mitterand in January, 1986.

Long before any decision as to the chosen form of fixed link, rumblings of opposition were building up, particularly in Kent. Soon protest meetings were being called, rumours abounded and the dockers of Dover were up in arms. I thought it sensible to spend an initial three days in the area and held a series of listening meetings picking up the views of councillors and the general public. One newspaper reported that I 'did not receive the kind of welcome normally reserved for visiting Tory dignitaries'. Indeed I did not! These meetings were universally hostile, not least a rowdy meeting in Dover dominated by angry dockers and seamen who had concluded that most of their jobs would disappear. My St Pancras soap box training came in useful. Happily a police presence stopped things from getting out of hand, although at the end I had to be smuggled out by a back door. To all at these meetings I undertook that their views would be reported back to government, although not those of the lady who complained that with an east wind the smell of garlic would be wafted through the Tunnel!

To me, three things came across very clearly: the genuine bewilderment and fear that the quiet pattern of people's lives would soon be dramatically disrupted,[7] the spate of rumours and exaggeration in circulation[8] and the lack of co-ordination between the different bodies who all had, or would have, 'a finger in the pie'. I discussed all this with John Noulton, the Department official mainly responsible for Channel Tunnel matters. He was an exceptionally perceptive man. Normally civil servants will produce a paper saying that xyz has occurred, here are the options, my recommendation is . . . John would say, 'I anticipate that next week so and so will happen, and this is how I suggest we prepare for it.' He was already in discussion with the Kent County Council on the need for some co-ordination. Out of this, we came up with the pioneering idea for a Joint Consultative Committee drawing together representatives of all the principal players, the Departments of Environment, Employment and Transport, the construction companies, and the three tiers of elected local councillors in the affected areas – Parish, District and County.

The first meeting of the 'Fixed Link Joint Consultation Committee' (or Mitchell Committee as it later became known) was held in

---

[7] Most of all, for both those whose houses would be compulsorily purchased and, importantly, those near to the terminal whose property would be blighted. I salute Michael Howard, Folkestone's MP, for persuading EuroTunnel to offer to buy blighted houses in the villages of Newington, Peene and Frogholt at their pre-existing prices. 2006 saw them sell off the last of them – at a profit.

[8] For example, a Phillips and Drew report spoke of a bloodbath among ferry services, knocking out fifteen routes from Hull to Plymouth.

the County Council Offices. Welcoming those attending I set out our purpose as, 'To consider the impact on Kent, to maximise the benefits to the County and minimise the damage . . . a forum for identifying problems and ways of solving them, but not the place to debate the principle of having a fixed link, that is for Parliament to decide, not us.' It was agreed after some hesitation that the meetings would be held in private, enabling discussion to be less inhibited and confidential matters to be discussed. I never had a complaint that this trust had been misplaced. Of course, all decisions were made public. This first meeting agreed to commission an impact study, to authorise officials to meet between Committee meetings to agree agendas and to prepare papers, also to pursue tasks remitted to them etc. Our future meetings would be monthly and move round the affected parts of Kent. I briefed local MPs after each meeting.

The agendas concentrated on environmental issues, including roads, disposal of spoil (sixty five options reduced by officials to seven), and the routeing of construction traffic, particularly to the adit at the foot of Shakespeare Cliff (named after a reference in the bard's *King Lear*). This was designed to provide entry to the two parts of the Tunnel, i.e. from the adit inland to the Folkestone terminal and from it out under the sea. One valuable initiative of ours was the appointment of an approachable man, an ex-Ambassador, Sir Donald Murray, as our Complaints Commissioner.

The Parliamentary Bill was termed Hybrid because, in addition to the generality of the project, it covered private individuals, for example compulsory purchase of their property. This procedure allowed anyone personally affected to petition the nine-member Select Committee for changes. It began hearings on 19 June, sat for thirty four days and heard four thousand, eight hundred and forty five petitions (many replicated) for changes in the Bill. In an unprecedented move, several days were spent on hearings away from Parliament. These away-days are recorded on a plaque which says 'The House of Commons Select Committee for the Channel Tunnel Bill sat for five days at the Hythe Imperial Hotel during September 1986. This was the first occasion on which any Parliamentary Select Committee had sat anywhere other than in the Palace of Westminster.' The tailpiece on the plaque reads 'In June the same year the Mitchell Committee met at this Hotel to consider the impact of the Tunnel on Kent'. A later meeting of 'my' Committee arranged for the impact study to be circulated with advice of a full day meeting of the Committee to hear representations from Parish Councils, environmental bodies and other interest groups. The disposal of chalk spoil was a vital issue because, if this was held up for any reason, tunnelling would have to halt. Eventually a seventy five acre landfill extension to the seaward side of Shakespeare Cliff was agreed and is now green common land. I understand that our Consultation Committee was deemed a considerable success in cooling tempers and ironing out problems, particularly on planning issues. Not least, it separated facts from persistent rumour! I am told ours was the first time a major construction project had been handled in this way. Our precedent, with some adjustment, was subsequently used years later for the new fast rail link to the Tunnel.

During preparation for the Treaty, the innovative idea emerged of juxtapositioning frontier controls, that is to say reversing the normal arrangement that you go through the English check for passenger and freight controls on entering the UK, and similar French controls on entering France. I gave enthusiastic support in the Department to reversing this, so that the British passport and customs etc. checks for the cross-channel shuttle trains are now in Sangatte and the French in Folkestone. Understandably this revolutionary concept had to go to Cabinet for approval. However, we did unearth an unexpected problem. French *Police de Mer et Frontière* and their customs officials would naturally wear full uniform. This included a loaded revolver. The idea of gun toting French officials in Kent was/would clearly be a bridge too far. After a somewhat sticky impasse, they were allowed to come armed for duty, but their arms were to be put in a locked cupboard controlled by the Chief Constable of Kent.

1987 was an important milestone. Robin Leigh Pemberton, Governor of the Bank of England, together with John Moore, our new Secretary of State, brought in Alastair Morton as the English Co-Chairman. He was made for the job, a man who loved a challenge and brought immense energy, enthusiasm and a steamroller-like determination to succeed. If his abrasive approach upset people, he undoubtedly got results and became the driving force behind the whole project. Personally I think that, but for him, the Tunnel would have foundered.

Difficulties arose with the French Government (supported by Alastair) on the issue of there being no new fast line programmed from London direct to the mouth of the Tunnel. The reason for this was simple. At the time the through train service opened, Eurostar would beat competitors through being quicker than the ferry and outclass flying, bringing passengers in comfort from the heart of London to the centre of Paris. This avoided traffic to Heathrow and its check-in times, and then getting from Charles de Gaulle airport into Paris. In this situation it did not make sense to incur a massive cost to shorten the journey time.[9] The French claimed they were spending out on a fast line from Paris and we should incur similar costs. This was spurious because they were already building the TGV line to Brussels and only needed to add a short link from Lille to Sangatte. I invited Monsieur Douffiagues, my opposite number, to come and see something of our difficulties compared to his. He was visibly surprised by the extent of London's built up area (in Paris it takes only five minutes from green fields to the Gare du Nord). We continued through the cuttings and tunnels in the Kent hills for him to see the difference from the flat Pas de Calais.

Earlier in June 1986 we had the Second Reading of the Tunnel Bill with its major vote on the principle of the legislation. My own rôle was to respond to points raised and wind up before the vote. The House did not divide on Party lines, much more on constituency concerns, particularly Kent Members fearing overload on the county's roads and Northern MPs who feared jobs would move to the South East. Happily British Rail had told me that they planned twenty freight trains a night in each direction, equating to the removal of a thousand lorries a day off Kent's roads. Also they already had six assembly depots in the North; these would enable manufacturers exporting to the continent to deliver their goods more quickly and more cheaply, for example, from Birmingham to Milan in two days instead of eight. I ended my own speech 'Future generations will not only look back on tonight as a historic occasion, but will ask themselves why the hell we did not do it before'. The Bill then moved to its Standing Committee stage. This lasted eight weeks and was principally chaired by Miss Betty Boothroyd, later a distinguished Speaker of the House. The first business was to confirm that the

---

[9] Subsequently this situation changed dramatically with the arrival of Easyjet and other cut-price air services. It has seemed to me that Eurostar was slow to respond to their challenge.

Committee would meet on Tuesdays and Thursdays at 10.30 a.m. It took over an hour to secure agreement on this. Proceedings started with the silver tongued Jonathan Aitken, MP for Thanet South, speaking of a 'surging controversy' surrounding the Bill, complaining that it had not been in our manifesto at the previous General Election, that both the Prime Minister and Nick Ridley had earlier expressed opposition, so, he claimed the Bill was a surprise which accelerated into a series of shocks etc. I responded that if 'My Honourable Friend' has genuine points to make, we shall all want to consider them most carefully. 'In addition I know he will have much joy mischief making during this Committee stage', and so it proved. I accused him of playing the rôle that ancient mariners feared, of the wrecker on the shore who put harbour lights in the wrong place to mislead the crew. When he tried to interrupt, apparently I snapped back 'I have not finished with you yet'. However, I enjoyed his Christmas card signed 'Jonathan, the loyal Opposition'.

James Sherwood, in concert with the Dover Harbour Board, employed the formidable Maureen Thomason to co-ordinate opposition in Committee. She sat at the front of the public seating area, picking up on points and passing notes to opponents of the Bill on both government and opposition sides of the Committee. One potentially important amendment I had to turn down concerned compulsory purchase (CPO) valuations. I supported the view that the CPO code was defective and offered to draw criticism by Mark Wolfson and others to the attention of the Minister concerned. As I see it, our system of valuation is unfair. It is based on the market value as between a willing seller and a willing buyer, but the seller is not 'willing'. The French do this rather better; an attractive price means a lot of time saved and, in business, time is money. Difficulties arose with the disclosure in a French newspaper that geological problems were holding up French tunnelling, hence extra spoil would come to Kent. This resulted in an ill thought out amendment requiring that the Tunnel meeting point be midway between the UK and France. Then new clauses to keep out rabid dogs, illegal immigrants, safeguards against terrorism, public health, checks on lorry weights, compatible fire fighting procedures and other safety amendments, a lengthy discussion on whether passengers should be allowed in their vehicles within the Tunnel. Sir George Young (later to become my successor as MP) successfully amended the Bill against my advice to

After the ratification of the Channel Tunnel Treaty with Monsieur Douffiagues

ensure bicycles are catered for; this was a loss making activity the Company could do without, and has been little used.

During Committee stages governments want to make progress, and the Opposition to delay proceedings. My earlier experience as a Whip had taught me the more time taken by debates on Clause 1, the quicker the Bill would ultimately be achieved. Discussion on our first clause, out of forty nine, was still continuing at 12.55 a.m. at the end of our fourth sitting. After that we double banked with afternoon sittings. As the last sitting came to an end, I thanked Betty Boothroyd on behalf of the whole Committee for presiding over our discussions with firmness and fairness. 'The Hon. Member for Thanet South at one point referred to a French proverb which says "It is a sad woman who has to buy her own perfume"; since you have presided so gracefully over our proceedings, Miss Boothroyd, I thought it would help to make you a happy Chairman if, on behalf of the Committee, I presented you with a small bottle of perfume.'

There were four highly enjoyable outings concerning the Channel Tunnel proceedings, the first on 12 February 1986. That day the Prime Minister hosted lunch in the precincts of Canterbury Cathedral for President Mitterand and some twenty four of his colleagues before the Heads of State signed the Channel Tunnel Fixed Link Treaty in the Chapter House. He was met by a couple of hundred noisy demonstrators and a few eggs splattered direct hits on his Rolls. At lunch I recall an interesting English white wine, followed by the fabulous Château Gruard Larose 1961.

In July the following year we were given lunch by President Mitterand at the Elysée Palace after ratification of the Treaty. This occasion was notable for me because the French appeared to misunderstand our protocol. I imagine they assumed a Minister to be senior to a Secretary (of State) and, as a result had seated me next to the President. We talked for a few minutes while I extolled the benefits of the Tunnel to France. There is an old expression that someone is 'boot-faced' i.e. bored and unsmiling, and this certainly applied. However, I discovered he was born at Jarnac, just north of Bordeaux, his wife came from near Pouilly Fuissé and, like me, he enjoyed the view from the top of the nearby hill of Solutré. Also his constituency was not far from Burgundy and, by then, he had become quite animated. Perhaps the Mâcon Villages Blanc and Château Angelus 1976 helped. Later that day Jacques Douffiagues and I carried out the official inauguration of the Intergovernmental Commission whose task was 'to supervise on behalf of both governments all matters concerning the construction and operation of the fixed link'.

The third party was in Dover Castle on 1 December 1990, a wonderful setting, to celebrate the breakthrough, joining the two halves of the Service Tunnel. I relished a grand spoof by the *Daily Mail* of 1 April reporting the extraordinary find of an old early 19th century tunnel from under the castle to just north of Boulogne.

The final party was unique in all of time. Out under the Channel, forty metres below the seabed are two gigantic caverns created to enable trains to cross from one tunnel to the other. On the 26 February 1994 I was one of seven hundred bidden to lunch in the UK crossover, which is about fifteen kilometres from the Folkestone portal. It would be churlish to rub in that the French were late, whilst the British arrived on time by a Network South East diesel. The guests of honour were the two Prime Ministers, Margaret Thatcher and Pierre Mauroy, at the time the Tunnel treaty was signed. At the end of the meal, Roger Lloyd Pack, playing the rôle of Brunel, dressed in a 'stove pipe' hat, entertained us with his views on the short sightedness of bankers and the politicos who had not the courage to grasp great opportunities. For me, one memory came from Tim Green who was seated at my table and recounted for me the history of Brunel's tunnel from Wapping to Rotherhithe. Apparently it was dogged by disasters; there was partial flooding, a strike, and then it ran out of money. A big reception was laid on in the Tunnel for the great, the good and investors. To prevent water seepage, the Tunnel was pressurised. Alas, the pressure was sufficient to banish the bubbles from the champagne – that was until the guests returned to normal air pressure whereupon there was a great deal of vulgar noise. My informant added it was fourteen years later before Brunel's tunnel (the first under water, for public use) was opened. My fellow guest then referred to the order for shuttle trains as being ominously late. Happily the Tunnel itself was completed pretty well on time.

Winding up the Third Reading and final debate on the legislation, I said it was just over a century since the first Bill was introduced, 'the longest pregnancy in the world' as Lord Palmerston described it. 'Now we are about to witness the birth of the greatest civil engineering project ever undertaken in this country down through the centuries.' That night Parliament played a small but significant part in turning a dream into reality.

Gloriously successful though the Tunnel is in engineering terms and in its physical operations (the largest undersea structure in the world), it is, alas, a financial disaster, not least for its shareholders. The reason for this is quite simple; the financing was based on substantial borrowing to be serviced, i.e. interest paid, from the income from train and shuttle operations. This all went horribly wrong, partly cost over-runs increasing the debt, but more from unforeseen delay in opening for business, hence no income to service the debt.

Considerable delay arose from heavy handed belt and braces requirements from the Safety Authority, for example its insistence that the width of the passage through 'pass doors' between the shuttle carriages should be no less than the seven hundred millimetres subsequently accepted by the Inter Government Commission; an increase of only ten centimetres, but this requirement was imposed when the shuttles were already in the process of being built and cost circa £40 million with, worse, a delay of up to nine months. Commissioning delays arose from the difficulties with the computer controlled trains which had to cope with overhead electricity in France, third rail south of London on a different voltage and overhead north of London, but a different voltage yet again. Opening for business was delayed from mid 1993 to June 1994, with full services delayed until early 1995. (No income to pay the interest on the borrowings led to additional loans being added to the debt to be serviced.)

Further problems arose from rail traffic through the Tunnel being less than forecast (the French are said to have inflated anticipated usage to justify investment in their fast line from Paris to Lille). Things would have been worse were it not for Alastair's Morton's brilliant negotiation with BR and SNCF for a contracted Minimum Usage Charge (MUC) paid every year until November 2006. Since traffic never reached the forecast level, Eurotunnel enjoyed an unrequited income for some thirteen years. The end of that guarantee must have presented significant financial problems during Eurotunnel's debt negotiation that year.

Eurotunnel has made an operating profit almost since commencing operations, but the burden of servicing the heightened debt, at one point £10 billion, has lost shareholders virtually all their money and the banks much of their loans. Let us hope the 2007 'restructuring' will be the last.

CHAPTER 18

Out of government

Out of government, with a 'K' and plenty still to do . . . /
I serve on Standards and Privileges Committee, including the
'Cash for Questions' affair also on the Public Accounts
Committee (close liaison with the National Audit
Office / Back at El Vino, by 2001 retirement beckoned

DURING THE SUMMER OF 1988, when I had been in the Department of Transport for five years, I came gradually to the conclusion that I ought to return to the backbenches, for a mixture of three reasons. I give them in no particular sequence.

My brother Christopher was understandably champing at the bit for me to come back to the family business. He had followed in our grandfather ALB's early footsteps as a Common Council member of the City of London Corporation and wanted to increase his commitment there. Secondly, I felt vulnerable as a shareholder in the family business; as matters stood, if I died there would be no shareholding member of my own family working in the business and I knew, alas, of other family businesses, including that of a Parliamentary colleague, where a similar situation had arisen with disastrous consequences. There, the interests of a shareholder not in the business had become virtually worthless. This was because valuation was based on the meagre dividend and most of the profit was either ploughed back into the business, or paid to the working directors as a bonus. For this reason I saw it as important to encourage Graham, my younger son, to join the firm as one of the team running a really interesting and successful business. Moreover, I felt I ought to be there to manage that change. Another very personal reason was that Pam was miserable, our marriage had been going through a rocky period which was largely my fault and I believed that, with more time at home, things would recover.

I was at a meeting with British Rail one afternoon in August 1988 when the expected government reshuffle occurred. The Prime Minister's call came at about 4.30. She asked me to go to Agriculture as number two to John MacGregor, along (although I did not know it at the time) with Russell Sanderson, my good friend who covered Agriculture in the Scottish Office. Naturally I was sorely tempted. Nevertheless I hastened back to the Commons and phoned to consult both Pam and Andrew. Neither was available[1] so, on arrival, I phoned Number Ten to say thank you, but no. Shortly after, Margaret asked me to come over to her and explain the situation. I said I had family and family business reasons for leaving government. She asked then, if I were to stay at Transport, whether it would make any difference, she supposed not. I concurred and walked disconsolately back to the Commons.

On arrival in the Members' Lobby, I was accosted by Murdo Maclean, the man known as 'the usual channels' oiling the wheels, as honest broker, between Government and Opposition. He said, 'You are to ring Number Ten'. I said, 'Thanks, but I am just back from seeing the PM'. He then said, 'You are to phone straight away,' seemingly deaf to what I had told him. He seized me by the elbow, marched me across to a telephone and rang the number connecting me to the PM. She said she was very sorry I was going, she had been on to the Palace and I was to have a 'K'.

Later I went back to my office in the Department, collected my own papers and overnight wrote personal letters of appreciation to my Private Office Secretary and a handful of senior officials with whom I had worked most closely. At about 10.00 a.m. next morning I walked over to go to my, now erstwhile, private office to leave the letters. Instead the ground floor doorman refused to admit me without a pass – such is real power! Someone came down to collect.

In due course Pam and I went with many others to the Honours ceremony at the Palace. Each knight takes it in turn to kneel and be dubbed on the shoulder by Her Majesty with the special sword presented to the Queen in 1953 by the Queen Mother. One is given thirty seconds of conversation in which, rather uselessly, I said that it was a happy coincidence that her grandfather had dubbed my grandfather, and away I went to rejoin Pam and then off to a celebratory lunch in the West End. That evening we had a light supper, mainly brown bread and butter, with nothing to distract from the flavours of a bottle of Château Latour 1945. Far and away the best wine in my cellar!

---

[1] Later both said that, if I had been able to contact them, they would have urged me to stay.

Subsequently my brother went on to complete thirty seven years as a member of the Common Council of the City Corporation, ending up with the bonus of being the Chief Commoner, having chaired the City Lands, Planning and Housing Committees, among others, and earning an OBE on the way.

In 2001, being of retirement age, my brother and I brought about a rearrangement of the capital structure of El Vino. This resulted in Chris and his two sons, Michael and Anthony, running the business and gave Graham the opportunity to set up his own independent company, now trading as Graham Mitchell Vintners Ltd. in Berkshire. This has all worked out rather well. El Vino remains a family business, and has recently expanded, taking over another restaurant in Mark Lane in the City, the street where Grandfather first set up in business. Graham's firm is proving a substantial success, particularly with his exclusive selections of French and New World wines. This gives me a particular sense of pride since he had learned from me how to taste and we had worked together on buying the French wines for El Vino.

I have retired (about time too!) but keep my interest alive by serving on the Wine committee of the Carlton Club, and continue to stay in touch through the Commanderie de Bordeaux, the Burgundian Chevaliers du Tastevin and old friends and former suppliers in France, not least through taking small groups round the vineyards and also tutored tastings for charities and Conservative Associations etc.

After I had ceased to be a Minister I served on a number of Parliamentary Committees. The most interesting of these were the Privileges Committee, later Standards and Privileges, and the Public Accounts Committee. Traditionally the law and custom of Parliament had been left very largely to the good sense of the individual Members to reconcile their private interest with their public duty. Bribing an MP or accepting a bribe were clearly unacceptable. However, the issues were more complex than that. For example, soon after I left the Whips' Office in 1967, I was approached on behalf of the trade association of a major and well respected industry to ask if I would become their Parliamentary adviser and defend their interests in Parliament; it was indicated that later I would be made a non-executive director of some lesser subsidiary of a major company. I refused. However, I do not doubt that someone else will have taken it on.

The 1994 Privileges Committee

The 1994 Privileges Committee was convened over allegations that two MPs had been entrapped by a journalist posing as a businessman for whom each agreed to table a question, for which they would be paid £1,000 – a bizarre amount for five minutes' work. I have to hand a letter which referred to many MPs being sponsored by industrial associations, trade unions, individual companies and pressure groups, 'Generally sponsorship will bring with it remuneration, it is likely the sponsoring MP will from time to time ask a Parliamentary Question for the benefit of the sponsor'. 'What, then,' the letter asked, 'Is the difference between an MP who is paid to ask several questions on behalf of the sponsor and an MP who is paid to ask a single question?' These matters were later to figure in new rules recommended by the Nolan report.

The first meeting of the 1994 Privileges Committee faced an unprecedented situation. There was a minority view vehemently espoused by Anthony Wedgwood Benn that both evidence to the Committee and its deliberations should be held in public. If the Committee did not concur, he would attend and personally issue a report of all its proceedings. Clearly this could not be acceptable. Meetings were called, Benn attended the Committee, which promptly adjourned. Eventually in December a debate was held on the floor of the House on a motion to expel him from the Committee. My own contribution referred to Benn as a distinguished but, at times, eccentric Parliamentarian.[2] This was one of his eccentricities: 'He is here because he was democratically elected . . . by voters in his constituency. He accepted then that the views of the majority should prevail. The Rt. Hon. Gentleman arrives in this place by a democratic process, but then behaves as an autocrat. He accepts democracy when it suits him, but rejects it when that suits him. This is the road to anarchy.'

The House removed him from the Committee and we were then able to get on with our business.

---

[2] I and my son Andrew had been the first father and son in the House at the same time since Harold Macmillan and his son Maurice. Later I passed this 'mantle' on to 'Wedgie', writing to congratulate him when his son Hilary joined him in the Commons.

The Public Accounts Committee (PAC)

The Public Accounts Committee (PAC) numbers fifteen or fewer MPs, a quorum being four in number. Its job is to follow up the spending of public money voted by Parliament. To do this, it works closely with the National Audit Office (NAO), indeed most of the Committee's investigations are based on its work. The NAO is answerable to Parliament, and totally independent of government. It is the external auditor of central government and its subsidiary spenders of public money.

I volunteered to be appointed to the Committee, not least for the opportunity to pursue the value for money reports which come to the Committee from the NAO. These include the economy, efficiency and effectiveness of government departments in their use of resources. The Committee has the power to send for papers, records and persons. The latter is generally the relevant Department's Permanent Secretary and Accounting Officer – the person who is the absolute boss in their Department. Cross examination is all done in a very urbane and civilised way. However, that is no barrier to effective exposure of deficiencies, I and others were especially ruthless when a problem continued into a second year. An example of one of our reports expressed grave concern that the Wessex Regional Health Authority had wasted at least £20 million in attempting to implement a new regional information system, later abandoned. The money should have been spent on health and care for sick people. In a later report we again condemned this Authority for using a secondee from IBM to advise on the purchase of an IBM computer for £3.3 million when it could have been bought at half to one million less cost! Going from large sums to small; in another example, the Welsh Development Agency was in hot water for providing cars to their Board members and senior executives without them having to reimburse their private motoring. They were similarly in trouble concerning tensions with their International Director. He had served only nine weeks of a four month posting in the US and was then sent home on eight months' 'gardening leave', which conveniently took him up to his fiftieth birthday when the total cost of his retirement package exceeded £228,000! If one wished to be caught up in a large scale can of worms, there was the report from the NAO on weaknesses in the Department of Social Security accounting and their control of expenditure. At the time, this Department had only nine qualified accountants (and twenty under training) to cover no less than £60 billion of expenditure.

In 2007 as I write, it is good to know that both the NAO and the Public Accounts Committee continue to be hard at work protecting the taxpayer. This is particularly important at this time of ever widening intervention by government, much of it incurring expenditure which needs to be monitored. When I left the Committee I felt that, at the margin, I had made a worthwhile contribution.

CHAPTER 19

Back bencher trips

Backbencher overseas trips, Canadian regional
conference / Election Observer in South Africa, I vote several
times / Leading IPU delegation to Argentina and Uruguay –
Falklands issue discussed – Las Malvinas Argentinian according
to local mythology / Riding in the foothills of Andes

BEFORE GOING INTO GOVERNMENT, I had always regarded an
overseas Parliamentary trip as a luxury and had been too busy to
put my name forward. Now that I was a backbencher again I started
to apply to the Commonwealth Parliamentary Association (CPA) and
the Inter Parliamentary Union (IPU). The first opportunity was a
Canadian Regional Conference of the CPA in New Brunswick and
Nova Scotia, for which Dr John Garrett, a congenial Labour
member, and I had been chosen. Events started with a reception new
world style, for the free food and drinks were provided by a range of
stallholders each promoting their own products. Later we had a
lobster supper – I could not match my neighbour's appetite as he
consumed four of them.

For us, as UK representatives, the interest divided between purely
Canadian matters and those common to both our countries such as
health care and its costs with an ageing population, environmental
management of toxic and nuclear waste on which John Garrett made
a well informed and well received contribution, and a discussion on
the extent to which opinion polls influence public opinion.

Unexpectedly I found many of the debates on purely Canadian
matters of great interest, not least the problems and aspirations of native
'aboriginals', known as First Nation people. Their extremely articulate
spokesman claimed that Canada supports human rights in other
countries but not self government for its own First Nationals, this
against the background of tear gas used in a riot over plans to expand a
golf course on to land claimed by the Mohawk tribe. The aspiration of
many Québécois for an independent state was a fascinating subject and
the passions aroused were a revelation (throughout our trip everything
was translated in both English **and** French).

There was a major discussion on the recently introduced Free Trade Agreement with the US. I contributed with an assessment of the effect on the UK of removing EC trade barriers. Both sides in this session claimed my remarks in support of their arguments.

We moved on to Halifax in Nova Scotia (New Scotland) where our programme included Grand Pré, the site where French settlers, the 'Arcadians' were rounded up by British troops, often with families separated, and deported by sea in 1755 to destinations unknown to them, down the American coast. The event is heartrendingly portrayed by Longfellow in his poem 'Evangeline' and commemorated in the local museum (with little explanation as to why).[1] It was difficult to escape without a tear.

Election Observer – South Africa 1994

The 'wind of change' had eventually brought South Africa its first multiracial election. I applied successfully to be one of the official Observers monitoring the election and was due to lead our group of twenty Parliamentarians. Later Neil Kinnock, former Labour Party Leader, decided to come; naturally, as a Privy Councillor, he took precedence. We would join a massive number of Observers from countries all round the world, ensuring sufficient coverage to deter election malpractice.

There had been a considerable amount of bloodshed in the period leading up to the election (four thousand political murders in the previous twelve months), so we were heavily briefed on personal security. Neil Kinnock and I were both to work out of Warmbad in the Afrikaner (Boer) dominated North Transvaal, so that if widespread violence raised the question of withdrawal, an instant, cross Party decision could be taken. Most of this violence involved the ANC (African National Party of Nelson Mandela) versus the Inkatha (Zulu) Party, led by Chief Buthelezi who had refused to participate in the election. On arrival at our hotel in Johannesburg we were advised not to wander outside (the previous week three Russian generals had been robbed of their medals on the hotel forecourt). I had just checked in and had a bath when the whole hotel shook from

---

[1] The reason was the refusal of the French settlers to sign a declaration of loyalty to the British Crown. They claimed this could have obliged them to fight against French troops in any renewal of Anglo French hostilities.

a bomb outside the nearby ANC headquarters, killing nine people and injuring about fifty others. Later that night the police decided to blow up a suspect car under my window, so I and my neighbour, Baroness Flather, had to spend some hours of the night together on the floor of the corridor (this later led to some suggestive banter).

Earlier our Ambassador had briefed us on the latest situation. He explained that much of the tension had been eased by a last minute reversal of Buthelezi's decision not to participate in the election. He had made this decision following a fortuitous meeting at Johannesburg airport with Professor Okuma, an old friend from Kenya, who had persuaded him that if he did not participate, he and his Party would be forever sidelined. Buthelezi needed an alibi for this *volte face* for his followers. So he had told them that he had flown out of Johannesburg on an aircraft which then had engine trouble and been forced to turn back. 'It was as though God has prevented me from leaving; my forced return was God sent'. The convenience of this explanation caused some hilarity amongst us Observers. Next day Neil Kinnock and Glenys would not arrive until 2 p.m., so I seized the opportunity to repay hospitality I had enjoyed from a retired paper manufacturer on a visit at Christmas two years earlier. Over lunch I repeated the briefing along with the laughing response to Buthelezi's excuse. There was a pause and my guest said very quietly 'David, it is absolutely true. My son-in-law was the pilot.'

As Observers, our job was to watch and report, not to get involved and never to make any comment to the press. After the poll closed and before any election result was declared, it was essential that we agree and report on whether the election had been reasonably free and fair in our area.

It was arranged with Neil that I would organise the route and timetable to cover our twenty polling stations. This was not easy, for the only large scale map showing these polling stations was stuck up on the wall of a seventy-one year old Irish nun's bedroom; I could look at it, but not take it down. Neil had problems hiring the six cars we needed. Headquarters had told him the going rate was seventy five rand per day; the local ANC chief owned the vehicles and demanded five hundred rand! It took over two hours to argue him down to reality, but negotiations moved more rapidly when I borrowed one car from a visiting doctor and called out to Neil we now needed only five and I had heard we could borrow others.

Polling Day, a solid breakfast, and we were away on the road by 5.45 a.m., complete with sandwiches and a bottle of water. Our first task was to check no-one had stuffed voting papers in the ballot box before it was sealed. No need to have worried. It was all being done properly but ponderously in Africa time, so polling started one and a half hours late. The ballot papers had been printed (in Basingstoke) but Buthelezi's decision came after printing had been completed, so we Observers had to check that the slips for his party were being stuck by hand on the bottom of each ballot paper. My timetabling had allotted forty five minutes for larger villages and twenty for hamlets such as Worthing. I was struck dumb on arrival there by the totally unexpected sight of nine hundred and fifty people queuing. One hopeful sign was the genuine degree of co-operation between white and black members of the community. Farm tractors were bringing in trailer loads of black workers. I met a farmer's wife who had brought together groups of them to demonstrate how to hold a pencil (hand one to an adult for the first time, and they will hold it at the top end which is NBG). My most memorable conversation was with an elderly white Afrikaner employing some hundred and fifty black workers who said 'For years my conscience troubled me over what we were doing and now I feel free'.

The very real difficulties which faced the IEC (Independent Electoral Commission) became ever more apparent. Forty five percent of the voters were said to be unable to read or write and there were nineteen Parties on the ballot paper. I recall vividly, arriving at one polling station to find the National Party candidate beside himself with rage over illiterate voters; the IEC system was that two of the polling station staff would go behind a curtain, discover the voter's wishes and one would vote accordingly. The furious candidate explained that at this polling station, every one of the staff was an ANC supporter and how did we think they would interpret illiterate voters' intentions? Observers were supposed only to observe and report, but we judged it right to use common sense, so our team took it in turns to be behind the curtain. I recall many a black face whisper to me 'Mandela' (not ANC) with a long, slow 'a'. I voted once for a Communist, once for the extreme right for a well dressed but totally illiterate white farmer, and many times for Mandela's ANC.

Our group had half a day to spare before flying back. We spent this on a thirteen thousand acre Game Park with the peculiarity that it had all the natural indigenous animals except those which were meat-eating, so we could ride horses quite close to the game. We gave a special cheer for Ivan Lawrence MP for not falling off, on this, the first time he had ever been on a horse.

The whole observer operation was thoroughly worthwhile because our collective worldwide reports gave genuine authority to the new government of South Africa.

P.S. I had not met Glenys Kinnock before and found her very Welsh, emotionally involved and charming. Neil wrote to thank me for my part, apparently impressed by the six car routes I had programmed and added that he was thinking of a summer holiday; any chance of me doing him an itinerary – it would be a simple trip, Denmark to Latvia to Gibraltar via Chad and . . .

I lead a parliamentary delegation to Argentina and Uruguay

I applied successfully to be part of a six-man Inter Parliamentary Union delegation to Argentina and Uruguay in September, 1996. Since the Falklands war, Argentina had changed from a dictatorship to a Parliamentary democracy, hence they were now able to rejoin the IPU. Happily this time I was chosen as leader. We were to be only the second delegation there since that war.

Things started to roll with the Argentine Ambassador to London inviting our group to lunch. He listened to our various interests and followed this up with a series of helpful suggestions for our schedule.

We arrived on 1 September and received a warm welcome from our Ambassador, a useful briefing on our programme and an agreeable meal. Next morning we met our hosts, the Argentina IPU, led by Señor Eduardo Menem, brother of their President. They filled in more information on our programme, followed by a welcoming lunch with, of course, appropriate speeches.

So far, so good, but of course the political temperature and postwar attitude would only become clear as we met with ministers and, later, the British Council, which had offices in Buenos Aires. In six packed days we met the Vice President, also their Foreign Minister, as well as the Minister of Health and a large number of Parliamentarians – both government and opposition supporters. An unexpected addition to our programme was a call on their Defence Chief of Staff, General Diaz. The benefit to us of this visit was his anxiety to stress that their much reduced armed forces were now finally and firmly under democratic civilian control.

It was inevitable that our hosts would at some time raise the Falkland issue – Las Malvinas and firmly Argentinian, according to local mythology. I generally parried this subject, pointing out that there are matters where even the best of friends agree to differ, and in any case, it was not on the agenda. There was, however, no escaping it when we met their Anglophile Foreign Minister, Guido di Tella at their Foreign Office. He explained that ninety eight percent of relations with the UK were excellent, and then spent most of the time on this delicate subject. At one point I intervened to express some bewilderment on the grounds that the Argentine was a keen supporter of the UN charter which had within it entrenched support for self determination. Di Tella, who had been educated at Cambridge and had a son at Oxford, responded with his view that self determination was not appropriate in this case. He called in support a Spanish Professor and the English Professor Higgins – a Judge at the International Court of Justice and a member of the UN Committee on Human Rights (actually Rosalyn, the wife of my parliamentary colleague, Terry Higgins). The discussion was throughout low key and intended to remain good-natured. We left after one and a half hours, having substantially overrun our allotted time.

We next moved on to a private dinner amongst ourselves. Interestingly when I got back to my hotel room there was a buff envelope under the door from Di Tella with the two opinions on self determination, and a personal note signed 'Guido' commending them. On return to London I accosted Terry Higgins on the subject; the reply came back that the passage was authentic but had been taken out of context.

Our visit to the British Council offices surprised us. Their figures showed a considerable appetite for British culture – a continuation of a long established relationship. Direct investment into the Argentine had been growing, particularly in response to their massive privatisation programme. At the Argentine Ambassador in London's suggestion, we had asked for a tour of the stunning architecture of the Colon Theatre. This was generously met by providing us with both the tour and the Presidential Box for a performance of Mozart's *Magic Flute*. I sat in Señora Peron's seat. (Don't cry for me!)

A visit up country to Mendoza in the shadow of the Andes was interesting, useful and enjoyable. We met the elected Provincial

Governor who arranged for us to meet local Senators, visited the Council Chamber which had been imported *in toto* from Britain in 1926, met local businessmen and lunched most agreeably at a wine lodge. Mendoza, with its tree-lined avenues, is actually an oasis in a desert interconnected by an old system of canals and ducts to mountainside reservoirs filled annually from melting snow. I managed to play truant one evening and dined with a wine grower and his family (third generation expats) to whom I had an introduction from a mutual friend. Their fifteen year old daughter raised the Malvinas in a spirited attack and vehemently refused to accept the possibility, which I gently pointed out, that at the time Argentina had its independence from Spain, the Falklands had never been occupied by Spain[2] and hence could not have been ceded by Spain to Argentina. I stayed overnight and had the memorable experience of a daybreak ride with my host in the foothills of the Andes, on one of the fast trotting Peruvian paso horses.

Back in Buenos Aires we were given a generous lunch by our IPU hosts, accompanied by those flowing phrases which exaggerated at some length the respect we had earned and the goodwill we had created. The flowing phrases nearly lost us our take-off time, so I had to make a very British minimal response, saying we had come as strangers and left as friends, ending '*Saludos mios Amigos.*'

On to Uruguay and a warm welcome from a country which still recognised its debt to Britain and to George Canning who as Foreign Secretary (later Prime Minister) was one of its main sponsors as a separate country. He remains a local hero. We called on their President, Dr Sanguinetti, and thanked him and later the Vice President and their Deputy Foreign Minister for assistance accorded to the RAF, and help with medical cases from the Falklands. We had an interesting meeting with the British Uruguayan Chamber of Commerce and a worthwhile visit to their National Veterinary

---

[2] The first recorded landing on the islands occurred in 1690 when an English expedition claimed the islands for the Crown. In 1820, the Buenos Aires government declared independence from Spain but did not at that time claim the Falklands. They did so in 1824, but it was not until 1828 they installed a settlement which we expelled in 1833. Ever since then there has always been open, continuous (apart from the Falklands war), effective possession and British administration of the islands. Indeed, it was not until the 1930s that revisionist historians began the campaign of indoctrination of school history books that has led subsequent generations of Argentinians to believe the islands to be theirs.

Laboratory, seeing research on cattle diseases (there is no indigenous BSE), and problems for beekeepers – this particularly interested me, as an erstwhile beekeeper, and also Tony Banks MP, surprisingly Secretary of the London Beekeepers Association. Uruguay has a population of three million people, twelve million cattle and twenty two million sheep.

The capital is the port of Montevideo (scene of the sinking of the German battleship, the *Graf Spee*). This city houses the secretariat for MERCOSUR, the then nearly new and significant Free Trade Area of Argentine, Brazil, Paraguay and Uruguay, with Chile then having associate status. I was greatly interested in this; unlike our EU, this had no powerful commission, but proceeded by intergovernment agreement. Uruguay saw itself as the gateway to this vast trading group. From this distance, I have not followed developments, but undoubtedly the later currency devaluation by Brazil must have had a significant effect in making their own goods cheaper within MERCOSUR, and presumably a step on the road to Argentina's subsequent economic woes.

There was a notable difference between the social and economic set up of the two countries we visited. As of then, Argentina had wide differences between rich and poor and a more thrusting and vigorous economy, whilst Uruguay had a more homogenous society but much less thrust and vigour. In both, I was impressed by the depth of goodwill towards Britain.

English Speaking Union

Later, when I had left the Commons, I carried out a number of overseas speaking engagements for the ESU. I gave them the title of 'A Life at Westminster' and in an amusing way covered the highlights of events described in this book. The initial tour covered visits along the East Coast of America, later to California. I met interesting people and enjoyed the trip immensely. Subsequently I have been invited back to California, visited Canada to talk in Vancouver and Victoria on Vancouver Island, and similarly in Australia and New Zealand. On most of these visits I have been put up for one or two nights by one of their ESU Committee with time to see the local sights. During these visits I was warmly welcomed and, in two or three cases, have been invited to come back and stay – all very agreeable.

CHAPTER 20

Constituency and county matters

Voting on Margaret Thatcher's Leadership / Constituents
plan to burn an effigy of me / I am made a DL / Boundary
changes / My political credo, retirement announced,
precedents, successor chosen

IT WAS TUESDAY, 20 NOVEMBER 1990, the week when Conservative
MPs voted on Michael Heseltine's audacious challenge to Margaret
Thatcher's leadership of the Conservative Party. By pure chance, that
Friday fell to be the night of my Constituency Party's Executive
Meeting in Andover's Guildhall. I was asked by the *Andover Advertiser*
how I had voted, and I responded that it was a secret ballot and added
the throw-away line 'that I had not even told my wife, much less
telling you'. These regular meetings of the Executive Committee had
an attendance of some forty or fifty, and covered constituency
business, reports from branches and the like, followed by my report
from Parliament. Normally these were very friendly occasions, as I
sat on the platform there would be smiles and nods of welcome. This
night was different. No smiles, a frigid coldness I had never
experienced before. Apparently the rumour had gone round that I
refused to say how I had voted because I had voted for Heseltine and
was frightened of the reaction if I admitted it. The attendance was
larger than usual, the constituency business completed in record time;
the Chairman called me to give my report.

I started by explaining that the previous week we had a big
meeting in Romsey Town Hall at which each time our visiting
speaker referred to Margaret, many of those present applauded, and
each time there was reference to a need for changes of policy, others
applauded. I recorded that the Association Chairman had, at my
request, carried out a poll of Branch Chairmen with the result of
fourteen for Heseltine to twenty one for Margaret, 'in short, we have
a deeply divided Association'. I added that I wanted to lead a united
Party into the next election and judged I would achieve this better if
I continued to remain silent, 'However, Mr Chairman, if this

meeting wishes me to divulge how I voted, I will do so. Please may I have a show of hands from those who want me to do that.' Five hands went up. People visibly relaxed and the normal smiles returned. Subsequently I heard of a number of MPs who disclosed and faced votes of censure by their Associations.

The fact is that at that time there was more vehement support for Margaret than ever – but from a shrinking proportion of the electorate; the radical nature and insensitive handling of the Poll Tax being pre-eminent in this loss of support. This was made worse by the crass stupidity of a Treasury cut-back on the expected level of finance for local authorities at a time they desperately needed extra funding to ameliorate poll tax hardship. There was widespread unease and protest in the constituency. This was most visible in the village of Bishops Green which declared itself a 'Poll Tax Free Zone' and planned a huge bonfire one Sunday in March 1990 where tax payment books would be publicly burnt. I was to be invited to light the bonfire and, if I declined, those present would burn an effigy of me (my memory now helpfully confirmed for me from the records of the *Newbury Weekly News*). In the event, I was not present and the protest fizzled down to rather less support and a smaller bonfire.

Deputy Lieutenant, County of Hampshire

For most of my early years I had assumed DL stood for Doctor of Law. Fortunately, well before 1994 I knew it stood for Deputy Lieutenant. The County of Hampshire is, as I write, extremely fortunate to have its first lady in the post of Lord Lieutenant. Mary Fagan has proved to be both highly respected and one of the most successful holders of this office in the long history of the Lieutenancy in Hampshire.

The Lord Lieutenant is the representative of the monarch in the County, as such welcoming the Queen on any visit she makes to Hampshire. It must be reassuring to Her Majesty to recognise someone she knows in the sea of faces wherever she makes an official visit in the UK. When the many calls on her time mean that the Queen cannot personally undertake an engagement, it will be the Lord Lieutenant, or the Vice Lieutenant, who will stand in her place and, should neither be available, it will be one of the supporting group of Deputies.

The role also involves a considerable amount of support for charities, for example inviting (urging!) me to become President of the Andover and District Medical Fund – an appeal for the purchase of medical equipment for our local hospital, starting with breast cancer screening. In 1994 I was honoured to become one of Hampshire's Deputy Lieutenants, the appointment being gazetted on 5 December that year.

Constituency boundary changes

The Boundary Commission is an independent body tasked with recommending the number and boundaries of constituencies in each county, their objective being to equalise as nearly as possible the numbers of voters per constituency. There has long been a drift out of the centre of major towns into suburban areas and beyond, so there is a real need for boundary changes. For example, it is unfair if twenty five thousand electors return a city centre MP, while eighty thousand or more are needed to return another. 1995 saw the implementation of the then Boundary Commission's Report. To err is human and, in my view, the Commission did a poor job when it failed to make Andover, with the neighbouring villages which look to it, into one constituency. Instead villages such as Barton Stacey and Longparish close to Andover were placed in the Romsey constituency; similarly it would have been better had there been East and West Basingstoke seats, with the surrounding villages attached to one or the other.

In July 1995 it was necessary to hold a Special General Meeting of the Association to deal with technical matters arising from boundary changes. This was chaired by our President, The Rt. Hon. Lord Boyd-Carpenter (at Westminster nicknamed 'Spring Heel Jack', also recognised as the best Speaker the Commons never had). These technical changes, although important, did not take up much time, so I was given the opportunity for a major speech. Normally I spoke from headings scribbled on the back of an envelope. This time, for reasons unknown, I have a full text; perhaps it was taped. Reading it now, it is clear it was my credo at the time and part of a lasting declaration of my political faith. Re-reading it I recognise that it is not a criterion of literary merit, to quote one's own words!

I spelled out some of the reasons I had wanted to become an MP; 'I did not want us to have Socialist governments because they always concentrate wealth in the hands of the State through excessive taxation and increased public ownership. I did not want to live in a society where more and more power is concentrated in the hands of civil servants in Whitehall for the benefit of their political masters. The more the State is aggrandised, the more the individual is diminished. Individuals should be more able to plan their own lives and make their own decisions, free of government intervention. You cannot build character by permanently doing for men and women that which they could and should do for themselves. You do not strengthen the weak by weakening the strong. However, I did not come into public life only to help destroy Socialism – that has been achieved; we all share in that achievement, we should be proud of the part each of us has played.' (Unhappily I fear the Blair and Brown years have proved me over-optimistic.)

'Now I want to see us continue building a society in which more and more of our people have a stake in our national wealth. Since 1979 home ownership is up from 59 per cent to 70 per cent, even now two hundred families a day buy their council houses, pension ownership is up with the independence that gives, there are now eight million pretty happy personal pension holders. [That was before Gordon Brown as Chancellor of the Exchequer stole £5 billion in tax out of their funds each year.] Share ownership was formerly three million people, mainly middle class, now it stands at ten million. The denationalisation of much of the public sector has lead to huge numbers of worker shareholders. On wealth creating small businesses, there are a net nine hundred thousand more since we came into office. I want a society in which power falls away from Whitehall. Here I recognise we have not done enough, particularly relating to local government, where we have some rethinking to do. So, I end my look back over past years and urge you to take pride in our achievements in changing society, that in itself is more important than whether people feel they have never had it so good.

'Next I want to look forward to the battles I see ahead. One big one concerns the sort of Europe we shall all live in. There should be trench warfare to make 'subsidiarity'[1] a reality, battles to keep us out of, or amend, the Social Chapter which would restore to the trade

---

[1] Decisions are taken at national or more local level, unless it is more effective that they be taken at EU level.

unions much of the opportunity for abuse of power which Margaret Thatcher and Jim Prior painstakingly took away from them. Ahead lie further battles over extended majority voting in Europe which could put at risk our essential national interests. That battle speaks of patriotism. I am old fashioned enough not to be ashamed of the word.'

It was at this meeting I went on to point out that this was the third time I had suffered from Boundary Commission changes during my thirty one years as an MP. 'It is always a wrench, one loses sight of good friends in the helter skelter of meeting new branches. At this point I want to clarify my own future intentions. Like a good parliamentarian, I have looked into precedent[2] and find that a predecessor, Sir Arthur Holbrook was elected in 1920 . . . he was then aged seventy, he lost the seat aged seventy three, won it back at seventy four and remained Member until he was seventy nine. On the other hand you, President, retired as an MP at the young age of sixty four. I find this a very difficult decision to make; if I stand again, I shall be sixty eight and I fear that, in the ensuing Parliament, I could be taking out rather than putting in, so I have reluctantly concluded, President, that yours is the better precedent and I shall not offer my name for the constituency at the next election. I would rather go, feeling that I have continued to the end doing a worthwhile job.'

P.S. This was the first time in my constituency I recall receiving a standing ovation – it came on my announcing my decision to retire!

I had made this announcement of my intention to retire some two years before a General Election might be expected. This was designed to give the Association sufficient time to select my successor and for him or her to make their mark and become known throughout the constituency.

---

[2] Anthony Henley, Member for Andover, set a different precedent in 1700 when the following infamous letter was sent to a constituent:

'I received yours and am surprised at your insolence in troubling me about the Excise. You know what I well know, that I bought you and I know what perhaps you think I do not know, that you are selling yourselves to somebody else.

But I know what you do not know, that I am buying another borough.

And may God's curse light on you all and may your homes be as open to the Excise Officers as your wives and daughters have been to me while I represented your rascally borough.'

My research in the Commons Library suggests that although published in the local paper, the letter was probably a hoax perpetrated by his son, also Anthony, the MP for Southampton.

Within three months they had set up their Selection Committee, refined the huge number of applicants down to twenty and then to six, finally to three. I had nothing to do with this process which was chaired by Paul Morgan, an exceptionally thorough Constituency Chairman, a fact well illustrated during the reduction from six to three stage. One candidate had homed in on small businesses for his ten minute speech. Towards the end (so it was reported to me) he had explained that he was not talking from theory since he ran a successful small firm and had indeed won some award for it. After his speech came questions; our Chairman asked if he would comment on the three summonses in the County Court his company had received for failing to pay their suppliers. Collapse of stout party!

Following the normal tradition, I was invited to attend the final selection with a view to praising the winner and calling on all the members to give him or her their united and enthusiastic support. The choice of Sir George Young, the 'bicycling baronet' proved a happy one and I had no difficulty introducing and commending him and his wife Aurelia to each of our wards and branches.

George had started his political life serving as a Councillor when the Conservatives took control of Lambeth Borough Council, along with Aurelia and also John Major. Amongst that borough's ineffic-iencies was 'totting' – a system where the dustmen had an additional cart for themselves, into which they put anything they thought saleable. This was a time and money wasting process. The new Councillors abolished it. The dustmen went on strike. George and John, in a strike-breaking operation, emptied the dustbins whilst Aurelia drove the dustcart.

I had long had a habit of warming up the start of meetings with a joke or amusing anecdote. Introducing George, I told of the Parochial Church Council whose vicar had retired. It was proving difficult to secure agreement on his successor. The rejects were said to be either too high-church, too low, too brash or too shy. Eventually the Archdeacon attended one of the meetings to try and persuade them. They remained, as he saw it, obstructive. In the Church of England, Parochial Council meetings are often closed with extemporary prayers. The Archdeacon's went 'Oh Lord, send down unto this Church and Parish the succour it so richly deserves.' George reciprocated with the tale of the circus proprietor whose big act was the human cannon ball. Alas, on one occasion too much

gunpowder was used and the human cannon ball shot into the next
world. Told of this, the circus proprietor said 'This is terrible, we'll
never find another man of the same calibre!' Our double act seemed
to go down well round the branches. George is an excellent MP, and
he and Aurelia have proved to be assiduous and popular throughout
the constituency. At the following Association AGM, George
presented me with a wonderful illustration of me dressed as an
Archdeacon and George shot in the air above the controversial
Newbury bypass.

I had to keep a careful record of which tale I told to which
audience so that no-one heard it twice. No-one, that is, except Janet
Butcher, my super agent for five years, and the kind people who
drove me during elections, particularly Evan Davies, erstwhile
bodyguard to Winston Churchill, also Sally Merison who threatened,
after nearly twenty times, to scream if she ever heard a particular one
of these stories again.

A year later in 1996 John Boyd-Carpenter wrote and said he felt
he was of an age when he should retire as President of the
Association. He asked if I would agree to become his successor. I was
delighted to concur and, when I stepped down as MP, a seamless
changeover occurred. John had been a huge success whenever the
Association needed support or advice. From my own selfish stand-
point I found myself in an enviable situation. My formal duties were
few, however it gave me a locus to turn up at any branch meeting
which often involved a reception, enabling me to keep in touch with
so many friends. Also, most welcome, many branch activities include
a supper – doubly welcome since I am not much good at cooking,
although always willing to share a bottle of wine with someone who
is.

As President, I have made it a firm rule to make only one speech
a year at the constituency AGM so as never to appear to be in a
conflict of opinion with Sir George. His safe election in 1997 gave
me much satisfaction. I lent Aurelia my blue-ribboned black cat, a
lucky mascot, which had, no doubt, played its part in my former
election successes and happily had not lost his touch.

CHAPTER 21

The Worshipful Company of Vintners

*My year as Master of this ancient Livery Company: activities
past and present, swans and swan upping, Prince Charles
opens Vintners' Place / Ups and downs of my 'year', a Court
visit to Bordeaux*

To BE MASTER OF ONE's Livery Company[1] is a privilege, doubly so
to be Master Vintner, one of the City of London Great Twelve,
the inner core of senior Companies. The Vintners are eleventh in their
pecking order. There has not always been unanimity on this sequence
since the Merchant Taylors and the Skinners quarrelled and would not
agree which was sixth and which seventh. This disarray produced the
phrase 'being all at sixes and sevens'. Now they take it in turn.

The Vintners' Company secured its first Royal Charter in 1363 for
three main purposes: to secure a trading monopoly, to provide care
for needy members and to maintain standards. Members ranged from
importers to hostelry keepers. As in other City Livery Companies,
those who failed to maintain standards risked expulsion and being
forbidden to trade within a hundred miles of the City. The nearest
significant town at that distance was Coventry (hence 'sent to
Coventry').

As previously mentioned, entry into the Company comes via one
of three routes, Patrimony, Apprenticeship or Redemption. The
progression within Companies after joining as a Freeman, is that some
are invited to join the Livery, and from amongst these a small number
are selected later to go forward as members of the Court. Membership Honoris Causa is granted occasionally to appropriately distinguished people. I was glad to be instrumental in Margaret Thatcher
(after she left office) becoming such a member. I joined the Freedom
by Redemption and the Livery in 1963. Twenty two years later I was
invited to join the Court, the ultimate ruling body of the Company.
After three or four years and provided one does not 'blot one's

---

[1] The term 'Livery Company' flows from the time each guild of craftsmen wore a distinctive
uniform – their Livery.

copybook' a new Court member progresses to be in turn (for one year only) Swan Warden, Renter Warden (Finance) then Upper Warden and finally Master. The Vintners' Court generally numbers between twenty and twenty six members.

The role of Swan Warden follows from the Company's historic and continuing connection with swans on the Thames. Early in Henry VIII's reign, the king fell into debt. The Vintners' and the Dyers' Companies helped him out and, in return, each Company was given a third of the swans on the Thames (then a sought-after delicacy). The decision as to which swans belonged to whom was determined sequentially by the crews of representational small boats (overseen by Court members from a more comfortable barge). This swan 'upping' allocated the swans by cutting one nick in the bill for a Dyers' bird, two nicks for a Vintners' bird and none for those of the King. The King was no fool, for birds which were missed up a backwater added to his total. Each year since, the small boats collectively move up the river, repeating history by marking cygnets according to their parentage; since 1997 the Vintners' two nicks have been replaced with rings twice engraved. The Company also assists financially with the care of sick swans, part of the responsibilities of the Swan Warden.

My turn to become Master was due in 1990. I was twice allowed to be bypassed because of the intensity of other commitments, and became Master for the year 1992/93. To be frank, I would have preferred to wait longer, but this would have upset the system. I cannot deny that being Chairman of El Vino, a busy MP and Master Vintner all at the same time was a pressurised schedule, but no more than Grandfather ALB who was Upper Warden and became Lord Mayor in 1924! I enjoyed it, I never let anyone down, but I would have enjoyed it much more had the pressure been less. It was all made possible and successful by the three superb secretaries who acted as the wonderfully cheerful and efficient team of Mavis and Karen, together with Jane Pittom at the Vintners, much helped by an understanding Clerk to the Company in the person of Brigadier Greg Read.

Normally the Master's spouse provides valuable support in a multitude of aspects in which a woman's judgment is much better, anyway, than mine. By 1992 Pam and I had separated, so I invited two ladies who graciously agreed to share the duties. Lady Donner, another Pam, the widow of a previous MP for my constituency, along with Judith Mayhew CC (later Dame Judith Mayhew Jonas), Chairman of the City Corporation's Policy and Resources Committee. They both made an enormous contribution to the success of my year as Master and I am indebted to both of them.

Some of the highlights of my year included the ride in the Lord Mayor's Procession, in the horse drawn 'Britska' carriage (which occurs every three years for a Vintners' Master). We stopped at the Law Courts where I recall the Lord Chief Justice's lovely turn of phrase referring to the new Lord Mayor who had been a civil engineering contractor, and later a barrister, as a 'Builder of sewers turned suer of builders'. Each Master of the Great Twelve entertains and is entertained once a year by the other eleven Masters. I was fascinated by the character of each hall and their varied traditions. From all of them came a heartening warmth of hospitality. When invited to speak at various functions, I paid tribute to Companies which retained a working relationship with their trade. This was partly from my own love of tradition and in part the fear that one day a left wing government might eye up the wealth and capital tax potential of Livery Companies, wondering what they do to justify their existence.

The Fishmongers continue to have responsibilities at London's great fishmarket of Billingsgate, now near Canary Wharf, the Goldsmiths still superintend the assaying and hallmarking of gold, silver and platinum. The Vintners founded and continue to help the Wine and Spirit Education Trust and the Institute of Masters of Wine, also during my time still contributed heavily to the Wine Standards Board which employs inspectors to ensure the authenticity of wine sold in the UK.

Undoubtedly the most prestigious event of my year concerned the opening of Vintners' Place, a building adjacent to the Vintners' Hall and backing onto the Thames. Some years before, the Court had a hand in choosing between a modern, conventional design and a gloriously neo-classical one. Specifically influenced by Prince Charles's known views, we had supported the latter. I understand it is rare for His Royal Highness to speak up supporting the design of a particular building. In our case, he came by barge and up the steps from the river and in officially declaring the building open, admired the architect's efforts to combine a classical design with contemporary requirements for office space. It was my privilege as Master to thank him and, in doing so, I recalled a piece of verse which seemed appropriate:

> Back of the beating hammer,
> Back of the workshop's clamour,
> The seeker may find the thought
> The thought that was ever master
> Of iron and steam and steel.
> But back of them all stands the dreamer
> Making his dreams come true.

and that was indeed true of the way that Prince Charles as the dreamer had influenced the choice of design.

My year was not all fun. The creation of Vintners' Place in which we had only a smallish interest had temporarily reduced our income and also involved additional building costs of our own. All would be well when the first rent cheque arrived from our share in the building. Meanwhile our bank balance shrank. Unenviably I had to lead the Company through a year of financial restraint. Never an easy or popular responsibility.

Happily, in spite of this, the traditional opportunity for the Master to lead a small group from the Court to a vineyard area was still within the budget. I chose Bordeaux, it being familiar territory to me, and it was fourteen years since the Vintners' last visit. The highlights of four and a half days there included Château Palmer where we were welcomed by Peter Sichel, an old friend and part owner of the Château. He had done a great deal in preparation for me 'on the ground'; after his conducted tour of the premises, we tasted the four most recent vintages of Palmer and enjoyed an excellent dinner accompanied by exceptional wines.

The next day we visited St Emilion, walking up a cobbled road made of stones brought as ship's ballast from Cornwall. Then an interesting tour of the cellars at Château Figeac, conducted with useful explanation by Eric d'Aramon. This famous vineyard is one of the best and largest of St Emilion, with an elegant style of its own. Our visit to Châteaux Langoa and Léoville Barton found the Wardens and myself being robed and 'intronised' as members of the Order of Bontemps du Médoc and then tasting wines from both Châteaux with Anthony Barton. He and his daughter, Lilian, were well known to several in our party and a relaxed and enjoyable visit ensued, with fine bottles of older vintages, but by this time my memory had become somewhat hazy! Before leaving Bordeaux we toured the Musée des Chartrons with its many exhibits of interest to those who love Bordeaux and its wines.

As my year drew to an end I took the Company's always helpful staff for a day in the House of Commons, coffee on the terrace, then we sat in on a Committee debate on 'Paralytic Shellfish Poisoning' – now that could not have been made up! Next a guided tour of the House of Lords as well as the Commons, followed by lunch in a room overlooking the terrace. My pre-lunch grace might not be approved by the chaplain: 'Oh Lord divine, who turnest water into wine, have mercy on us poor men who can only turn it back again'.

Following in Grandfather's footsteps as Master of the Company had given me a truly memorable year for which I am forever grateful to the Court and the Company.

CHAPTER 22

Travels with a Wallaby

Taking possession, forebodings, essential gifts, Armagnac and
a camel, night security, what if? / Wine breaks ice, the
scrapyard, a pair of crocks rejuvenated, role of a Minister

WHAT'S IN A PET NAME? Frequently a token of affection, rarely is a name so directly linked to her duties as in the case of this marsupial. A creature carrying young, protecting them from wind and rain, providing a secure, agreeable snuggery. Wallaby 1, a Volkswagen campervan safely carried a young Graham, Pam and me on many happy journeys both in the UK and in France and Spain – where its left hand drive was so much safer when overtaking.

One early decision was whether to go for the standard two berth vehicle or something a good deal bigger. One pays a lot more money for a larger one, hence you feel virtually obliged to live in it during a trip; moreover it can be a bit like driving a lorry. The smaller version we preferred was narrow enough for country lanes and gave us the diversity of a couple of nights on board, followed by a hotel or B&B and a blessed bath!

In the Aldwych, near Australia House, young Australians 'doing Europe' would line up their small campervans a few days before flying back home. Thus a mini buyers' market awaited new arrivals – and me. Here I found Wallaby 1. Its then owner was the son in an Australian family business of dental mechanics. He was much relieved to find a cash buyer. The deal was done; he took his personal possessions, had dinner with us, handed me the keys and headed for Heathrow. The most unexpected part of our inheritance was a good supply of tea and marmalade from Fortnum and Mason.

We were soon at work adding refinements and making lists of things to be done before setting out. Experience, over the years, has added up to thirty six items, from refilling the twenty gallon tank of water under the Wallaby's bottom to the provision of disposable instant barbecues, sunhats and my ankle length cowman's mac, the first aid kit etc. No point in stocking up with English food when one joy of travel is changing to, say, the foods of Provence or the Basque country.

One chronic mistake to which I am prone is not being good at saying 'No'. As a result I take on too much which, whilst it is no doubt better than having nothing to do, easily ends up with me battling against the clock, imprisoned behind a wall of work until I become desperate to escape. I recall vividly the first Wallaby trip to France and the vast relief and delight of having an open, undated return ticket.

We landed at Le Havre that evening amidst the puddles of an afternoon of rain. Not unreasonably, explanation was sought from me as to where we would spend the night. 'We can always turn off the road into a field entrance', I suggested. Every such gateway turned out to be a short, slippery, wet slope, easy to slide into but not to back out. Fortunately we found an abandoned piece of road which had been superseded by a new one, importantly it was level. The back seat was swiftly converted into a bed for us, while Graham, still short enough, slept across the front seat. The morning saw me dress, put on my mackintosh and stand outside in gentle rain, leaving room for the others to get up. It was then that my hidden but growing doubts became a foreboding about the whole enterprise. Later that morning we set off to the small port of Honfleur. The sun came out, the town turned out to be an enchanting artists' paradise and soon my forebodings evaporated and have not returned – yet. We made our way to the best hotel in town for coffee, croissants and other facilities, which set us up for the day.

I am now on Wallaby 3 with her name in distinct letters on front and back. I gossiped about this when on the phone renewing my vehicle insurance and the company promptly took £30 off the charge for comprehensive cover. I had conjectured that no-one would steal a vehicle so distinctive, however, the downside is the unquestionable identification of any traffic misdemeanour. My instant response when a gendarme stopped me at the entrance to Beaune was, 'Do you speak English?' Alas, he did, dressed me down and told me not to jump the lights again.

Wallaby 3 is a considerable improvement on my earlier models; in them the roof could be lifted up enabling the occupants to stand – just. Number 3 has a permanently raised roof, giving much more storage space. As with a small yacht, everything must be stored in its correct place; under the back seat, things for the vehicle from oil to

My Volkswagen campervan, Wallaby 3

spanners, plus a cool place for selected bottles of picnic wines. Above the driver's head, storage for bedclothes and a small cupboard with my best china teacups and saucers, cake plates and wine glasses etc. so that visitors can be agreeably surprised and properly entertained. The upper back section has ample space for a collapsible picnic table and chairs, two suitcases with liftable lids perform as clothes drawers and, below, a library of books I hope I shall have time to read. One corner of this shelf is reserved, VIP, for small gifts to those who render assistance en route – such as the farmer whose tractor pulled me out of a ditch and refused payment. There are packets of tea for the lesser kindnesses of filling my five gallon can with drinking water etc.; not to overlook a bottle for the good Samaritan in the hamlet of St Pantaléon in the Lot valley who rescued me from a breakdown. This on my way to visit my good friends, Bruce and Elizabeth, with their small vineyard where, each year, I am invited to help pick, and make, the wine.

Beginning a recent trip, I slammed on the brakes to avoid a collision, and there was a loud crash behind me as the half closed catch to the library shelf gave way and out tumbled an assortment of guide books (out of date), and classics I ought to have read long ago. Along with them, Schama's *History of Britain*, Leo Walmsley's *Three Fevers*, Peter Mayle's *A Year in Provence*, Patrick O'Brien's HMS *Surprise* and a couple of Alexander Kent's glorious historical sea novels, together with the *Times Guide to Le Lunch*, all wildly scattered around the interior of the Wallaby, a sharp reminder to check everything is secured when moving off.

I must not leave Wallabies 1 and 2 without recalling some incidents. As a Minister in the Department of Industry, I looked forward to the great release of my summer break. You will appreciate that I was somewhat disconcerted when my private office insisted I give them address and phone number even whilst I was on holiday in the UK. I explained my intended gipsy-like existence which was incompatible with this request. Eventually pinned down, I said,

'The orange dormobile on the far side of Fox Tor mires near Princetown on Dartmoor'.

'And how do we get in touch with you there?'

'Difficult, but I can give you the phone number of a farmer's wife, Mrs Rosemary Mudge, and she would send her daughter on a pony.'

A look of sad resignation ended the conversation.

The next year saw us in Normandy. One night we parked beside a farm track through a field, taking care to leave space for a farm tractor to pass. I woke to a curious 'swish swish' sound unlike anything I could immediately recall. I pulled back the curtain to see, adjacent to Wallaby's flank, an elderly bewhiskered peasant lady sitting on a three legged stool, milking a cow into a bucket. I should have recognised that distinctive sound.

Another time I was in the wine village of Pouilly-sur-Loire. I recall an excellent dinner of good, home cooking. Pam and I enjoyed a bottle of Sancerre rouge from that nearby village. Then I spotted a remarkable old Armagnac, reasonably priced, and brought two glasses to our table. Pam declined and I declined Graham's offer of assistance . . . later I successfully navigated an extremely narrow road down to a spread of flat land beside the great Loire river. We all slept rather well but, in the morning, I realised I must have over-imbibed when I heard a noise outside, pulled back a corner of the curtain and thought I saw a camel! A bit later, an odd noise, a quick peep, this time there were two camels – too much of that fabulous Armagnac.

I vowed 'never again' and put my head under the pillow. Shortly after, there was a loud banging on the door. I opened it cautiously to find a red faced gendarme gesticulating, '*Allez Monsieur, allez, allez tout de suite!*' We were parked in the middle of the circus site just where the big top was about to be erected.

I am often surprised by the number of people jealous of the freedom to roam inherent in my Wallaby. Other times, I am asked anxiously about security, particularly when I admit I rarely go into a proper campsite. I am not enamoured of queuing among strangers for the 'facilities', especially since I know a good hotel in the nearest town will be cleaner, devoid of queues and all this for the price of a coffee. At night I take a few sensible precautions, e.g. I never park facing a dead end, always stop where I can drive out, keys in the ignition, by my bedside a police whistle, mobile phone and, probably most important, a loaded camera, on the contention that anyone trying the doors will not hang around after its flash. We did have one scare in Portugal. Imprudently I had parked beside some bushes at the back of a lorry park on the edge of an industrial town. By this time Graham was too tall to sleep fully stretched across the front seat, so we took it in turns. This night, Pam was in front, Graham beside me in the back. In the early hours, his hand grabbed me as he whispered, 'There's someone outside', adding he had heard a twig break. I listened intently and heard for myself. I think it took less than a minute to be driving away. Of course, it may have been only a dog . . . I am not saying my defences will always work, but certainly I live in hope.

Now in retirement, a kaleidoscope of recent trips has taken me to lovely Salcombe in South Devon with glorious sea views from cliff top walks, then up on to Dartmoor to a hidden valley where the farmer lets me park by the river – what can be nicer that to drift off to sleep to the sound of a murmuring stream? The Plymouth ferry to Santander speeds me to Northern Spain. Going west some fifty miles along the coast near San Vicente de la Barquera, I park close to a beach, sleep to the sound of the waves and enjoy the warm sea. In the next bay I find a café with a barbecue four feet long. I do not speak Spanish, but discover what is on offer by a mixture of, 'Baa Baa', 'Moo Moo' and a snorting noise, all of which causes much hilarity, and a larger portion of pork comes my way. I spend an afternoon and a night at the 'Los Infantes' hotel in the interesting small mediaeval town of Santillana del Mar, before journeying into South West France.

I arrive there near to lovely St Jean de Luz with its restaurants spilling out into the sunlit street, then head inland to rediscover the unique Basque culture and architecture. I wend my way through the foothills of the Pyrenees, add a few more entries to my private good loo guide, note characterful villages, also restaurants with genuine regional foods of their locality, not least delicious Gâteau Basque, and the Brebis des Pyrenées (sheep cheese).

A few days on find me in Cucugnac, one of the centres of Corbières wine production and the Sichel's vineyard. Nearby are the impressive hilltop fortresses where the supporters of the breakaway Albigensian sect defended themselves from the attacks of orthodox Catholicism led by Simon de Montfort. Later the delightful tale of a new priest arriving in Cucugnac, taking the morning service in the presence of one old man and two geese. He preaches about the hidden treasure whose whereabouts he will divulge the following Sunday. The church is then packed full, he tells the congregation of a dream of a blissful existence, but alas the Parish of Cucugnac is not included because only churchgoers can find the happiness and contentment of soul to be found there. Even today this church's services are well attended. I remain envious of those whose religious conviction leaves no room for doubts.

I find my way back to the Mediterranean coast, turn north, skirt Nîmes with its huge amphitheatre and press on to Avignon to the wee flat I have there. It is a glorious city with its historic Popes' Palace (especially striking when floodlit at night), endless architectural discoveries and an outstanding covered food market. On another occasion I came in July to go to the opera in the magnificent Roman theatre in Orange, capacity nearly nine thousand (I have a photo-graphic memory of *Aida* with its grandest of grand marches right across the stage, the orchestra augmented with trumpeters high up above, to left and right). Spectacular! Pause to imagine the traffic jam at the end of the evening. I escape by a lane which leads out to Châteauneuf du Pape and park by the ruin of the Popes' summer château, then waken to morning sunshine over the famous vineyards.

It is an opportunity to look back and reminisce to myself over a busy life and to conjecture on some 'what ifs'. What if my father had accepted his father-in-law's offer to pay for my brother and my entire

education? What if I had become a barrister? What if I had not
rebelled when Whip on the Leasehold Reform Bill? What if I had
accepted the Prime Minister's invitation to become number two
Minister in the Department of Agriculture? (I would have liked that.)
One does what seems right at the time, so I can dream on – it costs
nothing!

I return to my journey home from Châteauneuf. This small town
has been made famous by its unique wine, not cheap, for the
vineyards of this Appellation are in demand throughout the civilised
world. Driving from the shadow of its ruined château, I am still
astonished by its 'soil'; this has a preponderance of 'pudding stones',
many large enough to fill the palm of my hand. Elsewhere, most
stones have sharp edges but these are smooth, having been rolled by
the glaciers from the mountains of Haute Savoie and deposited here
as the glaciers melted. A casual glance leaves the impression that
nothing would grow in such soil. Indeed, nowhere exemplifies more
the fact that many of the best wines come from poor soil. This forces
the vine to develop an astonishingly large network of roots as it
searches for moisture and its nutrients. Here the principal grape is
Grenache, augmented by much lesser amounts of Syrah, Mourvèdre
and any of seven others. One under-recognised feature of the
pudding stones is that they absorb the daytime heat of the sun and,
like a night storage heater, release it during the hours of darkness, so
in some years the buyer needs to take care to avoid wines with a
burnt flavour.

I lunch in my favourite local restaurant, Les Florets in Gigondas,
to which I had brought a group from the Carlton Club Wine
Committee. I then drive eighty miles north, with scarcely a vine in
sight until reaching the small towns of Tournon and Tain. The latter
has attached 'L'Hermitage' to its name so it can bask in the glory of
its most famous wine. This, with Crozes Hermitage from the
surrounding vineyards, along with St Joseph and Cornas, is made
from the Syrah grape, a cousin of Shiraz in the New World. I press
on, not stopping as I pass the vineyards of the Cru Beaujolais and
White Mâconnais and into the Côte d'Or. I have in my memory a
track beside a vineyard above the hillside village of Pernand
Vergelesses, just outside Beaune. It is dusk – would anyone know or
care if the Wallaby stops the night here? Suddenly the vineyard
proprietor appears, exercising his dog. I ask his consent which is

readily given with an invitation to taste his wine in the morning. It is then I explain that I am a *'marchand de vin en retraite'*. He claps me on the shoulder and says, 'We are bound together by the common heritage of wine'. As I drive on, this sets me thinking of the camaraderie, almost freemasonry, of wine and the barriers it has broken down for me on visits abroad – even breaking the ice with President Mitterand – also, in both Bulgaria and Hungary when I went behind the Iron Curtain promoting aircraft sales to their Ministers of Transport. Another aspect of mixing the 'endless adventures of wine with politics'.

I continued my return but, alas, at one point a red light indicated the battery was not charging. I turned off the autoroute at the first layby; as I got out, a large cloud of white smoke came pouring out of the back of the camper – I hastily started to unload and, as I did so, the 'fire', as I assumed it to be, died down. Fortunately it was steam from overheated water spurting past a broken gasket on to the exhaust cylinder. On French autoroutes you are not allowed to choose your tow away for repair; the police arrange it, after having the damage assessed. I asked for a Volkswagen garage, to be told it would be an 'appropriate' firm which covered all types of vehicle. The Wallaby was duly wound up on to the low loader and away we went to the chosen repairer. Imagine my shock and the Wallaby's indignation when we arrived at a breaker's yard! All of this because, unrecognised by me, the fan belt had gone, and I had continued to drive an overheated engine for three or four kilometres. A temporary gasket was found from an abandoned VW in the scrapyard and we limped home to Hampshire. My VW garage proclaimed the engine as beyond economic repair. During the recent weeks I had been feeling increasingly tired as if I, too, was running out of steam. Dr John Coltart, an eminent cardiologist, found my heartbeats per minute had become too slow. Wallaby and me, a pair of crocks! Wallaby is now reinvigorated with a new engine and my heartbeats restored to normal. So we can both look forward to whatever opportunities lie ahead.

I turn my thoughts to the 'endless adventure' of my political life and ponder on how extraordinarily lucky I have been: a constituency with an historic town and many attractive villages, each with its group of loyal friends and supporters. My time in the Whips' Office learning what goes on behind the scenes, and my foolhardy exit. The campaign, almost a crusade, to help change our business culture and have the potential of new and small firms recognised. Then working with Sir Keith Joseph as PPS and later as a Minister in the Department of Industry, the experiences and fascination of Northern Ireland, my varied responsibilities at Transport, and my involvement in the Channel Tunnel project.

So, what should be the true role of a Minister? Surely not to be an expert, that is for advisers, but to stand back and apply common sense. It was Lord Salisbury in 1877 who wrote, 'No lesson seems so deeply inculcated by the experiences of life, that you should never rely on experts . . . they all require to have their strong wine diluted by a very large admixture of insipid common sense.'

My recollections turn to the products of the vine, the style and character of vintages I have purchased (and those I wish I had), and the interesting, often inexpensive, wines in store for me with El Vino. (I prefer a lesser wine ready to drink to a raw great wine.) Surprisingly often, when I open a bottle, I smile to myself as I recall the circumstances and the personality of those whose wine I have bought.

Enough of my reminiscences on the endless adventure of politics and wine, more important to me is the legacy of three happily married children and nine grandchildren with whom our family is blessed.

Alfred Bower as Lord Mayor

ALB – Grandfather Sir Alfred Bower Bt as Lord Mayor

T HE LORD MAYOR'S SHOW with its procession round the City is the
public's first sight of a new Lord Mayor. All Sheriffs and Lord
Mayors have to belong to one of the traditional City Livery
Companies. ALB had just completed his year as Upper Warden of
the Vintners' Company. The 1924 procession was enlivened by a
specially colourful input with the banners of the Company, of the
Swan Warden and of Bacchus, then the Bargemaster and Swan
Marker in full uniform et al. Then came personages, each in the dress
of his period, to represent the seventeen Lord Mayors who, since
1270, had been Masters of the Vintners. Next the two Sheriffs in

My grandfather, Sir Alfred Bower Bt

State carriages each drawn by four horses, the Band of the Life Guards, the State Trumpeters and, only then, a smiling ALB in the Lord Mayor's coach drawn by six horses and attended by his chaplain (was this in case he burst with pride and needed the last rites?).

The Lord Mayor's banquet is the second major function in his calendar; here a unique situation arose because the 1924 general election had been in full swing when the invitations went out. Only at the last minute was it certain that the Prime Minister as chief guest would be Stanley Baldwin and not Ramsay MacDonald. This heralded a particularly amusing speech by Neville Chamberlain who parodied the bible reference to those Ministers (of the previous government) 'invited to the feast who with one accord began to make excuses, one saying he had lost a seat, another he must attend a rally on the Clyde and yet another that his mood was not attuned to high festivities at this moment'. The proceedings were broadcast by the BBC for the first time. The traditional menu started with turtle soup and continued in gastronomic glory. Happily, early that evening, another tradition continued with two thousand one hundred and fifty of the poor from London's East End being provided with a substantial high tea and musical entertainment (at the expense of ALB and his two Sheriffs) in the Great Assembly Hall on the Mile End Road.

During the Mayoral year ALB lunched or dined several members of the royal family, also Stanley Baldwin, Asquith, Balfour, Winston Churchill, Douglas Hogg, an Archbishop, the Chief Rabbi, Baden-Powell, Lord Lucan and leaders in many aspects of UK and Empire life. These are recorded in his bound volume of Mansion House visitors along with, I regret to say, Graham Mitchell in the childlike writing of our younger son – on the page for Edward, the then Prince of Wales!

Of course his year was packed with civic activity and the odd crisis – such as when his City Surveyor served a Dangerous Structure Notice on the Dean and Chapter of St Paul's in respect of the cathedral's sixty thousand ton dome. This was supported by columns originally filled with rubble which, over the years, had crumbled and slipped down, leaving only the outer ring of the columns loadbearing. Although a Catholic, ALB was, as Lord Mayor, a Trustee of St Paul's, and in the thick of the subsequent controversy between his City official and the Cathedral authorities. Happily an appeal *The Times*

Times newspaper raised the £250,000 for essential works required by the City Surveyor.

A brouhaha occurred later when, in June, 1925, he invited leading Catholic clergy from the Cardinal Archbishop of Westminster down, together with RC peers and MPs, to a Mansion House dinner. When asked about the toasts to be proposed, he let it be known these would be, first to the King, and second to the Pope. This went down badly with the Catholic hierarchy, a number of whom refused to attend.

One interesting break involved a ceremonial visit to Paris, Rheims and Verdun (a town on the front line which had been of enormous strategic importance during the First World War). Here ALB was the first Englishman to receive the Life Freedom of that city, and later was made a Grand Officier of the Légion d'Honneur. A big Champagne Syndicat dinner in Rheims presided over by the Marquis de Polignac (Pommery) was enlivened by an amusing incident when the uniformed footmen were mistaken for the Sheriffs and called upon for a speech. Eventually one rose to his feet and, in good voice, called out 'Vive la France and down with those that don't drink!'

During their time at the Mansion House, Darly, as Lady Mayoress, earned herself a reputation as a cheerful and apt speaker bringing humour, sympathy and practical suggestions as she fulfilled her own programme of opening sales of work, bazaars and fetes, distributing prizes, attending events and giving support to a range of appropriate charities.

10 DOWNING STREET
LONDON SW1A 2AA

THE PRIME MINISTER   25 July 1988

Dear David,

    I was very sad when you told me today that you wanted to
resign. You have been with me from the beginning and I very
much wanted you to carry on in Government. But of course I
fully appreciate that you have other duties to think of, in
particular your family.

    You have been an excellent Minister, first at Industry,
then in Northern Ireland and finally in Transport where you
did wonders in steering through deregulation of buses. I
shall miss you tremendously, but you were good enough to say
that you would continue to give us your full support from the
back benches.

    With warm regards and good wishes,

Yours ever

Margaret

David Mitchell, Esq., M.P.

Index

Individuals' titles used below are generally those pertaining at the time of the events described in 'House to House'.